WALKING IN
BULGARIA'S NATIONAL PARKS

About the Author

Julian Perry was born and raised on the southeast coast of England, but for the last 20 years has spent most of his time in the Bulgarian mountains, where he now runs a specialist eco-tourism company, Balkan Trek, organising walking and wildlife-watching holidays. Julian's passionate interest in the flora, fauna and culture of Bulgaria has quickly gained him recognition as one of the leading authorities on the region. His photographs and articles have appeared in a variety of newspapers, magazines and other publications, and he is also the author of *The Mountains of Bulgaria: A Walker's Companion*, the first ever English-language guidebook to long-distance hiking trails in Bulgaria. When not writing or guiding groups, Julian's greatest pleasure is exploring the wildlife of the Rodopi Mountains in the company of his young son, Alex.

WALKING IN
BULGARIA'S NATIONAL PARKS

by
Julian Perry

JUNIPER HOUSE, MURLEY MOSS,
OXENHOLME ROAD, KENDAL, CUMBRIA LA9 7RL
www.cicerone.co.uk

© Julian Perry 2010
First edition 2010
ISBN 978 1 85284 574 2
Reprinted 2017 (with updates)

Printed by KHL Printing, Singapore

A catalogue record for this book is available from the British Library.
All photographs are by the author unless otherwise stated.

Acknowledgements

I would like to express my gratitude to all those who have helped with this project, in particular all the members of my family who have once again provided essential encouragement and support. I would also like to offer special thanks to Mihaela Yordanova, Siya Cholakova, Svetlana Drumeva and Svetoslava Toncheva, who have accompanied me on some of the walks and patiently posed as 'foreground interest' in many of the photos! Two other people who deserve my thanks are Kalina Petrova for helping check current bus schedules to and from the mountains, and Milen Marinov, for his expert advice and comments on the dragonfly fauna of the Bulgarian national parks.

Updates to this Guide

While every effort is made by our authors to ensure the accuracy of guidebooks as they go to print, changes can occur during the lifetime of an edition. Any updates that we know of for this guide will be on the Cicerone website (www.cicerone.co.uk/574/updates), so please check before planning your trip. We also advise that you check information about such things as transport, accommodation and shops locally. Even rights of way can be altered over time. We are always grateful for information about any discrepancies between a guidebook and the facts on the ground, sent by email to updates@cicerone.co.uk or by post to Cicerone, Juniper House, Murley Moss, Oxenholme Road, Kendal, LA9 7RL.

Register your book: To sign up to receive free updates, special offers and GPX files where available, register your book at www.cicerone.co.uk.

Front cover: View towards Vihren (2914m) in the Pirin National Park

CONTENTS

Location of Bulgaria's National Parks 7
Map Key. 8

PREFACE 9

INTRODUCTION 11
Geography 12
Climate. 12
Biodiversity 13
Protected Territories 15
History 15
Culture. 18
Cuisine. 18
Language 20
Money 20
Communications 20
Travelling to Bulgaria 21
Travelling to the Mountains 22
Walking in Bulgaria 23
Accommodation. 24
Food and Water 25
Maps 25
Mountain Rescue 27
About this Guidebook 28
Key Facts and Figures 28

PART 1 THE CENTRAL BALKAN NATIONAL PARK 29
Introduction 31
Walk 1   The Boatin, Tsarichina and Kozya Stena Reserves. 40
Walk 2   The Severen Dzhendem, Stara Reka and Steneto Reserves 58
Walk 3   The Dzhendema and Stara Reka Reserves 76
Walk 4   The Peeshtite Skali and Sokolna Reserves. 92

PART 2 THE RILA NATIONAL PARK. 105
Introduction 107
Walk 5   The Rila Monastery Nature Park and Forest Reserve 118
Walk 6   Sedemte Ezera and Zeleni Rid 136
Walk 7   The Central Rila Reserve. 149
Walk 8   The Ibar Reserve. 171

PART 3 THE PIRIN NATIONAL PARK 181
Introduction 183
Walk 9   The Pirin Wine Trail 192
Walk 10 The Yulen Reserve. 216
Walk 11 Mount Vihren 227
Walk 12 The Bayvuvi Dupki–Dzhindzhiritsa Reserve and Koncheto 235

Appendix 1   Route Summary Table 246
Appendix 2   English–Bulgarian Glossary and Pronunciation Guide 247
Appendix 3   Further Reading 250
Appendix 4   Mountain Huts and Other Useful Contacts 251

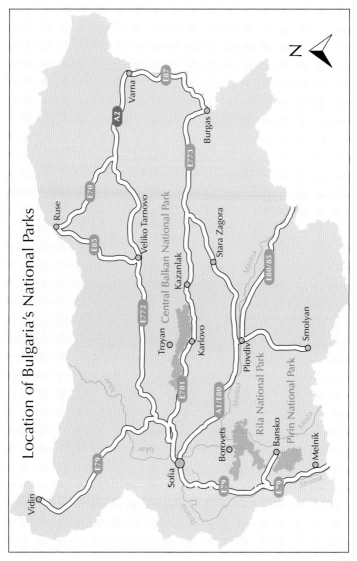

Location of Bulgaria's National Parks

Map key

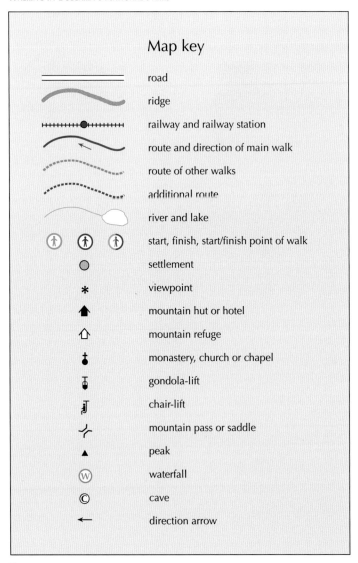

road
ridge
railway and railway station
route and direction of main walk
route of other walks
additional route
river and lake
start, finish, start/finish point of walk
settlement
viewpoint
mountain hut or hotel
mountain refuge
monastery, church or chapel
gondola-lift
chair-lift
mountain pass or saddle
peak
waterfall
cave
direction arrow

PREFACE

Descending from Todorina Porta into the Banderitsa valley with Vihren (2914m) on horizon (Walk 10)

According to an old Bulgarian legend, when God had made the world and was partitioning out the land, the Bulgarian people ended up at the back of the queue. By the time their turn finally came, there was nothing left, so God decided to stitch together a tiny piece from all the other countries and give them this patchwork as their homeland. Indeed, despite its small area, just under 111,000km^2 (less than half the size of the United Kingdom), Bulgaria is one of the most geographically and biologically diverse countries in Europe.

During the 20 or so years that I have been exploring Bulgaria, I have witnessed many changes. Not only has the country emerged from behind the Iron Curtain, it has also successfully thrown off the shackles of its communist legacy to become a fully-fledged member of the European Union. Furthermore, in the last few years alone, Bulgaria has developed from being a country usually described as 'forgotten', 'unknown' and 'secret', to a place that is now regularly declared to be 'one of the hottest new destinations' for both tourists and property investors alike. However, despite these dramatic developments, one thing has not changed – Bulgaria still remains a paradise for walkers and naturalists.

Cascade formed by the Retizhe river near Popovo Ezero (Walk 10, Day 1)

INTRODUCTION

Blessed with a favourable climate, a wonderful variety of landscapes, a uniquely rich flora and fauna and a wealth of hiking trails, the choice of where to walk in Bulgaria is pretty much limitless. For the author of a guidebook such as this, it also makes the choice of what to include and what to leave out very difficult. In the end, I decided to limit the focus to Bulgaria's three national parks – Rila, Pirin and Central Balkan. These national parks not only occupy the highest and wildest mountains in the country, but they are also threaded with a network of well-marked hiking trails. These paths typically lead through spectacular scenery and offer an unrivalled opportunity to encounter some of Europe's rarest plants and animals.

As well as providing detailed route descriptions for many of the most outstanding walks offered by these three national parks, I have also included a great deal of background information about the history and geography of places passed along the trails, along with comprehensive details of the wildlife likely to be seen. Mountain walking in Bulgaria's national parks provides more than simply a physical challenge – it is a unique opportunity to experience wilderness and to glimpse the rare flora and fauna that still manages to find a safe refuge there.

View towards Popovo Ezero, with Sivriya (2593m) to the left and Dzhengal (2730m) to the right (Walk 10, Day 1)

GEOGRAPHY

Bulgaria lies in the southeastern corner of Europe, and has the rough outline of a large irregular rectangle some 520km from west to east and 330km from north to south. The country makes up about one-fifth of the Balkan Peninsula, and is bordered by Romania to the north, Serbia and Macedonia to the west, and Greece and Turkey to the south. Its eastern boundary is formed by a 378km stretch of the Black Sea's western shore.

Bulgaria has 37 distinct mountain ranges, of which 14 can be classed as 'high mountains' over 1600m. These include eight mountain ranges which reach altitudes of over 2000m – Rila (2925m), Pirin (2914m), Stara Planina (2376m), Vitosha (2290m), Osogovo (2254m), Slavyanka (2212m), Rodopi (2191m) and Belasitsa (2029m).

CLIMATE

Bulgaria lies on the boundary between continental and Mediterranean climatic zones. The significance of these competing climatic influences is, however, greatly controlled and modified by the country's mountains. Most significant is the Stara Planina range, which runs west to east right across Bulgaria, helping to hinder cooler and wetter continental air masses as they move in from the north. Likewise, the Rodopi Mountains, which occupy a large part of southern Bulgaria, tend to hold up any Mediterranean weather systems coming in from the south. This means that the central part of the country, between these two major mountain ranges, represents a transitional climatic zone. Surprisingly, the influence of the Black Sea on Bulgaria's overall

Cascade formed by the River Odzhovitsa below hizha Belmeken (Walk 8, Day 1)

climate is very limited, and really only has an impact on a narrow coastal strip.

In northern parts of Bulgaria, where a moderate continental climate predominates, the wettest months are May and June, and the driest is February, while in the south, the Mediterranean influence means maximum precipitation tends to be in November and December, and minimum in August and September.

In the lowlands of northern Bulgaria, precipitation regularly falls as snow between December and March, while along the Black Sea coast and the lowlands of southern Bulgaria this tends to be limited to January and February. However, snowfall in these lowland regions usually only results in intermittent cover, because the temperature frequently rises above zero. In the mountains, of course, the situation is very different, and above 2000m snow can last between four and nine months depending on altitude.

The average annual temperature in Bulgaria is between 10°C and 14°C. In the lowlands, January tends to be the coldest month with an average temperature in northern Bulgaria of -1.4°C to -2°C, and in the south between 0°C to 2°C. In the mountains it varies from -2°C to -10°C depending on altitude. Highest average temperatures are in July or August, reaching 21°C to 24°C degrees in the lowlands, but dropping from 16°C to 5°C in the mountains as the altitude increases. Interestingly, however, the lowest temperatures ever recorded in Bulgaria have not been high up in the mountains, but actually in lower-lying basins, which in winter frequently experience dramatic temperature inversions.

In general, from the point of view of walkers, Bulgaria's climatic peculiarities make weather conditions in the mountains very pleasant during summer. Temperatures rarely rise too high to become uncomfortable for walking, and rain, when it falls, tends to be in the form of a short sharp downpour, which often quickly gives away to another prolonged spell of fine dry weather.

In the high mountains, June and July are wonderfully fresh and green, with the alpine flowers at their best, though you may find late-lying snow patches a hindrance on some of the highest peaks and passes, particularly their shaded northern flanks. August and September offer long days and stable sunny weather, ideal for major hikes, while October tends to be great for photography, the air crisp and clear, the deciduous forests turning gold, and perhaps a dusting of early snow on the highest tops to add some extra contrast.

BIODIVERSITY

Located as it is, in the far southeastern corner of Europe, Bulgaria straddles the boundaries between the Central European forest, Eurasian steppe and Mediterranean bio-geographic zones, and is thus one of the most important countries on the continent in terms of its biodiversity.

Bulgaria is blessed with a unique natural heritage and an amazing variety of landscapes and eco-systems. To the east lies the Black Sea, with its rocky capes, sandy beaches and sheltered bays, while to the north is the Danube, fringed by lakes and marshes, and bordered by an ever-alternating succession of low hills, elevated plateaus and broad steppe-like plains. But it is the majestic mountains that dominate Bulgaria, forming the physical heartland of the country. There you will find rugged alpine peaks and ridges with deep caves and precipitous gorges, surrounded by an extensive cloak of sub-alpine pastures, scrubs and peat-bogs. These then give way to ancient coniferous and beech forests, and lower still a zone of oak and hornbeam, as well as lush flower-filled meadows that surround small rural settlements where the local people still live a traditional pastoral life.

Because of its location, varied climate, relief and geological structure, Bulgaria has an outstandingly rich flora, with more than 3900 species of higher plants, made up of Central European, Carpathian, Mediterranean and Pontic species, as well as many unique Balkan and Bulgarian endemics which constitute about eight per cent of Bulgaria's flora. There are also some 52 species of ferns, 4000 species of algae, 670 species of moss and 600 species of lichen.

The fauna too is extremely interesting and diverse, a meeting place for European and Asiatic species, including 100 of mammal, of which 33 are bats, 421 of bird, 207 of fish, some 37 of reptile, 18 of amphibian, and an estimated 27,000 species of invertebrate, which includes over 200 species of butterfly and 68 species of dragonfly.

Sokolna Reserve information boards (Walk 4)

PROTECTED TERRITORIES

Bulgaria has a long tradition of nature conservation. Its first protected area, the Silkosiya Reserve was created in the Strandzha Mountains in 1931. Three years later, in 1934, a People's Park was established on the Vitosha Mountains, becoming the first such 'national nature park' on the Balkan Peninsula. Today, Bulgaria's protected areas encompass approximately 4.3 per cent of the country's territory, and include 90 nature reserves, 10 nature parks and three national parks. It is these three national parks – Pirin, Rila and Central Balkan – that are the focus of this guidebook, for they not only represent some of the finest wilderness regions in Europe, they are also conveniently accessible, being crisscrossed with a well-marked and well-maintained network of hiking trails.

HISTORY

Situated at the edge of Europe, Bulgaria has long been an important eastern gateway to the continent, and a melting pot for a range of different peoples and cultures, all of whom have left their mark on the country, and helped to shape its development and rich historical legacy.

The earliest traces of human life on Bulgarian territory date back to Palaeolithic (Stone Age) times, and archaeologists from the Bulgarian Academy of Science are currently investigating a cave encampment in northwestern Bulgaria, which has been dated to between 1.6 million and 1.4 million years ago. This has led to claims that the initial 'conquest' of the European continent by humans was through what are today Bulgarian lands. Later, during the Neolithic (New Stone Age) and Eneolithic (Stone-Copper Age) periods, people began to settle in the plains, cultivating the fertile soil and domesticating livestock.

By the Middle Bronze Age, about 2000BC, a distinct people, known as the Thracians, had become established. An amalgamation of independent tribes rather than a united kingdom, they were not only farmers and shepherds, but also accomplished craftsmen, producing what are today world-renowned golden treasures. However, during the fourth century BC, Philip II of Macedon temporarily over-ran the region, and after another brief spell of independence, the Thracian tribes were finally subjugated by the Romans in the first century AD. Eventually, during the fourth century, and after the separation of the Western and Eastern Roman Empires, the territory of present day Bulgaria fell under Byzantine control.

During the sixth century the Slavic tribes started to penetrate into the region and, despite the efforts of the Byzantine Empire to prevent them, by the beginning of the seventh century the region had become settled with a new Slavic population, which quickly merged with and assimilated what remained of the original Thracian inhabitants. The Slavs were then followed by new invaders, the Bulgars, a Turkic people from Central Asia who by 681 had pushed south of the Danube and established the First Bulgarian Kingdom (681–1018) under the leadership of Khan Asparuh (681–700).

Bulgaria's golden age

A couple of centuries later, during the reign of Tsar Boris I (852–899), Christianity was officially adopted as the state religion, and a new Slavonic alphabet was created, enabling Bulgaria to become the leading centre of Slavonic literature and culture. This period of development reached its zenith in the reign of Tsar Simeon I (893–927), the so-called 'golden age' of both Bulgarian culture and territorial expansion.

A period of decline then set in, until finally in 1018 Byzantium managed to achieve its long dreamed-of goal, the re-annexation of Bulgaria. This lasted for just over 150 years, until, following an uprising led by the brothers Petar and Asen, Byzantine control was overthrown, and the Second Bulgarian Kingdom (1186–1396) was established under the rule of Tsar Petar II (1186–1196).

The Ottoman era

This second kingdom reached its height during the reign of Tsar Ivan II (1218–1241) and marked a new high point in Bulgarian art and cultural development. However, a period of internal strife and unrest soon set in, and this took its toll on the Bulgarian state, so that by the middle of the 14th century it was in no condition to resist the advancing Ottoman Turks. They penetrated into Europe in 1354, and by 1396 had snuffed out the last pocket of Bulgarian resistance.

The Ottoman 'yoke', as it is usually called, lasted for over 500 years, and was a black period for Bulgaria, bringing great suffering to the ordinary people and, for several centuries, stifling the development of the nation. Finally, during the 18th century, something of a renaissance began to take place. Driven forward on the one side by patriotic monks such as Paisius of Hilendar (Paisiy Hilendarski) and later Neophyt of Rila (Neofit Rilski), and on the other by increasingly wealthy Bulgarian merchants, Bulgaria began its National Revival Period. This not only saw the flourishing of arts and crafts such as woodcarving and icon painting, but also inspired a new collective Bulgarian pride and ignited the desire for independence, first educational and religious, and finally political.

In April 1876, a long-planned but premature uprising broke out in the Sredna Gora Mountains, which was quickly and brutally crushed by the Ottoman Turks. However, although a failure in itself, it awoke European attention, and the following year Russia declared war on Turkey, eventually liberating Bulgaria in early 1878 after an epic winter campaign.

The Treaty of San Stefano that followed in March 1878 reinstated much of Bulgaria's traditional lands in Macedonia, Thrace and Moesia. However, the western powers (Britain amongst them) feared the establishment of a Greater Bulgaria that would be closely allied to Russia, and in July 1878 convened the Congress of Berlin. At this, it was decided to do away with the earlier agreement and instead directly hand back to the Turks the territories of Macedonia and Aegean Thrace, while carving up what was left of the country into an independent Principality of Bulgaria in the north, and a Turkish-controlled region known as Eastern Rumelia in the south. Not surprisingly,

Rila Monastery (Walk 5)

the Bulgarian people felt betrayed, and this unjust and ill-conceived decision sowed the seeds for Bulgaria's subsequent involvement in the 1912–13 Balkan Wars, and ultimately in the First and Second World Wars as well, when the lure of regaining former territories of which they had been robbed led them into siding first with the central powers and then with Germany.

The Soviet era

At the beginning of September 1944, the Soviet Union declared war on and invaded Bulgaria, allowing the communist-backed Bulgarian resistance organisation known as the Fatherland Front to assume power on 9 September. An armistice with the Soviet Union, Great Britain and the United States quickly followed,

and two years later, in September 1946, following a rigged referendum, Bulgaria became a people's republic, forcing the former royal family into exile.

For the next four decades Bulgaria quietly functioned as a loyal Soviet-backed satellite state. However, by the late 1980s, with Gorbachev's *perestroika* in full swing, the Bulgarian Communist Party was in disarray, enfeebled and unsure of its next move. With the outbreak of demonstrations in November 1989, the Communist Party had an internal shake-up, which saw the end of Todor Zhivkov's 27-year reign. However, seeing the way the political wind was now blowing throughout Eastern Europe, the Bulgarian Communist Party cleverly decided to give up power without a fight, and instead remodelled itself as the Bulgarian Socialist Party to contest the country's first free elections for almost 60 years. These were held in June 1990, and in their new guise the former communists did indeed find themselves immediately elected back into power.

Democratic Bulgaria

The ensuing years saw a whole string of governments come and go, as the balance of power shifted back and forth between the Bulgarian Socialist Party and their main rivals, the Union of Democratic Forces. With successive governments failing to deliver on their promises, or to prevent increasing economic hardships and surging unemployment, the Bulgarian people, impatient for change and an improvement in their lot, were unsure of which way to turn. Then, suddenly in June 2001, it seemed as though they had found their salvation, when the exiled heir to the Bulgarian throne, Tsar Simeon II, led his own political party, the National Movement Simeon II, to victory in the parliamentary elections, and formed a government backed by the minority Turkish party Movement for Rights and Freedoms.

However, once again the Bulgarian people were very quickly disappointed and became disenchanted with their leader, and not surprisingly Simeon and his party failed to gain a second term after the 2005 elections, which saw the Bulgarian Socialist Party return to power headed by Sergey Stanishev.

On 1 January 2007, the history of Bulgaria entered a new phase, with accession into the European Union. What it will actually mean for Bulgaria and the Bulgarian people is hard to predict, but for walkers it makes the country more accessible than ever before. Now is the ideal time to go there and explore this fascinating country on foot, for wherever you walk you will not only come across reminders of Bulgaria's historic past, but in your meetings with ordinary people you will gain an insight into the society as a whole, and perhaps get a glimpse of its future direction and destiny.

CULTURE

Rural Bulgaria is a land of villages and hamlets, a pastoral paradise where picturesque stone and timber cottages lie scattered on the mountainsides, tucked in amongst extensive forests and lush green meadows. Here, over the centuries, the local people have not only eked out a living from the land, but also developed a rich and important tradition of crafts, costumes and customs.

As you explore Bulgaria you will come across beautifully crafted ceramic bowls and plates, all lovingly decorated by hand, and wonderful home-spun textiles in the form of brightly coloured costumes, carpets, blankets and rugs. Undoubtedly you will hear the complex lively rhythms of traditional music, as well as hauntingly atmospheric Bulgarian folk songs, and perhaps even find yourself swept off your feet and invited to join a long snaking line of locals enjoying an energetic dance (*horo*) while dining and drinking at a local inn (*mehana*).

CUISINE

Bulgaria's historic legacy and geographical location have had a direct influence

Traditional Bulgarian cuisine

on its cuisine, which incorporates Turkish, Greek and Slavic influences, as well as numerous unique regional dishes and specialities.

Meals usually start with a salad, which depending on season, is typically made from vegetables such as tomatoes, cucumbers, roasted peppers, cabbage, onions, carrots and lettuce. Bread, potatoes and rice are the staple carbohydrates, while pulses such as lentils and beans are made into wonderful thick rich soups flavoured with herbs. Pork, beef, veal, lamb and chicken are all widely available, as well as trout in the mountains, and other varieties of fish along the coast and in northern Bulgaria.

However, the real staples of Bulgarian cuisine are dairy products, with yoghurt (*kiselo mlyako*) and particularly white cheese (*sirene*) turning up as key ingredients in many dishes. With plenty of fruit, such as cherries, strawberries, apples, pears, apricots, peaches, yellow melons and water melons, available during their seasons, traditional Bulgarian cuisine is great for vegetarians, but extremely difficult for vegans.

While slowly eating their salads, many Bulgarians also enjoy drinking a glass of *rakiya*, a brandy-type liquor made from distilled fruit such as grapes, plums or apricots. Commercial varieties normally have an alcohol content of about 40%, but home-made brews are sometimes nearer 50%. The other drink for which Bulgaria is famous, of course, is its wine. Some archaeologists believe that the territory of present day Bulgaria was the first place where vines were cultivated and wine produced. Today, one can still enjoy some traditional indigenous Bulgarian wines, such as mavrud, pamid, shevka and broad melnik, the latter reputed to have been a great favourite of Winston Churchill.

LANGUAGE

Bulgarian is a South Slavonic language written in the Cyrillic alphabet. Although more and more young people are learning and speaking English, and many signs are starting to appear in Latin letters, you will certainly find it helpful if you familiarise yourself with the Cyrillic alphabet and carry with you a small phrasebook or dictionary such as the *Chambers Bulgarian Phrasebook* (Chambers Harrap, 2007) or *Bulgarian: Lonely Planet Phrasebook* by Ronelle Alexander (Lonely Planet, 2008).

The Ministry of State Administration and Reform has recently implemented an initiative entitled 'Comprehensible Bulgarian', along with a new law on the official standardised transliteration of Bulgarian into Latin letters (http://transliteration.mdaar.government.bg/alphabet.php). This is summarised in Appendix 2, which also includes a short Bulgarian–English glossary.

MONEY

The local currency used in Bulgaria is the *lev* (plural *leva*). At the time of writing this is fixed to the euro at a rate of 1 euro to 1.95583 leva. All major currencies can be exchanged in Bulgaria, but Euros are easiest. Be aware that travellers' cheques are of little use, since they can only be exchanged in Sofia.

Most banks now have ATM machines, and these are also found at Sofia Airport. However, if you are arriving at Sofia Airport and plan on changing cash, then you should be aware that the banks located within the airport arrivals hall are usually closed at weekends, so make sure you obtain Bulgarian currency either in your home country or before going through customs into the arrivals hall.

When you are travelling around Bulgaria itself, you will find banks and ATM machines in most major towns. The latter are usually more convenient, as bank opening hours tend to be fairly restricted, normally Monday to Friday, 9am to 5pm.

Bulgaria is still a very good-value destination, although accession to the European Union and fairly highly inflation means it is no longer as cheap as it was. To aid you with budgeting, here are some current (2009) average prices:

- bus from Sofia to the mountains (€7–10)
- dormitory bed in mountain hut (€5–10)
- room in family hotel or guesthouse (€15)
- loaf of bread (€0.5)
- salad (€2)
- evening meal (€10)
- bottle of wine (€7.5)
- bottle of beer (€1).

COMMUNICATIONS

Mobile phone coverage is surprisingly good over much of Bulgaria, although – not surprisingly – connections are more difficult in the heart of the mountains. Roaming is available for most international mobile phones in Bulgaria, but the cost of calls can be very high.

If you are likely to want to use your phone a lot, it is possible to buy yourself a Bulgarian SIM card (Mtel and Globul are the most popular providers) from newsagents, bookshops and mobile phone outlets. However, you may need your phone to be unlocked to operate with a Bulgarian SIM.

Public card-operated telephones can be found in towns throughout Bulgaria and these can be used for both domestic and international calls – the latter are made by first dialling 00, then the country code. Cards for these can be purchased from street kiosks and bookshops, but bear in mind the orange Bulfon phones and blue Mobika phones each require their special cards. Telephone calls can also be made from special phone cabins in almost all post offices. Having asked for and been assigned your cabin, you make your call in the normal way, then when you have finished go and pay in cash at the counter. Although post office counter services have restricted opening hours, normally 8.30am to 5.30pm, the telephone section is usually open every day and has longer hours.

Most Bulgarian towns, and even many villages, now have internet clubs. These are mainly frequented by children playing computer games, but they do offer an opportunity to check and send e-mails, as well as communicate via Skype.

TRAVELLING TO BULGARIA

With the country's recent accession to the European Union, Bulgaria no longer seems such a remote and daunting destination. For independent travellers wishing to walk in the country, there are an ever-growing number of cheap flights available to Bulgaria. Most major European airlines now operate regular services, including British Airways (www.britishairways.com) and Bulgaria Air (www.air.bg/en), while several smaller 'no-frills' airlines such as Easyjet (www.easyjet.com) and Wizz Air (http://wizzair.com), are also steadily opening up new routes to the country.

Although there are some flights to Varna and Burgas on the Bulgarian coast, Sofia Airport (www.sofia-airport.bg) is the most convenient point of arrival for those planning on walking in the Bulgarian mountains, as all three national parks can be easily reached by public transport from the Bulgarian capital.

Entrance Formalities

To enter Bulgaria you require a full passport that must be valid for three months beyond the intended length of stay. Visas are not necessary for British or other EU citizens. Other nationalities should check current requirements. There are no statutory vaccinations needed for Bulgaria when travelling from the UK, but up-to-date tetanus and polio immunisations are recommended. Useful sources of information are:

- The Embassy of the Republic of Bulgaria in London (0207 5849400) www.bulgarianembassy-london.org
- The British Embassy in Sofia (02-9339222) http://ukinbulgaria.fco.gov.uk/en
- Foreign and Commonwealth Office Travel Advice for Bulgaria http://www.fco.gov.uk/en/travelling-and-living-overseas/travel-advice-by-country/europe/bulgaria

TRAVELLING TO THE MOUNTAINS

Useful up-to-date information about buses and trains can be obtained from the following sources: Sofia Central Bus Station (www.centralnaavtogara.bg) and Bulgarian State Railways (http://razpisanie.bdz.bg/site/search.jsp). The simplest way to reach the central bus station (*tsentralna avtogara*) or central station (*tsentralna gara*) from Sofia Airiport is to take a taxi.

Be warned there are very many unscrupulous taxi operators hanging around the airport terminals ready to whisk you off at an extortionate price! You can quite simply avoid any problems by making certain that you order a taxi from the OK Supertrans (www.oktaxi.net) booking offices, which are located in the arrivals hall of both Terminal 1 and Terminal 2. Don't be tempted simply to walk outside and try to hail an 'OK' taxi yourself – there are now at least half a dozen other taxi companies in Sofia who are using the initials 'OK' in some form or other, deliberately to catch out unsuspecting tourists.

The current tariff for genuine OK Supertrans taxis is 0.59 leva/km (6am to 10pm) and 0.70 leva/km (10pm to 6am), so the ride to the bus or train stations shouldn't cost more than 20 leva (€10). The drive normally takes about 30 minutes, but it is good to allow yourself an hour for your connection.

Crossing the River Marinkovitsa (Walk 7, Day 4)

Details of how to reach the relevant trailheads by public transport are given at the start of each walk. The following distances and timings should give you a rough idea of how long it's going to get to each place from Sofia.

Walk start	Time from Sofia	Distance from Sofia
Divchovoto (Walk 1)	3hrs 30mins	130km
Mazaneto (Walk 2)	4hrs	215km
Kalofer (Walk 3)	2hrs 30mins	165km
Lagat (Walk 4)	4hrs	210km
Rila Monastery (Walk 5)	2hrs 30mins	155km
Malyovitsa (Walk 6)	2hrs 30mins	100km
Borovets (Walk 7)	1hr 30mins	80km
Kostenets (Walk 8)	1hr 30mins	68km
Bansko (Walks 9, 10, 11 and 12)	3hrs 30mins	200km

WALKING IN BULGARIA

The origins of recreational hiking in Bulgaria can be traced back to the end of the 19th century and one man, Aleko Konstantinov, the founding father of the Bulgarian hiking movement. An author and journalist with an intense love of the mountains, he decided to awaken his compatriots' appreciation of the natural beauties that lay hitherto unnoticed around them. To do so, he organised a mass excursion on the Vitosha Mountains in the summer of 1895, exhorting the citizens of Sofia to leave behind the smoke and dust of the city and experience for themselves the peace and pleasure of the countryside. More than 400 people responded to an advertisement he placed in a newspaper, and on 28 August they set off from Dragalevtsi to climb Cherni Vrah (2290m), the highest peak in the range.

For Konstantinov the outing proved an enormous success, and over the following years more and more people took to the hills and started to explore the country, eventually opening up an extensive network of huts and routes throughout the Bulgarian mountains. Today it is estimated that there are some 40,000km of marked hiking trails spanning the length and breadth of Bulgaria.

Naturally, there are two ways of enjoying a walking holiday in Bulgaria – either independently or on an organised tour. It is hoped that this guidebook will prove useful for both categories of hiker, giving comprehensive route descriptions for those going it alone, but also plenty of supplementary information and background details for those on a guided tour. Furthermore, by providing a detailed account of the flora and fauna of the three national parks through which the trails lead, I hope that this guidebook will also be of use to the growing number of birdwatchers, botanists and other naturalists who are venturing deeper into the mountains on foot.

For those who would prefer to join an organised walking holiday in Bulgaria, there are several companies offering such tours. In the UK, Exodus Travels (www.exodus.co.uk) is at the forefront, and for many years has been operating a range of excellent walking holidays in different parts of country, including a one-week hiking trip in the Pirin and Rila national parks. The German company Kia Ora-Reisen (www.kia-ora-reisen.de) has a two-week trip that takes in all three of the national parks, while the Dutch company Go For Nature (www.gofornature.nl) offers one-week walking and wildlife tours in both the Central Balkan and Rila national parks.

For those who would prefer to join a more specialist group wildlife holiday, then the British-Bulgarian Friendship Society (www.bbfs.org.uk), Nature Trek (www.naturetrek.co.uk), Quest for Nature (www.questfornature.co.uk) and Greentours (www.greentours.co.uk) offer a selection of botanic, butterfly, dragonfly and birding tours in Bulgaria which include visits to the national parks.

Within Bulgaria itself, Balkan Trek (www.balkantrek.com) is one of the country's leading and most highly respected adventure and eco-tour operators, organising and operating a wide variety of specialist holidays for walkers, birdwatchers, botanists and all lovers of nature. They can also provide local guides and help tailor-make unique walking and wildlife tours for private groups, societies and individuals.

ACCOMMODATION

There is no shortage of accommodation in Bulgaria, with alternatives for every taste and budget. Almost all towns have at least one hotel, and many of the mountain villages have small family-run guesthouses (*semeini hoteli*) or offer B&B (*chastni kvartiri*) accommodation. Such places tend to be comfortable, welcoming, and offer delicious homemade food.

Hizha Ray is a typical mountain hut (Walk 3)

Once into the mountains themselves, you will find an extensive network of mountain huts (*hizhi*). Standards of facilities and cleanliness tend to vary quite considerably, but they all offer a bed with sheets, pillow-cases and blankets. There are also quite a number of small 'refuges' (*zasloni*), usually unmanned, that offer a roof over your head if nothing else.

Note that the walks described in this guidebook are all focused in Bulgaria's national parks, where **wild camping is forbidden**.

Most of the mountain huts are owned and operated by the Bulgarian Hiking Association (www.btsbg.org), but some are now in private hands. Usually it is possible for individual walkers simply to turn up and find a free bed in larger huts, but during August the huts can occasionally fill up. The Bulgarian Hiking Association does offer a central reservation service for its own huts, so it might be worth trying to book ahead if you are planning your hike for the peak season, and at the same time trying to order an evening meal and/or breakfast if required. You can contact them by e-mail (centerbts@btsbg.org) or by telephone (02-9801285). Normally the person answering calls to this number will be able to speak some English.

FOOD AND WATER

Some of the mountain huts do have restaurants, but whether they are functioning or actually willing or able to provide a meal is another matter. It is always best, therefore, to **carry your own food supplies** with you for a walk, and if you find a hot meal being served at a hut, to enjoy it as a bonus. The vast majority of mountain huts do have water (*voda*) available on tap, and throughout the mountains you will also come across drinking fountains (*cheshmi*), many of which flow throughout the summer, though some do dry up in August and September. In general, water from such sources is regarded as safe to drink. Those with more fragile constitutions should take with them a means of purification along with their other supplies.

Most basic food provisions (*hranitelni stoki*) can be purchased before setting off from the numerous little general stores (*hranitelni magazini*) that are found in towns and the majority of villages. However, be aware that you are extremely unlikely to find other more technical items, such as specialist clothing or other mountain equipment outside Sofia, and even there, such supplies are often extremely difficult and time-consuming to track down. The best advice is to bring everything you need from home, and be properly equipped to set off straight for the hills.

MAPS

It is also a good idea to get hold of your maps before you go. Hiking maps at varying scales, and even more varying accuracy, have been produced for most of the major mountain ranges in Bulgaria, but it is often a rather hit-and-miss affair trying to obtain them. Your best first point of contact for maps is Balkan Trek (www.balkantrek.com), as they usually maintain a stock and sell them by mail

Traditional costume from the Pirin region

Typical trail markings: winter poles and summer blazes (Walk 1)

order. Something to bear in mind is that these maps are nowhere near the same standard or accuracy of British Ordnance Survey or French IGN maps. They are not proper topographic maps, and even those at a scale of 1:50 000 should be treated as schematic, and not relied on for critical navigation with a compass.

Thankfully, the majority of hiking trails are very well marked. Summer routes are indicated with coloured blazes (usually red, green, yellow or blue) painted onto rocks or trees, while the safest winter routes are delineated by lines of tall metal poles.

One other thing to be aware of when studying Bulgarian maps is that over the years many of the peaks, passes and other important topographic points, have had their names changed, often more than once. In this guidebook I have tended

to use the most traditional names as my preferred choice, and included any other widely used title in parenthesis.

MOUNTAIN RESCUE

In the event of something going wrong, Bulgaria does have an efficient and effective mountain rescue service (*planinska spasitelna sluzhba*), which although underfunded does a great job assisting and rescuing injured walkers and climbers. Bear in mind that if you do need their help, you will be expected to pay for it in cash, and then claim the cost back later from your own travel insurance. Once in the country itself, it is possible to purchase specialist Bulgarian mountain rescue insurance from the main mountain rescue bases (www.pss.bg/base.html).

It is very reasonably priced, and not only helps to simplify administrative procedures in the event of an accident, but also helps provide much-needed extra funds direct to the mountain rescue services. The emergency telephone number for mountain rescue is 02-9632000.

ABOUT THIS GUIDEBOOK

This guidebook focuses on walking in the Rila, Pirin and Central Balkan national parks. Each of these regions has its own section, which begins with a detailed overview of its geography, climate, flora and fauna. There then follow detailed descriptions of the walks themselves, including background information and trail notes, as well as a summary of walking time, distance, ascent, descent and the highest point of the day. Be aware that the walking times given in this book refer to 'pure' walking times, without pauses for rest, meals, or to enjoy the views and abundant wildlife.

For clarity and convenience each walk is broken down into separate daily stages, each stage finishing at either a mountain hut (*hizha*), or some other suitable source of accommodation. I have also set out to provide clear and concise details of how best to reach, and indeed leave, the mountains at the start and end of every walk.

The walks in this book are challenging, and aimed at fit, experienced mountain walkers. Trails are often physically demanding, with long steep ascents and descents, often over rocks and boulders. Furthermore, most of the ridge walks require a good head for heights – especially the exposed scramble along the Koncheto crest (Walk 12). Be sure to read the route description carefully before setting out.

KEY FACTS AND FIGURES

Country name	Republic of Bulgaria
Capital	Sofia
Surface Area	110,993.6km²
Population (2007)	7,640,238
Ethnicity (2001)	Bulgarian 83.9%, Turkish 9.4%, Roma 4.7%, other 2%
Religion (2001)	Bulgarian Orthodox 82.6%, Muslim 12.2%, other 5.2%
Language	Bulgarian 84.5%, other 15.5%
Alphabet	Cyrillic
Currency	lev
Time Zone	GMT + 2hrs
National Day	3 March (Liberation from the Ottoman Turks)
International Dialing Code	+359
Mountain Rescue Telephone	02-9632000

PART 1
THE CENTRAL BALKAN
NATIONAL PARK

Cascade in valley of Kostina Reka along trail to Hizha Benkovski (Walk 1)

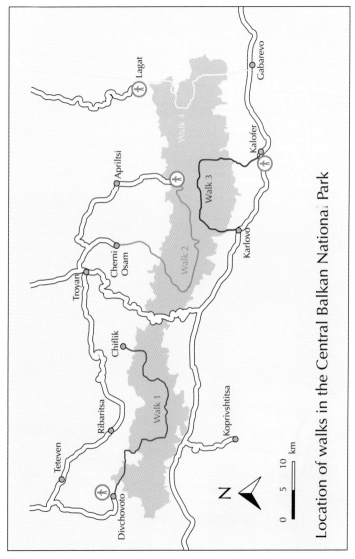

Location of walks in the Central Balkan National Park

INTRODUCTION

With stern and frowning brow, behind a cloak of cloud,
The Balkan Range arises in the distance, high and proud...
Pencho Slaveykov, *The Song of Blood* (1913)

TOPOGRAPHY

Stretching right across Bulgaria for about 520km, from the Serbian border in the west to Cape Emine on the Black Sea coast in the east, the Stara Planina (meaning 'old mountains'), or Balkan Mountains as they are often known, form the backbone of Bulgaria, both physically as well as in the nation's psyche. The range as a whole covers an area of some 11,600km², about one-tenth of Bulgaria's total land mass, and has 29 peaks that top 2000m.

The Stara Planina comprises many individual massifs, which geographers group into three distinct sections. The Western Stara Planina extends for 190km between the Belogradchik pass and Zlatitsa pass and includes four peaks over 2000m, of which Midzhar (2168m) is the highest. Beyond the Zlatitsa pass begins the Central Stara Planina. This stretches for a distance of 185km, as far as the Vratnik pass, and boasts 25 peaks over 2000m, including Botev (2376m), the highest summit of the entire range. The final section is the Eastern Stara Planina, which runs for 155km between the Vratnik pass and Cape Emine. This is the lowest section of

On the main ridge of the Stara Planina at the edge of the Tsarichina Reserve (Walk 1, Day 2)

31

the range, scarcely topping 1000m. Its highest top is Balgarka (1181m).

Founded in 1991, the Central Balkan national park, as its name suggests, is located in heart of the Central Stara Planina, covering an 85km stretch of the main ridge. It is the second largest protected territory in Bulgaria, with a total area of 71,670ha, and encompasses the three highest and wildest massifs of the range, the Zlatishko-Tetevenska Planina, Troyanska Planina and Kaloferska Planina, including 20 of the Stara Planina's 2000m peaks. About 60 per cent of the national park is covered in forest, while the rest comprises a patchwork of high-mountain meadows, pastures and rock outcrops.

There are nine nature reserves within the boundaries of the national park, accounting for about 30 per cent of its total area. These are the Boatin, Tsarichina, Kozya Stena, Steneto, Stara Reka, Dzhendema, Severen Dzhendem, Peeshtite Skali and Sokolna reserves. In 2003 the Central Balkan national park became the fourth national park in Europe to be awarded the prestigious title PAN park, recognising it as the best of Europe's wilderness. A PAN park offers real wilderness with outstanding nature and high-quality tourism facilities, well

 balanced with wilderness protection and sustainable local development. See www.panparks.org.

GEOLOGY

The name Stara Planina – 'old mountains' – is something of a misnomer, as this is in fact the youngest mountain range in the country, one of the so-called 'new fold-mountains' that were uplifted at the same time as the Alps and Himalayas as a result of tectonic pressures from the south. As a whole, the Central Balkan national park has a complex geological history and structure, and this helps to give the region its charm, and an ever-changing succession of landscapes. In places the main ridge is narrow, bristling with rugged peaks, its flanks lined with cliffs and pierced by deeply cut valleys. Elsewhere it is broad and mellow, with gently domed summits separated by shallow grassy saddles, the slopes swathed by pastures and ancient forests

Granites and crystalline schist are the dominant types of rock, most apparent in the highest parts of the range, where they burst to the surface along the backbone of the ridge like an array of jagged vertebrae. However, there are also sandstones, gneiss and marls, as well as a small but striking area of karst limestone. This forms the heart of the Steneto Reserve, where the river Cherni Osam has carved out a dramatic gorge flanked by cave-studded cliffs and precipices. Here is Raychova Dupka, which at 377m is the deepest cave in Bulgaria.

HYDROLOGY

Running right across Bulgaria from west to east, the Stara Planina forms part of one of the most important watersheds on the Balkan Peninsula, dividing rivers between the Black Sea and Aegean basins. Rivers running down north from the mountains flow towards the Danube, and hence into the Black Sea, while those that drop south feed into

Cascade along the trail to hizha Dobrila (Walk 2, Day 2)

the Maritsa and eventually out into the Aegean Sea. The main rivers of the Black Sea basin originating in the Central Balkan national park are the Vit, Osam, Vidima and Rositsa, while the most important rivers of the Aegean basin are the Topolnitsa, Stryama and Tundzha.

The Central Balkan national park has only one small lake, Saragyol ('the yellow pool'), which lies tucked in at the southern foot of the peaks Malak Kupen and Golyam Kupen in the Kaloferska Planina. However, the national park is rich in streams on both sides of the watershed. The upper reaches of these streams tend to be steep and fast flowing, frequently cascading over rocks, and in several places plunging over high precipices to form beautiful waterfalls which are known locally as *praskala* (sprinklers). These include Karlovsko Praskalo,

Babsko Praskalo, Kademliysko Praskalo and Raysko Praskalo, the latter being the highest waterfall in Bulgaria, with a drop of 125m. The majority of waterfalls are found tumbling down the southern flank of the mountains, but there is one major waterfall, Vidimsko Praskalo, which is located on the northern flank of the ridge in the Severen Dzhendem Reserve.

CLIMATE

Not surprisingly, on account of its west–east alignment across the length of Bulgaria, the Stara Planina forms a significant climatic barrier whose influence is felt throughout the country. The northern slopes of the range experience a moderate-continental climate, while the southern slopes experience a transitional-continental climate with some

Mediterranean influences. Within the Central Balkan national park itself, factors such as altitude and slope exposition also have a profound influence on the local micro-climate.

The average annual temperature within the national park is 7°C, but this figure is lower at higher altitudes, dropping to between zero and 2°C at altitudes above 2000m. Summer temperatures are often surprisingly warm, with a July average varying between 16°C and 22°C at lower altitudes, and between 7°C and 17°C at altitudes over 1000m. Winters, by contrast, tend to be very cold, with average January temperatures of between -1°C to -3°C at lower altitudes and between -3°C and -9°C above 1000m.

For walkers, one of the most important climatic characteristics that must be taken into account when venturing into the Central Balkan national park is fog. The Stara Planina as a whole is notorious for this, with the region of the national park experiencing on average some 270 days per year with foggy conditions. This figure rises to a staggering 305 days on the highest peak Botev. May and June tend to be worst in this respect, and the winter months of January and February are also fairly bad. For those in search of the sunniest and clearest weather, then August is usually the best bet.

At lower altitudes, the average annual precipitation within the Central Balkan national park varies from 550mm to 1000mm, with the southern slopes being notably drier than those to the north. At altitudes above 1000m, the average annual precipitation reaches 1200mm, and at hizha Ambaritsa on the northern flank of the range it is 1360mm, making this one of the wettest places in Bulgaria. Maximum precipitation occurs in early summer (typically during June) and is lowest in winter (usually in February).

During winter, precipitation tends to fall as snow. The first fleeting flurries can often be seen in September or October, but it is not usually until November that any dusting of snow is likely to remain permanent. The snow cover then gradually accumulates over the ensuing months, in March reaching a maximum depth of between 150cm and 220cm at altitudes above 2000m. At higher altitudes, the snow cover tends to last between 150 to 180 days, while in lower parts of the national park the duration is typically 75 to 80 days. Avalanches are a serious menace in the region during the winter months, typically in the high mountain treeless zone between 1500m and 2200m.

Another feature of the climate in the Stara Planina is the wind. The summit of Murgash (1687m) in the Western Stara Planina has the highest average annual wind speed in the country, with Botev (2376m) in the Central Balkan national park coming in a close second. In general, the average annual wind speed on the main ridge typically tops 10m/s, but it is not unusual for even stronger winds to be experienced in the region. One such wind is the *föhn*, a warm dry spring wind that whips up from the south and then gusts over the ridge, at times reaching speeds of between 18m/s and 20m/s. There is also a biting northerly wind, know as the *bora*, which blasts across the ridge and sweeps down over the southern slopes. Typical winds, however, tend to be northwesterly and of moderate strength.

Up-to-date weather information and forecasts for the Central Balkan region can be found at http://vremeto.v.bg, and then follow the link for Peak Botev.

PLANT LIFE

The flora of the Central Balkan national park is extremely rich and varied, with approximately 1900 species and sub-species of higher plants found growing in the region. These include 67 Balkan endemics, 10 Bulgarian endemics, and 10 local endemics that are unique to this part of the Stara Planina. The latter include three species of lady's mantle *Alchemilla achtarowii*, *Alchemilla jumrukczalica* and *Alchemilla asteroantha*, as well as Ognyanov's knapweed (*Centaurea ognianoffi*), Urumov's hawkweed (*Hieraceum urumoffii*), Bulgarian seseli (*Seseli bulgaricum*), two catchflies *Silene balcanica* and *Silene trojanensis*,

Central Balkan endemic flora: Balkan primrose (Priumla frondosa) (Walk 2)

the mullein *Verbascum boevae* and the beautiful little primrose *Primula frondosa*.

While walking through the Central Balkan national park you will pass through six distinct vegetation zones. Around the lowest edge of the national park, between about 550m and 900m, there are patches of oak forest. Typically these comprise Turkey oak (*Quercus cerris*), Hungarian oak (*Quercus frainetto*) or downy oak (*Quercus pubescens*), and also include secondary associations of eastern hornbeam (*Carpinus orientalis*), prickly juniper (*Juniperus oxycedrus*), hop-hornbeam (*Ostrya carpinifolia*), manna ash (*Fraxinus ornus*) and Tartar maple (*Acer tartaricum*). Many of the trees in this zone are stunted by decades of cutting and grazing, and resemble thickets rather than mature woodland.

The oak zone is found exclusively on the southern flank of the mountains. Here too, and again reaching up to altitudes of about 900m, there is also a somewhat similar oak-hornbeam zone. This is dominated by communities of the Balkan durmast oak (*Quercus dalechampii*) in conjunction with hornbeam (*Carpinus betulus*) and eastern hornbeam (*Carpinus orientalis*). Manna ash (*Fraxinus ornus*) and hop-hornbeam (*Ostrya carpinifolia*) again both also often occur in this zone, as well as silver lime (*Tilia tomentosa*), hazel (*Corylus avellana*) and blackthorn (*Prunus spinosa*).

Between about 800m and 1600m, on both sides of the ridge, it is beech forests that dominate the national park, covering over 40 per cent of its total area. Indeed, about 70 per cent of all trees growing within the national park are beech (*Fagus sylvatica*), and these have an average age of 135 years. Not only do they play a fundamental role in terms of local climate, hydrology and biodiversity, they also make up the most extensive and least degraded block of beech forest in Europe. Within this zone one also frequently finds examples of sycamore (*Acer pseudoplatanus*), hornbeam (*Carpinus betulus*), Balkan maple (*Acer heldreichii*), Norway maple (*Acer platanoides*) and silver fir (*Abies alba*), as well as the occasional common ash (*Fraxinus excelsior*), rowan (*Sorbus aucuparia*) and hazel (*Corylus avellana*).

Within the Central Balkan national park, coniferous forests are highly fragmented and do not form a distinct zone as they do in the Rila and Pirin mountains. Isolated blocks of Norway spruce (*Picea abies*) are found in and around the Boatin, Tsarichina, Stara Reka and Dzhendema reserves, with the average age of trees being 120 years. Of particular interest is the occurrence of Macedonian pine (*Pinus peuce*) within the national park. Not only is the region of the Tsarichina Reserve the sole location of this Balkan endemic species in the Stara Planina, it also represents the most extreme northerly outpost of its worldwide geographical distribution.

As the beech or coniferous forests finally give way, somewhere between 1500m and 1850m, you enter into the sub-alpine zone. Here the vegetation is dominated by low scrubby formations of Siberian juniper (*Juniperus sibirica*), whortleberry (*Vaccinium myrtillus*) and Balkan spike-heath (*Bruckenthalia spiculifolia*). In places you can also find patches of dwarf mountain pine (*Pinus mugo*), but the occurrence of this species within the Central Balkan national park is far more restricted than it is in the Rila or Pirin mountains.

WILDLIFE

Dragonflies

The dragonflies of the Central Balkan national park have not yet been studied in detail, with records only from one small region. So far nine species have been reported: robust spreadwing (*Lestes dryas*), common bluetail (*Ischnura elegans*), azure bluet (*Coenagrion puella*), blue featherleg (*Platycnemis pennipes*), blue hawker (*Aeschna cyanea*), sombre goldenring (*Cordulegaster bidentatus*), broad-bodied chaser (*Libellula depressa*), southern skimmer (*Orthetrum brunneum*) and ruddy darter (*Sympetrum sanguineum*). It is likely, however, that after further research, especially along the upper courses of some of the streams, more species will be discovered.

Butterflies

The butterflies of the Central Balkan national park have been the focus of scientific research for almost 100 years. So far almost 60 species have been recorded in the region, and it has recently been recognised as a Prime Butterfly Area. Important species found within the national park include Apollo (*Parnassius apollo*), clouded Apollo (*Parnassius mnemosyne*), large blue (*Maculinea arion*), false Eros blue (*Polyommatus eroides*), purple emperor (*Apatura iris*), eastern large heath (*Coenonympha rhodopensis*), lesser spotted fritillary (*Melitaea* trivia), bog fritillary (*Boloria eunomia*), and a variety of high mountain ringlets such as Bulgarian ringlet (*Erebia orientalis*), woodland ringlet (*Erebia medusa*), almond-eyed ringlet (*Erebia alberganus*), Nicholl's ringlet (*Erebia rhodopensis*), water ringlet (*Erebia pronoe*) and black ringlet (*Erebia melas*).

Fire salamander (*Salamandra salamandra*)

Fish

Lacking lakes or other large areas of open water, the variety of fish found within the Central Balkan national park is rather limited, with only six species recorded in the region. Most typical are the brown trout (*Salmo trutta fario*) and the minnow (*Phoxinus phoxinus*), while the miller's thumb (*Cottus gobio*), Balkan barbel (*Barbus meridionalis petenyi*) and rainbow trout (*Oncorhynchus mykiss*) have been reported in rivers at the periphery of the national park. There is also a record of brook trout (*Salvelinus fontinalis*) from the river Zavodna from the 1970s, but this species has not since been recorded in the region.

Amphibians

There are eight species of amphibian currently known to be present within the Central Balkan national park. These are fire salamander (*Salamandra salamandra*), yellow-bellied toad (*Bombina variegata*), green toad (*Epidalea viridis*), common toad (*Bufo bufo*), European tree frog (*Hyla arborea*), marsh frog (*Pelophylax ridibundus*), common frog (*Rana temporaria*) and agile frog (*Rana dalmatina*).

Reptiles

Reptiles are well represented, with 14 species having been recorded within the

national park. Most often seen by walkers are the slow worm (*Anguis fragilis*), viviparous lizard (*Zootoca vivipara*) and common wall lizard (*Podarcis muralis*). However, if you are lucky you may also spot green lizard (*Lacerta viridis*) and sand lizard (*Lacerta agilis*), and there are old records of Balkan wall lizard (*Podarcis tauricus*) and snake-eyed skink (*Ablepharus kitaibelii*) from the Stara Reka Reserve above Karlovo.

The Central Balkan national park also has seven species of snake. These include the common viper (*Vipera berus*) and nose-horned viper (*Vipera ammodytes*), as well as the grass snake (*Natrix natrix*), dice snake (*Natrix tessellata*), Aesculapian snake (*Zamenis longissimus*) and smooth snake (*Coronella austriaca*). Most interesting of all is the large whip snake (*Dolichophis caspius*), which has been recorded in both the Boatin and Stara Reka reserves.

Birds

Over 220 species of bird have been recorded within the Central Balkan national park, of which over 120 are

37

thought to breed. Not surprisingly, the region has been internationally recognised as an Important Bird Area. In the beech forests, chaffinch (*Fringilla coelebs*), robin (*Erithacus rubecula*), wren (*Troglodytes troglodytes*) and blackcap (*Sylvia atricapilla*) are dominant, with other typical species being song thrush (*Turdus philomelos*), blackbird (*Turdus merula*), chiffchaff (*Phylloscopus collybita*), coal tit (*Parus ater*), nuthatch (*Sitta europaea*), great tit (*Parus major*), treecreeper (*Certhia familiaris*), woodpigeon (*Columba palumbus*), bullfinch (*Pyrrhula pyrrhula*), marsh tit (*Parus palustris*) and blue tit (*Parus caeruleus*). Also present in the beech forests, but less often seen, are red-breasted flycatcher (*Ficedula parva*), collared flycatcher (*Ficedula albicollis*), wood warbler (*Phylloscopus sibilatrix*), white-backed woodpecker (*Dendrocopos leucotos* ssp. *lilfordi*) and lesser spotted woodpecker (*Dendrocopos minor*).

Many of the commoner beech forest species can also be seen in the spruce and mixed coniferous forests, along with firecrest (*Regulus ignicapillus*), goldcrest

White stork (*Ciconia ciconia*)

(*Regulus regulus*), mistle thrush (*Turdus viscivorus*), nutcracker (*Nucifraga caryocatactes*), common crossbill (*Loxia curvirostra*), black woodpecker (*Dryocopus martius*) and willow tit (*Parus montanus*). Then, emerging from the forest belt into the scrub of the sub-alpine zone, you typically encounter dunnock (*Prunella modularis*), whinchat (*Saxicola rubetra*), stonechat (*Saxicola torquata*), ring ouzel (*Turdus torquatus*) and linnet (*Carduelis cannabina*). In places you can also find yellow bunting (*Emberiza citrinella*), goldfinch (*Carduelis carduelis*) and red-backed shrike (*Lanius collurio*).

On meadows in the high-mountain treeless zone there are water pipit (*Anthus spinoletta*), Balkan horned lark (*Eremophila alpestris* ssp. *balcanica*) and skylark (*Alauda arvensis*), while streams are frequented by grey wagtail (*Motacilla cinerea*) and dipper (*Cinclus cinclus*), and more rocky terrain by black redstart (*Phoenicurus ochruros*), northern wheatear (*Oenanthe oenanthe*), alpine accentor (*Prunella collaris* ssp. *subalpina*), rock partridge (*Alectoris graeca*) and wallcreeper (*Tichodroma muraria*).

Finally, you should always keep an eye on the sky overhead where, as well as being able to spot red-rumped swallow (*Hirundo daurica*), crag martin (*Ptyonoprogne rupestris*), alpine swift (*Tachymarptis melba*), raven (*Corvus corax*) and alpine chough (*Pyrrhocorax graculus*), there is always a chance of glimpsing a bird of prey. Possible raptors that could be seen in the national park include common buzzard (*Buteo buteo*), long-legged buzzard (*Buteo rufinus*), golden eagle (*Aquila chrysaetos*), kestrel (*Falco tinnunculus*), saker falcon (*Falco cherrug*) and peregrine (*Falco peregrinus*), as well as the occasional foraging imperial eagle (*Aquila heliaca*).

Mammals

There have been 63 species of mammal recorded within the national park, including 22 species of bat. There are also 17 species of large mammal, of which 13 species are carnivores. Data from 1999 suggests there are about 60 brown bears (*Ursus arctos*) roaming within the national park, as well as nine packs of wolves (*Canis lupus*) totalling about 25 to 30 individuals. Deer are very important prey for the latter, and the national park is home to about 1000–1200 roe deer (*Capreolus capreolus*) and 400 red deer (*Cervus elaphus*), although unfortunately the red deer population is declining badly due to poaching. The same is true for the Balkan chamois (*Rupicapra rupicapra* ssp. *balcanica*), which now numbers less than 80 individuals. Wild boar (*Sus scrofa*), on the other hand, seem to be doing well, with a population of 350–400 animals.

WALKING OPPORTUNITIES

The Central Balkan national park has a good network of well-maintained hiking trails, including a section of the E3 European long-distance walking route, which follows the main ridge of the Stara Planina from the Serbian border in the west to Cape Emine in the east. The national park authorities have also established several interpretative routes in the region, as well as a number of special eco-trails. For accommodation within the national park, walkers also have at their disposal 21 mountain huts and several small refuges, not to mention the numerous hotels and guest-houses that are found in settlements around the foot of the mountains.

For the purposes of this guidebook, I have linked together some of what I consider to be the most interesting, picturesque and representative trails, to form four multi-stage walks each with durations of between three and four days (33 to 51km). These walks are not only beautiful mountain routes in their own rights, but the trails have been specifically chosen to take you through the nine nature reserves of the national park, thereby providing the perfect opportunity to discover more about the rich flora and fauna of the region.

MAPS

- Central Balkan National Park Tourist Map (1:50 000) – a 64 page atlas published by Directorate of the Central Balkan National Park

- Troyan Balkan (1:65 000) – published by the Bulgarian mountain rescue service

- Sredna Stara Planina (1:100 000) – published by Kartografiya EOOD

WALK 1

The Boatin, Tsarichina and Kozya Stena Reserves

42.5km/3 days

Looking out over the Kozya Stena Reserve (Day 3)

This wonderfully varied walk explores the western part of the Central Balkan National Park, taking in three nature reserves that are rich in flora and fauna. The trail starts off in the ancient beech forests of the Boatin Reserve, a rugged and steeply sloping region formed around the catchment area of the Cherni Vit, whose headstreams lie deeply cut into the northern flank of the mountains beneath Tetevenska Baba (2071m). On the second day, the route skirts the southern edge of the Tsarichina Reserve, renowned for its expansive sub-alpine pastures as well as its coniferous forests. Then, on the third day of the walk, the trail continues its spectacular course along the crest of the Stara Planina, before dropping down north to the village and spa resort of Chiflik. Much of this day you are walking in the Kozya Stena Reserve, a wild region formed around the head-streams of the Beli Osam. The reserve

is named 'the goat wall', after its most impressive peak, Kozya Stena (1670m), whose northwestern flank forms a dramatic 100m high cliff.

GETTING TO THE START

The starting point for this walk is the tiny village of Divchovoto, which lies about 24km south of Teteven. On weekdays there are three buses daily between the bus station in Teteven (0678-2557) and Divchovoto, currently departing at 11.30am, 2.30pm and 5.00pm. On Saturday there is just one bus at 12.30pm and on Sunday a single bus at 2.30pm. Teteven itself is served by seven buses each day from the *tsentralna avtogara* (central bus station) in Sofia, at 9.00am, 12.30pm, 2.30pm, 4.00pm, 5.00pm, 6.00pm and 6.40pm.

DAY 1
Divchovoto to Hizha Benkovski

Time	5hrs 15mins
Distance	15.5km
Ascent	1235m
Descent	350m
Highest point	1535m (hizha Benkovski)

The day begins with a gentle climb through the beautiful ancient beech forests of the Boatin Reserve, home to red squirrel, wild boar, red deer and roe deer, as well as carnivores such as brown bear, beech marten, pine marten, badger and wild cat. After crossing the saddle Klimashka Prevlaka, the trail leaves the reserve and drops steadily down into the valley of the Kostina Reka. There then follows a long ascent to hizha Benkovski, with the climb along the valley of the Ravna Reka being particularly steep and demanding.

From the final bus stop in the village of **Divchovoto** (650m), set off upstream along the asphalt lane signed 'Kordela 5km'. The road runs gently up the valley, and after about 20mins reaches a drinking fountain and shelter. Continue upstream, after another 10mins passing an imposing white building tucked away on the left behind a high wall. Some 15mins further on you reach the entrance to the Central Balkan National Park and the boundary of the Boatin Reserve. The trail proper begins here, breaking off left from the road into the beech forest. However, if it is late in the day and you need accommodation, you could keep on up the road for 5mins to **vila Kordela**. ▶

Vila Kordela (06905-228) is a former hunting lodge that is now open to all. It has 10 rooms, but doesn't offer food unless ordered in advance.

If you do stay the night, it is well worth venturing out after dark to listen for owls. The tawny owl, Tengmalm's owl and the Ural owl all inhabit the region.

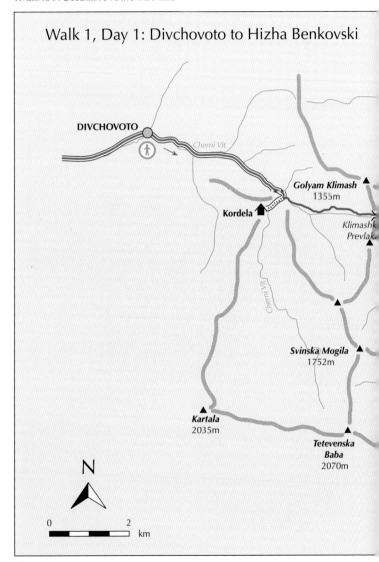

Walk 1, Day 1: Divchovoto to Hizha Benkovski

DIVCHOVOTO

Cherni Vit

Golyam Klimash
1355m

Kordela

Klimashk
Prevlak

Cherni Vit

Svinska Mogila
1752m

Kartala
2035m

Tetevenska
Baba
2070m

N

0   2
         km

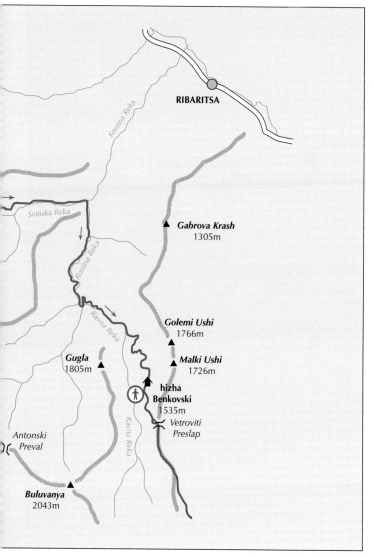

Leaving the road and entering the Boatin Reserve, follow the yellow-blazed trail across a couple of wooden footbridges before climbing up to join an old forest path marked '**Putya na Benkovski**' ('the track of Benkovski').

The old forest path takes you in the footsteps of **Georgi Benkovski** (1843–76), a famous revolutionary leader who fled this way into the mountains after the collapse of the 1876 April Rising. The surrounding forests are full of birds, particularly woodpeckers, including middle spotted woodpecker, lesser spotted woodpecker, black woodpecker and white-backed woodpecker. It is also worth keeping an eye out for red-breasted flycatcher and semi-collared flycatcher.

The path leads on upstream along the true right bank, but soon becomes overgrown with brambles. Thankfully, it's easy to skirt the obstruction, after which the trail becomes clearer once again. One important thing to be aware of is that although the official colour of the trail markings is yellow, as shown on maps, the path has been recently re-marked with green blazes, and these are what you should follow.

The trail now starts to climb, and after about 25mins you emerge into a glade that you head straight across east. On re-entering the forest, the path leads on via thinned beech wood, with small open areas covered with spike-heath, whortleberry, juniper and some thicker patches of bracken. After 20mins you emerge at a second glade, where you need to keep slightly left, heading on east back into the beech forest. Finally, after another 15mins, you emerge at the large open saddle **Klimashka Prevlaka** (1070m).

From the saddle, resume straight on east into the forest. The trail immediately bends left and starts descending via more wonderful beech forest. After 5mins you cross the right edge of a large bracken-clad clearing before re-entering the forest, where the path once again becomes broad and clear. Having passed an old broken footbridge over a dry gully, the trail then becomes steeper and stonier, eventually dropping to join a track. Follow this straight on down east, passing a small wooden hunters' refuge some 30mins from the saddle. Continue straight on downstream along the **Svinska Reka** for another 20mins to arrive at an important junction in the valley of the **Kostina Reka**.

The green blazes now continue left downstream, bound for the village of Ribaritsa, about a 1hr walk away. However, you turn right, following the track south upstream. After 10mins you pass a national park information board, then 5mins further on ignore the minor track that breaks off right. Keep on the main dirt road up the valley, here and there marked with some faint green blazes, and after 15mins pass a water fountain. Some 15mins beyond the water fountain there is a pretty cascade on the right.

A couple of minutes beyond that, the dirt road makes a sharp bend left, crossing a bridge at the confluence of the Dalboko Dere (Dyasna Reka) and Ravna Reka (Lyava Reka) to enter the national park. Although it is now possible to save 5mins by climbing straight up and cutting off a bend, the easiest thing with a large pack is simply to stay on the main track and follow it on as it hairpins up and round. The important junction comes about 15mins later, when the track bends sharp right over a second bridge. Here you finally leave the track behind for good by keeping straight

Walking through the ancient beech forests of the Boatin Reserve

on along the green-blazed trail into the forest on the true right bank of the **Ravna Reka**.

The trail, overgrown in places with brambles and nettles, follows what resembles an old track, but after a little over 10mins the stony track bends right to ford the river, and you keep left, following a faintly marked green-blazed path. This makes a very steep and stony zigzag climb, before dropping back down towards the river near a pretty forest pool after about 10mins. Some 5mins later you will come to an old, rather incongruous, drag-lift sign on a tree within a deep forest gully. Here fork up left, climbing a stony path still on the true right bank of the stream.

After 10mins fork left again, climbing so steeply through the forest that you will be forced to find hand-holds on roots and rocks. To make matters even more awkward, large trees also lie strewn across the trail, so you will need to keep a careful eye on the blazes and what little there is in the way of a path. Eventually, after about 45mins, the trail levels off and becomes clearer. Contouring on, you now get a first glimpse right through the forest towards the high mountain pastures and sheepfolds on the flank of **Gugla** (1805m). Then finally, having crossed a forest brook and with a gentle climb, you emerge after 25mins at **hizha Benkovski** (1535m).

The hut stands at the upper edge of the treeline on the southern flank of the so-called Bratanishki Ushi, the two peaks of Golemi Ushi (1766m) and Malki Ushi (1726m). The latter can be climbed in less than 30mins from the hut, and offers a fine view towards the main ridge of the Stara Planina, on which the peaks Tetevenska Baba (2070m), Buluvanya (2043m) and Bratanitsa (1992m) stand out clearly.

Hizha Benkovski is permanently manned and it is usually possible to buy a bowl of hot soup from the kitchen.

DAY 2
Hizha Benkovski to Hizha Eho

Time	5hrs 15mins
Distance	16km
Ascent	750m
Descent	650m
Highest point	2198m (Vezhen)

Today's stage involves some fine open ridge-walking along the backbone of the Stara Planina, crossing extensive high mountain pastures at the southern edge of the Tsarichina Reserve. This reserve is renowned for its rich flora, with over 600 species having been recorded here, including some rare Bulgarian endemics such as *Alchemilla catachnoa*, *Anthemis sancti-johannis* and *Viola balcanica*. The reserve takes its name from the beautiful red-flowered *Geum coccineum*, which can be seen blooming in damp places. According to legend, this flower was the favourite of a princess (*tsaritsa*) who spent much time convalescing from a serious illness in the region. In good weather the gently undulating trail is easy to follow and a true delight to walk. However, in poor visibility navigation would become difficult.

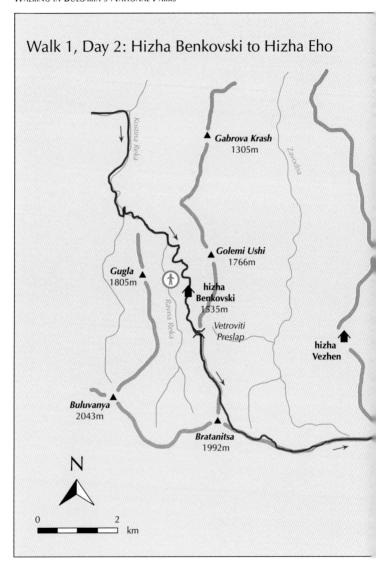

Walk 1, Day 2: Hizha Benkovski to Hizha Eho

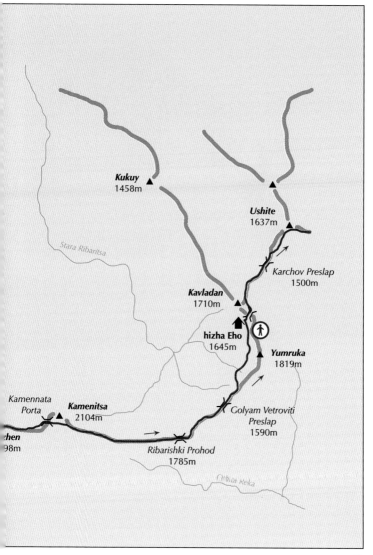

Kukuy ▲
1458m

Ushite
1637m

Karchov Preslap
1500m

Stara Ribaritsa

Kavladan ▲
1710m

hizha Eho
1645m

Yumruka ▲
1819m

Kamennata
Porta
Kamenitsa ▲
2104m

hen
98m

Golyam Vetroviti
Preslap
1590m

Ribarishki Prohod
1785m

Tilhui Reka

On the main ridge of the Stara Planina at the edge of the Tsarichina Reserve

From **hizha Benkovski** (1535m) set off into the trees. The trail crosses a shallow gully and then runs on southeast through the top edge of the beech forest. After 10mins you emerge at a junction of tracks. The right-hand track, marked in green, curves round the head of a deep valley, passing the now defunct Dom na Ovchari ('house of shepherds'), once the centre of a substantial high-mountain livestock-rearing complex. This trail climbs up and over the ridge saddle Antonski Preval, ultimately bound for the village of Anton, but you go left, following a stony track with red and green blazes that climbs to the saddle **Vetroviti Preslap** (1610m) after 10mins.

The green-blazed trail now continues on along the track, descending east into the valley of the Suvatski Dol en route for hizha Vezhen. However, you fork off right, following the winter pole-markers south up the grassy spur of Bratanashki Rid. After about 20mins the slope levels off slightly, and some 10mins later you bend away left on the red-blazed summer trail, contouring across an avalanche slope on the northeastern flank of **Bratanitsa** (1992m). After about 15mins the path becomes quite faint, and overgrown with dwarf juniper. Your best option now is simply to climb straight on up to the main ridgeback after about 5mins. There you can pick up the winter pole-markers at the start of a narrow rocky crest known as the Staroplaninsko Konche.

The trail along the crest is a delight, threading its way over and between rock outcrops as it skirts along the southern border of the Tsarichina Reserve. After 20mins you reach a col and reunite with the red-blazed summer path, following it on left to skirt north of Papa (1976m). Another 20mins then brings you to the next saddle, where you begin a steady climb.

On reaching a junction some 30mins later, ignore the grassy path that breaks off left, and simply keep straight on up the main ridge following the pole-markers. After a couple more minutes a second junction is reached, where a yellow-blazed trail cuts back left past the source of the River Zavodna bound for hizha Vezhen. You keep straight on along the red-blazed pole-marked ridge trail, and after 10mins reach a third junction. Ignore the winter trail to hizha Vezhen, which breaks off left, and keep straight on east-northeast to arrive in a little under 10mins on the summit of **Vezhen** (2198m).

> The peak itself is unimpressive – a broad grassy plateau-like dome that is often bleak and windswept – but in fine weather it does offer some **impressive views**, in particular east-northeast towards hizha Eho, which can be seen perched on the ridge between the peaks of Yumruka (1819m) and Kavladan (1710m).

From the summit, keep gently on along the ridge. You pass a memorial cross, then skirt north of a rocky peak before eventually uniting with a broad blue-blazed packhorse track. Climbing on along this, you then arrive at the saddle **Kamennata Porta** (2080m), some 20mins from the summit of Vezhen. From the saddle, the blue-blazed trail, known as the Klisurskata Pateka ('the Klisura path'), drops southeast over the ridge bound for Klisura. However, you continue straight on east along the main ridge, skirting south of **Kamenitsa** (2104m).

After about 40mins, ignore the unmarked path that crosses over the ridge, and continue along the main trail, a wonderful ridge-walk skirting a succession of rocky outcrops.

Some 15mins later you reach a col where there is a memorial below the path to the right. The trail now switches to the northern flank of the ridge and, after another 10mins, brings you to the **Ribarishki Prohod** (1735m), the highest pass in the Stara Planina.

Ignore a clear path that forks down left, and continue straight on along the red-blazed summer trail, first along the left flank of the ridge, then on the right flank, while the ridge itself gradually bends northeast. Eventually the path drops steeply, and after 15mins brings you to a col from which you then climb gently across the shoulder of the next peak. Finally, after 10mins you reach the saddle **Golyam Vetroviti Prelsap** (1570m), where you ignore the yellow-blazed summer path that cuts back on the right, bound for Klisura.

On reaching pole no. 307, you now begin a steep ascent towards the next peak, but thankfully, after only about 5mins climb, you can bend away left on the summer trail to cut more gently across the northwestern flank of the ridge. Then 10mins later, having passed above a rocky spur, you arrive at the fountain Sladkoto Izvorche (1660m). ◀

Continuing north-northeast across the western flank of **Yumruka** (1819m), loop through the top edge of the beech forest high above the valley of the Ribaritsa, to emerge after 25mins at the saddle Zhelyazna Vrata. Here, above the path, is the small stone Holy Trinity chapel and a junction – a green-blazed trail cuts back right leading to Rozino, while a yellow-blazed trail that also breaks off right leads to Hristo Danovo. You keep straight on along the ridge for another 5mins to arrive at **hizha Eho** (1645m).

Hizha Eho, which can accommodate about 40 people, is beautifully sited. It stands tucked in beneath Kavladan (1710m) at the far side of the saddle, looking west across the Tsarichina Reserve and the labyrinthine network of forested valleys that mark the headwaters of the River Ribaritsa. You will need to bring your own food and, more importantly, enough water, just in case the hut's supplies have run low.

Fill up your bottles here, as the water supply at hizha Eho is not always reliable.

DAY 3
Hizha Eho to Chiflik (via Hizha Kozya Stena)

Time	4hrs
Distance	11km
Ascent	125m
Descent	1050m
Highest point	1645m (hizha Eho)

This lovely stage continues along the main ridgeback of the Stara Planina, the trail threading its way amongst a succession of beautiful limestone outcrops at the southern edge of the Kozya Stena Reserve. These outcrops are not only a favourite haunt for Balkan chamois, but also a refuge for many rare plants, including Bulgarian endemics such as *Silene trojanensis*, *Silene balcanica*, *Seseli degenii* and *Viola balcanica*, as well as the Balkan endemics *Alchemilla gracillima*, *Sempervivum velenovsyi* and *Haberlea rhodopensis*. Eventually, beyond hizha Kozya Stena, you drop north from the main ridge towards the enticing mineral pools in the village of Chiflik.

Setting off from **hizha Eho**, cross over to the eastern side of the ridge, and follow the summer trail north-northeast as it skirts below **Kavladan** (1710m). A pole-marked route forks right down a side spur, but you stick with the red- and green-blazed path that bends left towards the main ridge, passing through the top edge of the beech forest.

After 25mins you reach the elongated ridge saddle **Karchov Prelsap** (1500m), where the green-blazed trail breaks off left leading to Ribaritsa. You continue with the red-blazed path across the bracken- and raspberry-clad glade, and begin to climb the next peak. However, you can soon bend away right from the poles on the summer trail to cut across the southeastern flank of **Ushite** (1637m).

Beyond the peak, about 1hr from hizha Eho, you reach the next col, where a blue-blazed trail breaks off left towards hizha Haydushki Pesen. Ignore this and continue on along the rocky crest of the main ridge, getting wonderful views down left into the heart of the Kozya Stena Reserve. After a

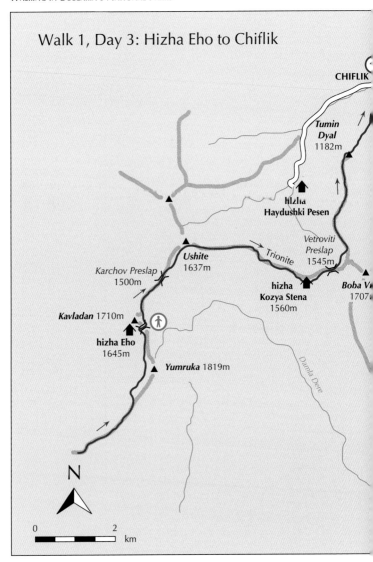

Walk 1, Day 3: Hizha Eho to Chiflik

CHIFLIK

Tumin Dyal 1182m

hizha **Haydushki Pesen**

Vetroviti Preslap 1545m

Trionite

Ushite 1637m

Karchov Preslap 1500m

hizha **Kozya Stena** 1560m

Boba V 1707

Kavladan 1710m

hizha Eho 1645m

Yumruka 1819m

Danila Dere

N

0   2   km

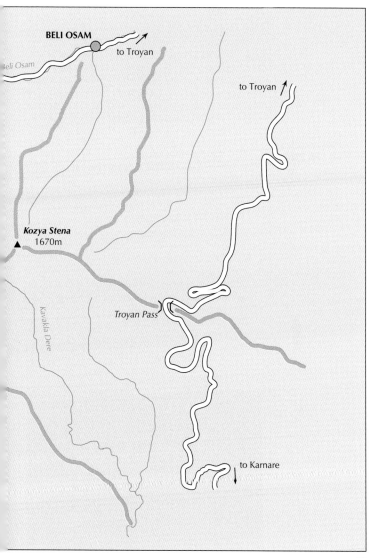

short time the summer path bends left to skirt the northern flank of the ridge, but in good weather it's fun to follow the poles along the rocky ridge crest.

After about 30mins you rejoin the summer trail and follow it on along the ridge, crisscrossing backwards and forwards between the northern and southern flanks. This beautiful jagged section of crest is often referred to as **Trionite** ('the saws'). Finally, after about 45mins, the trail loops down southeast to arrive at **hizha Kozya Stena** (1560m). ◄

A green-blazed path cuts down right just before the hut, leading southeast towards Hristo Danovo.

Hizha Kozya Stena is a large hut that can accommodate about 100 people. It is beautifully sited on the southern flank of the ridge overlooking the deeply cut valley of the Damla Dere ('valley of mist')

Continuing northeast along the main trail, you climb gently, cutting across the southern flank of Kucheto to arrive after 15mins at the saddle **Vetroviti Preslap** (1545m). ◄ The saddle is an important junction, where you now say goodbye to the red-blazed ridge route, which carries on east towards the Troyan Pass. Instead, break off left on the yellow- and green-blazed trail, which climbs gently over the northwestern shoulder of **Boba Vrah** (1707m). The path soon dips to the

At the saddle there is a memorial to Petko Dachev, a former warden of hizha Kozya Stena who perished nearby in an avalanche.

View back towards Yumruka (1819m) and Kavladan (1707m)

top edge of the beech forest, and then runs on north down the open back of the side spur Tumin Dyal.

Eventually the trail bends right into the beech forest, and after a couple of zigzags runs on down the forested crest to arrive, after about 25mins from Vetroviti Preslap, at the next important junction. Here, ignore the green-blazed trail for hizha Haydushki Pesen, which keeps straight on past a forest shelter and information boards, and instead fork down right on the yellow-blazed trail. This runs on gently north along the beech-clad ridgeback. After about 10mins ignore the forest track that breaks off right, and simply keep straight on down the ridge to emerge 10mins later at a large open saddle clearing.

Directly ahead rises **Tumin Dyal** (1182m), but by keeping left as you cross the clearing you can pick up a lovely gentle path across the western flank of the peak. Eventually the trail gets steeper, making a steady descent down the back of the ridge. After about 20mins, when the track you are following bends left, watch out for a junction that is easy to overlook. Here fork off right with the yellow-blazed path to continue a steep northerly descent.

The blazes soon disappear completely, and the trail underfoot becomes less clear beneath a deep covering of leaf litter. However, the line of descent is obvious enough – straight on north down the spur. Eventually, after about 25mins, you reach the edge of **Chiflik**, and passing right of two small bungalows, meet a track by a wire fence and villas. Here go left, to arrive after a total of about 4hrs in front of **hotel Diva** (720m).

Hotel Diva is a pleasant spa hotel (0670-60935) that makes an ideal place to end the hike and soothe away your aches and pains. The bus stop lies just below, opposite the entrance of hotel Balkan (0670-62222), but be aware that there are only a couple of buses each day that make the half-hour journey to the bus station in Troyan (0670-62172), currently at 7.00am and 1.00pm. The hotel receptionists should be able to provide up-to-date timetable information, or even order you a taxi if you need one.

WALK 2
The Severen Dzhendem, Stara Reka and Steneto Reserves

51km/4 days

On the trail to Hizha Dobrila (Day 2)

This challenging walk leads through the heart of the Central Balkan National Park, giving an opportunity to encounter the amazing variety of landscapes and habitats that the national park has to offer. The first day is short and fairly gentle, skirting the edge of the Severen Dzhendem Reserve. At times, particularly from hizha Pleven at the end of the day, there are wonderful views towards the inaccessible cliffs that bristle along the northern flank of the ridge. It is these that have given the reserve its name – 'northern hell'.

On the second day there is a long steady climb up and over the spine of the Stara Planina, before contouring on along its southern flank at the upper edge of the Stara Reka Reserve. After a short

third day, which leads through a mix of ancient forest and open ridgeback pastures, there follows a long, demanding descent through the heart of the Steneto Reserve. This is a truly wild region – a rugged limestone gorge formed by the rivers Cherni Osam and Kumanitsa. For much of the time, the 100m-high cliffs lie hidden away under a thick blanket of ancient forest, a remote and undisturbed paradise for large carnivores and many secretive woodland birds.

GETTING TO THE START

The starting point for this walk is the car park below hizha Pleven, at Mazaneto. This lies at the end of the road, 7km upstream from the Vidima district of Apriltisi. The easiest way to get there is by taxi, either from Troyan (about 50km) or from the centre of Apriltsi itself. There are a couple of local taxi companies operating in Apriltisi: ET E. Radeva (0877-577377) and Taxi Miami (0885-108282; 0897-865111). Currently there are five buses a day from the avtogara in Troyan (0670-62172) to Apriltsi, at 8.00am, 10.00am, 1.00pm, 5.10pm and 7.00pm, and one bus daily at 12.30pm from the tsentralna avtogara in Sofia.

DAY 1
Mazaneto to Hizha Pleven

Time	1hr 15mins
Distance	3km
Ascent	430m
Descent	20m
Highest point	1390m (hizha Pleven)

This short, simple opening stage leads steadily up through the forest to emerge on an open ridge spur by hizha Pleven. The trail is well used and clearly marked.

From the end of the road and parking place at **Mazaneto** set off right, across the stream, and enter the forest. After just over 5mins you reach a junction where the summer trail for hizha Pleven forks right; however, I recommend you ignore this, and keep straight on for a couple more minutes to the next junction. Here fork left over a wooden footbridge to follow the so-called Vodni Dupki eco-trail.

The path is very pleasant, climbing steadily yet not too steeply through beech forest along the along the eastern flank of a side spur known as Bazyov Dyal. After 10mins a steep path breaks off right to short-cut a bend, but you might as well ignore this and keep on the main trail, which is gentler and only a couple of minutes longer.

About 10mins later, and having passed a small concrete building, fork left on the main path, following it along the eastern flank of the spur. This brings you after 10mins to a bench and an important junction. The eco-trail now continues left, leading southwest towards the **Vodnite Dupki cave**, and if the weather is fine and you have the time, it is worth making a half-hour detour along this path to enjoy some fine views into the Severen Dzhendem Reserve.

The Vodnite Dupki cave is renowned for its **bats** and should not be entered without a permit. Seventeen species of bat have been recorded there, including the

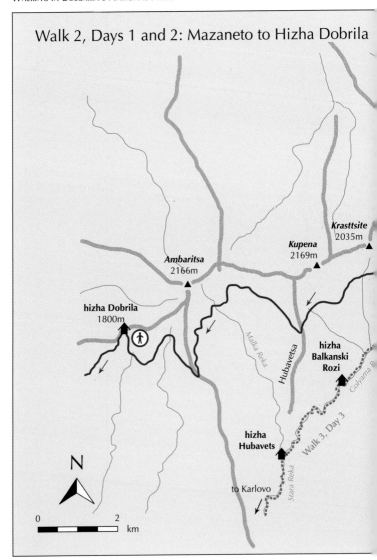

Walk 2, Days 1 and 2: Mazaneto to Hizha Dobrila

Krasttsite
2035m

Kupena
2169m

Ambaritsa
2166m

hizha Dobrila
1800m

hizha
Balkanski
Rozi

Malka Reka

Hubavetsa

Golyama R.

hizha
Hubavets

Walk 3, Day 3

Stara Reka

to Karlovo

N

0   2 km

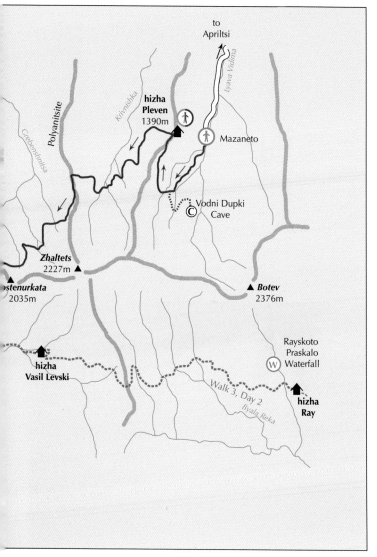

cryptic Alcathoe whiskered bat (*Myotis alcathoe*), for which this was the first known site in Bulgaria.

From the bench resume right, picking up blue blazes and then dropping down to cross a stream after 5mins. A short climb follows, leading up to a small glade that you cut across diagonally right, following a very faint path, before re-entering the forest. The trail is now clear and gentle once again, and having crossed a brook you emerge after less than 30mins on the open ridgeback just a short distance south of **hizha Pleven** (1390m).

The Severen Dzhendem Reserve and Botev (2376m)

Hizha Pleven is a large hut that actually comprises two buildings accommodating a total of about 180 people. The location is superb, offering a stunning view towards the dramatic 400m high crags of the Severen Dzhendem Reserve. Scarred by avalanche gullies, these form an imposing 10km long curtain along the northern flank of the Stara Planina, between Botev (2376m) and Yurushka Gramada (2136m).

DAY 2
Hizha Pleven to Hizha Dobrila

Time	7hrs 20mins
Distance	18.5km
Ascent	925m
Descent	530m
Highest point	1925m (col below Kostenurkata)

Despite being long and tiring, this is a wonderfully wild walk. You start the day by following a little-used trail across the northern folds of the Stara Planina, before climbing steadily up and over the main crest. There then follows an undulating walk west along the southern flank of the ridge at the upper edge of the Stara Reka Reserve, before ending the day at hizha Dobrila. The walk offers a good chance of seeing typical montane birds such as alpine chough, alpine accentor, water pipit, rock partridge, ring ouzel, nutcracker and golden eagle, as well as mammals such as Balkan chamois, wild boar, red deer and roe deer. Wolves and brown bears also roam this region.

From **hizha Pleven** (1390m) set off west following a pole-marked trail that leads past a large dairy (*mandra*). ▶ Beyond, after about 10mins, you reach an open pasture on the back of the Murgata spur. The trail now bends south-southwest across the pasture, and then enters the forest following a yellow-blazed path directly along the spur. The path is broad and stony and runs on gently through the beech forest, crossing a couple of dry gullies. After about 40mins you cross a stream that flows through an avalanche gully and loop right round a fallen tree. Some 10mins later you cross the **Krivnishka** (Krivinishka) **Reka** and a second avalanche gully, with an array of imposing rocky teeth rising up on the left.

Beyond the gully, the path crosses above a small rock outcrop and re-enters the beech forest. Then, after 15mins, you emerge at a junction. Ignore the yellow-blazed trail that leads straight on towards more sheepfolds, as this is eventually bound for the now defunct hizha Yavorova Laka in the valley of the Krayovitsa. Instead, resume left on the green-blazed

The sheepdogs at the dairy need to be treated with caution, so rather than walk directly past the buildings, it may be prudent to skirt round the sheepfolds by dropping down to cross the stream in the gully below.

Crossing a headstream of the Krivnishka Reka

trail. This follows a couple of pole-markers before bending right and running steadily on.

After 20mins you reach a second major junction located directly on the back of the open ridge spur **Polyanitsite** (Polenitsite). Again, ignore the yellow-blazed route north along the ridge towards the sheepfolds, and stick with the green-blazed trail that slants off south-south-west onto the western flank of the spur, entering the forest below two rocky peaks.

The next section of the walk is a delight, as you skirt round the northwestern flank of **Zhaltets** (2227m; Sarakaya). The path has a truly wild feel and seems to be little frequented by walkers. However, judging by the number of animal droppings, it is well used by both red deer and roe deer. Having threaded your way on across a couple of rocky spurs, you pass a water source after about 25mins. Some 5mins later you then cross a stream that forms tiny cascades, and 5mins beyond that, pass below a rock wall that is a botanist's dream, being covered in beautiful flowers such as *Geum coccineum*, *Primula frondosa*, *Pinguicula balcanica*, and *Anemone narcissiflora*.

The trail runs steadily on, and after 15mins crosses one of the headstreams of the Krayovitsa Reka, and about 5mins later passes just below an attractive cascade. Care is now needed, for just beyond you must fork up left on a very faint, green-arrowed trail, ignoring the clearer, more tempting path straight on. The true trail climbs up between small rock outcrops and then, when it disappears in the grass, you simply keep on south-southwest, slanting slightly up left towards a small eroded patch after 15mins. From there, continue slanting west, and after 5mins you reach the back of a grassy spur.

The trail continues climbing up the spur south-southeast; however, once more you need to be careful. After 5mins, at a point where a green blaze on a rock suggests that the route simply leads straight on, you actually need to fork off right on a faint path that cuts diagonally onto the western flank of the spur. Following it down for 10mins, you then cross a stream, before gradually climbing again across the northern flank of **Kostenurkata** (2035m). Finally, after 15mins, you arrive at a small col (1925m) situated on the main ridge of the Stara Planina at the northwestern foot of the peak.

From the col, drop south over the ridge, passing below some rock outcrops. The path then starts a succession of zigzags, which bring you down after about 25mins to a flat grassy area at the southern foot of **Krasttsite** (2035m). Here the path splits, with both branches ill-defined. The simplest thing is to keep straight on west-northwest for 10mins through ankle-high dwarf juniper to reach a large boulder. Then, heading south-southwest from this, past some old broken piping, you can eventually, after about 10mins, pick up the clear blue-blazed path connecting hizha Vasil Levski and hizha Dobrila.

Climbing steeply with pole-markers for 10mins, you cross the back of a spur and then continue west, passing below rock outcrops on the southern flank of **Kupena** (2169m). After 15mins you cross an eroded gully, and 10mins later pass a pretty cascade formed by the Kurnaderesi. Eventually, having skirted right of a boggy patch, and after a gentle climb, you arrive after 15mins at a pole-marker on the back of the **Hubavetsa** spur. The trail now bends sharply and runs on northwest for 30mins, to arrive at a junction. Here, ignore the green-blazed route that descends south from the main ridge towards hizha Hubavets in the valley of the Stara Reka. ▶

Be aware that there are often large flocks of sheep grazing on the high mountain pastures in this region, and that these flocks are guarded by extremely fierce dogs.

Beyond the junction keep following the blue-blazed trail as it steadily contours its way on around the avalanche-scoured southeastern flank of **Ambaritsa** (2166m; Levski). The trail crosses a succession of gullies, and after about 30mins passes a beautiful cascade formed by the **Malka Reka**, one of the main tributaries of the Stara Reka. In fact, you are now threading your way round the top edge of the Stara Reka Reserve.

The trail leads on through a belt of spruce, to emerge after about 5mins at a glade on a rocky spur. It then contours on, and after 5mins passes another smaller cascade, with a rocky avalanche gully visible below. Climbing on via another stand of spruce, you emerge 5mins later at the next spur, before contouring on and heading back into the spruce forest. After a gentle 10mins climb you reach an avalanche zone strewn with old dead trees. There then follows another 10mins of spruce forest before you emerge at a junction on the long watershed spur that drops south from Ambaritsa.

A green-blazed trail heads south from the junction, passing a small refuge tucked away in the trees at the foot of Ireltiyata (1839m), before descending along the spur to

The Stara Reka Reserve en route to hizha Dobrila

Karlovo. However, for hizha Dobrila you keep northwest on the blue-blazed trail, skirting across the western flank of Zalamtsa (1902m). The path contours steadily on, crossing a succession of small brooks, before arriving after about 30mins on a grassy ridge spur. Go straight across, northwest, for 10mins to reach a stream below an eroded slope. From here you climb up to arrive at **hizha Dobrila** (1800m) in about 10mins.

Hizha Dobrila is probably the most comfortable hut in the Stara Planina. It can accommodate about 60 people and includes a hotel-type annexe with eight en-suite centrally heated rooms. The hut restaurant also functions efficiently and offers the chance of a good hot meal.

DAY 3
Hizha Dobrila to Hizha Dermenka

Time	3hrs 10mins
Distance	11km
Ascent	185m
Descent	455m
Highest point	1713m (Gerdektepe)

The usual route between hizha Dobrila and hizha Dermenka is simply to follow the main red-blazed ridge trail, a gentle walk of just over 2hrs. However, the first part of the route described below offers a slightly longer and less used alternative that leads through some ancient coniferous forest. In general, it is a fairly gentle and straightforward walk, apart from a couple of places in the forest where the line of the path has been slightly obscured by fallen trees.

From **hizha Dobrila** (1800m) set off south on the dirt road, reaching a junction after about 20mins. Ignore the yellow-blazed trail that forks left and follow the green-blazed trail

Walk 2, Days 3 and 4: Hizha Dobrila to Cherni Osam

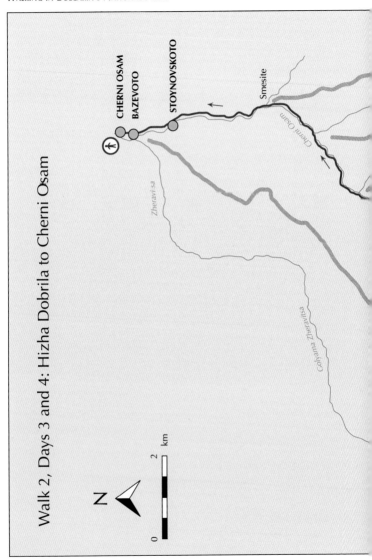

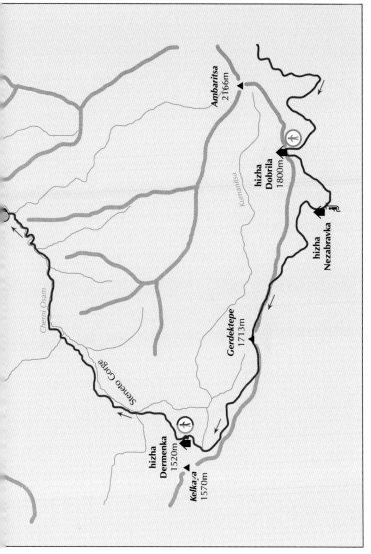

right, to arrive after 10mins at the upper station of the Sopot chairlift. From here, continue north-northwest along a track that descends gently via spruce forest. After 5mins you reach a junction where you ignore the left fork, which leads in a couple of minutes to **hizha Nezabravka**, and instead go right to follow the green-blazed trail along the main track. This bends left, climbing gradually to enter pine forest.

After 10mins the trail forks left off the track onto a forest path, crossing a couple of brooks, then a somewhat wet and boggy area overgrown with thistles and nettles, and finally, after about 10mins, some fallen trees. The trail leads gently on, passing a boulder and then crossing a glade and a couple more streams.

Some 10mins later you cross another stream and a muddy area, after which you bend left via a patch overgrown with nettles, ignoring what looks like a good path cutting back right above the stream. Then, after 5mins, there is another confusing point where fallen trees have made the continuation hard to see. Here, don't bend left into a small glade, but keep straight on west-southwest over a fallen tree.

Route-finding now becomes easier again, and after a little over 5mins you join a track and follow it left through a succession of pretty glades. Finally, after 20mins, you meet up with the main red-blazed ridge trail in the centre of a long open meadow. Follow this west across more meadows, with a small bare domed peak rising directly ahead.

After about 10mins you reach the saddle at the eastern foot of the peak, where there is a memorial plaque. The trail now climbs, steeply at first, following a stony track that cuts across the northern flank of the peak to reach the small col beyond. From here it is then a short climb to the summit of **Gerdektepe** (1713m), some 20mins from the plaque. ◀

As well as offering a fine view back towards Ambaritsa, you also get a first glimpse of hizha Dermenka over to the northwest.

Continue following the track along the ridgeback over the next minor top. The track then starts to drop, bending right onto the northeastern flank of the ridge beneath some attractive rock outcrops, before entering beautiful ancient beech forest. Here, some 30mins from Gerdektepe, you reach a junction where a green-blazed trail breaks off left, bound for the village of Iganovo. You keep straight on, descending through the forest on the main track.

Eventually, after 20mins, you emerge onto open pastures, an area known as Mecho Pole. Here, fork off right from

the track on a red-blazed path that drops down to cross a stream. Then, climbing through another belt of trees and past a water source, you arrive after 15mins at **hizha Dermenka** (1520m). As this is a short stage, you should arrive at hizha Dermenka nice and early, so it is well worth having a wander in the vicinity of the hut, perhaps climbing **Kelkaya** (1570m; Dermenka), a small peak rising just to the west.

Hizha Dermenka

The region around hizha Dermenka is excellent for **butterflies**, so keep an eye open for species such as large grizzled skipper, eastern pale clouded yellow, clouded yellow, scarce copper, Balkan copper, large blue, northern wall brown, Russian heath, eastern large heath, woodland ringlet, almond-eyed ringlet, comma, Glanville fritillary, heath fritillary, high brown fritillary, pearl-bordered fritillary and weaver's fritillary.

Hizha Dermenka is a large, well-maintained hut that can accommodate over 100 people.

DAY 4
Hizha Dermenka to Cherni Osam

Time	7hrs
Distance	18.5km
Ascent	135m
Descent	1100m
Highest point	1520m (hizha Dermenka)

This stage is unexpectedly demanding. Not only is the walk longer and more undulating than it appears on the map, it also leads through a wild, little-visited gorge where, in places, the rugged terrain and thick forests call for careful route-finding. It is not uncommon for people to go astray in this labyrinthine region. For most of the day you are walking through the heart of the Steneto Reserve, one of the most important refuges in the Stara Planina for brown bear. It is also the haunt of other elusive mammals such as wolf, wild boar, pine marten, otter and red deer. The shady beech forests have a limited flora, but in June and July it is worth looking out for the pale violet flowers of *Haberlea rhodopensis*, a Balkan endemic that grows profusely on damp rock walls in the very depths of the gorge.

From **hizha Dermenka** (1520m) set off north on a blue-blazed trail into the beech forest below the hut. After 20mins the path splits and you fork left through an overgrown patch of brambles, raspberries and wild garlic. Descending steadily, some 30mins later you bend right, running on northeast along the flank of a gully. You soon bend right again, crossing over a spur and negotiating a side stream. On descending to the main river 15mins later, keep straight on downstream on the true left bank, passing rock outcrops clad in *Haberlea rhodopensis*. Then, just over 5mins later, cross a side stream and reach a wooden barrier that has been placed here to try and prevent hikers from going astray.

The correct continuation is to follow the blazed trail, which now suddenly climbs steeply left, swiftly gaining height above the river. The ascent lasts for about 30mins, after which you dip down for 10mins to cross a dry rocky gully. Then, having climbed again slightly, contour on to reach a small spur and viewpoint after another 10mins. A short steep drop now follows, then another climb, before you contour on to arrive after 10mins at the broad flat rocky promontory known as Haydushkoto Igrishte. It is the best viewpoint along the trail, offering a rare glimpse into the depths of the **Steneto Gorge**.

The trail now cuts back sharp left, climbing west-northwest for 5mins, before beginning to drop. After less than 10mins you reach the foot of the rock wall Skoka (Hayduka), where there is a water source and memorial plaque. Continue on behind a large boulder, then a few minutes later cross a small stream. For a time you now contour on beneath outcrops, then drop gently down to a broad spur in an airy beech wood, before finally passing a big weedy glade after about 15mins.

For the next 20mins the path continues gently, making a gradual descent to reach a small spur, after which you start to drop more steeply once again. Having passed beneath a rock outcrop with *Haberlea rhodopensis*, it gets steeper

View down into the depths of the Steneto Reserve

still, dropping down the right side of a dry gully. After about 20mins you cross the gully, then undulate on, eventually passing a rock fall and crossing a rocky, boulder-strewn stream. Finally, after another 20mins, you reach a point where the trail suddenly cuts back sharp left to climb above rocks.

Care is now needed, for you reach an eroded outcrop where the trail markings temporarily disappear. The continuation is not immediately obvious, as there are several faint paths fanning out in different directions. The actual trail makes a couple of zigzags up left above the rock outcrop, at the top of which you will pick up the marked trail once again. Keep straight on over the gravelly slope, and then descend the spur east to reach a rocky viewpoint. The trail now zigzags down, dropping to the right bank of a strong side stream, then arriving after 15mins at a small metal footbridge by the confluence of the stream and the **Cherni Osam** river.

> The **confluence** is a pretty spot, with the river Cherni Osam forming several cascades and pools. The water may look tempting for a dip, but remember that this is a special water protection zone, and bathing in or polluting the river in any way is absolutley forbidden. You will see signs constantly reminding you of this as you make your way on down the valley.

Resume following the clear track downstream. It is soft and grassy to start with, but soon becomes stonier. After about 35mins you reach an information board about the Steneto Reserve, then continuing downstream, pass a couple of memorial plaques. Eventually, after 30mins and having passed a barrier and an old shack, you exit the national park.

Information board in the Steneto Reserve

Keep left on the main track, crossing a bridge to the left bank of the river, then continue straight on downstream, ignoring a track that breaks off left towards the tiny hamlet of **Neshkovtsi**. After 15mins ignore another grassy track that again forks off left, and keep on down the valley to arrive after 5mins at a large, and apparently abandoned, forestry settlement. The dirt road leads on and on downstream, to arrive after 30mins at a building and barrier at the edge of the water protection zone.

Keep straight on down the road, ignoring the green-blazed trail that forks off right beside some ruins, and after

5mins you reach the road junction at **Smesite**. To reach the village of Cherni Osam, simply keep straight on north along the main road. After 5mins you pass a small hydro-electric power station, known as VETs Cherni Osam, where there is an impressive drinking fountain with a lion-headed spout. ▶

Keeping on down the main road for 25mins, you pass the hamlet of **Stoynovskoto**, which lies across the river on the left bank, then 20mins later reach the next hamlet, **Bazevoto**. Beside the road at Bazevoto there is a pretty cottage called vila Ani (06962-575), offering rooms to rent. Finally, 10mins beyond, you reach the bus turning circle at the southern edge of Cherni Osam village. If you have timed your walk right, you should be able to catch the last bus of the day to Troyan, which departs at 7.00pm. Alternatively, you can walk on for another 10mins into the heart of **Cherni Osam** and stay the night there.

Just beyond the drinking fountain a blue-blazed trail forks off right. This leads to the hamlet of Glushka and then on towards the former monastery Zelenikovski Manastir.

There are several places to stay in the village, including Hotel Sherpa (06962-269), located right in the centre and owned and run by Radyu Minkov, a well-known local mountaineer.

Cherni Osam has two interesting **museums**, the Natural Science Museum, which displays exhibits about the fauna of the Central Stara Planina, and the Photo Archive and Ethnographic Collection of Docho Neshkov, which contains a fascinating collection of old photos illustrating both life in the village and the natural wonders of the Steneto Reserve.

GETTING BACK

When the time comes to move on, there are seven buses a day between Cherni Osam and Troyan, currently departing at 8.00am, 11.00am, 1.00pm, 2.00pm, 4.15pm, 5.00pm and 7.00pm. Be aware that the 2.00pm and 4.15pm do not operate at weekends. From the avtogara in Troyan (0670-62172) you can then get an onward connection to Sofia. Weekday buses to the capital currently depart at 6.30am, 8.20am and 10.00am, while on Saturdays they run at 6.30am and 5.10pm, and on Sundays at 1.00pm and 5.10pm.

WALK 3
The Dzhendema and Stara Reka Reserves

38km/3 days

This lovely walk is located on the southern flank of the Stara Planina, above the towns of Kalofer and Karlovo. The focus of the first two days is the Dzhendema Reserve, a large part of which is covered by ancient mixed forests of silver fir, Norway spruce, beech and oak. However, above the treeline there are extensive high mountain pastures and a spectacular backcloth of precipitous cliffs and rock outcrops. On the third day, almost the entire descent towards Karlovo is through the heart of the Stara Reka Reserve. This was established to preserve the ancient forest eco-systems that surround the River Stara Reka and its two main headstreams, the Malka Reka and Golyama Reka. Beech forests predominate, but there is also plenty of hornbeam, oak, sycamore and field maple.

GETTING TO THE START

The starting point for this walk is the small mountain town of Kalofer, which lies tucked in at the southern foot of the Stara Planina on the banks of the River Tundzha. It is a tranquil and picturesque place, boasting some fine examples of traditional National Revival Style architecture, several churches, two monasteries and three museums, including one in honour of the great revolutionary poet Hristo Botev. The Central Balkan National Park maintains a tourist information centre (03133-2988) on the main square. There are also plenty of pleasant places to stay, including the pretty family-run guesthouse Tsatsovata Kashta (03133-2483). Kalofer is only served by one direct bus each day, from the tsentralna avtogara in Sofia, at 3.00pm. However, there are six other buses running daily between Sofia and Kazanlak – at 9.00am, 10.30am, 12 noon, 2.00pm, 4.00pm and 5.30pm – which although not actually detouring into Kalofer itself, will drop passengers off at the nearest road junction, from where it is only about 20mins walk to the town centre.

View towards the Central Balkan National Park from Kalofer (Day 1)

DAY 1
Kalofer to Hizha Ray

Time	4hrs 10mins
Distance	16.5km
Ascent	1030m
Descent	220m
Highest point	1479m (Malkiya Kupen)

The walk begins gently, leading past a couple of monasteries as it makes its way out of Kalofer and on towards the very foot of the mountains. There, on entering the Central Balkan National Park, you have the option to spend an extra hour or so exploring the specially created Byala Reka eco-trail, before beginning what is a prolonged climb towards hizha Ray. Route-finding during the first half of the ascent is somewhat tricky, and would be difficult in poor visibility.

From the centre of **Kalofer** (600m) set off northwest beside the **Tundzha river**, following a sign marked 'Devechevski Manastir'. The path narrows and runs on beside the stream, but after 5mins you break off left on an asphalt lane, and then fork right along *ulitsa* Tundzha (Tundzha street). This leads on in under 5mins to *ploshtad* Rayko Daskolov (Rayko Daskolov square), where the Holy Archangel Michael church stands imposingly on the hillside above the old stone bridge. ▸

From the square, branch left uphill along ulitsa Kozloduy, from where you can then make a short detour to visit the **Presentation of the Virgin Nunnery**, which was founded in the 18th century.

The original wooden **church** was destroyed by fire and replaced by a stone building in 1862. However, this was also destroyed just 15 years later when Ottoman troops ransacked the town. Finally, in 1881, the nunnery was rebuilt, and today the church holds several interesting Russian icons, as well as some relics of Saint Mina and Saint Nektarios.

The church was originally founded in 1714, but the building you see today dates from 1869. The main altar, screened off by an unusual masonry iconostasis, preserves some fine frescoes painted in 1870–71.

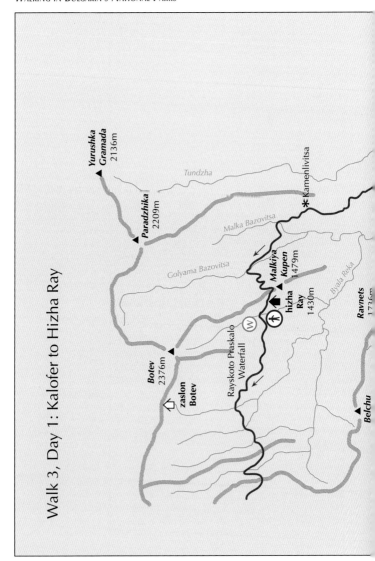

Walk 3, Day 1: Kalofer to Hizha Ray

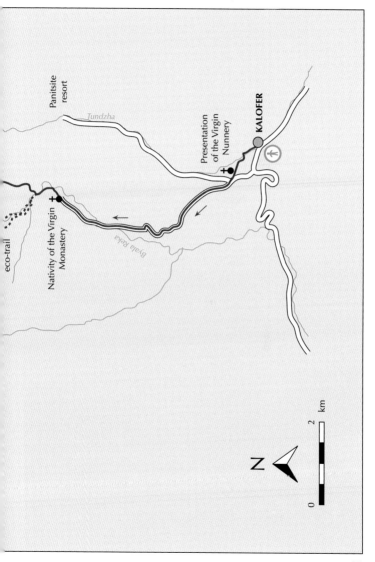

Continue up to join *ulitsa* Yumrukchal, and follow this right. After about 5mins, at the edge of town, ignore the road that heads straight on right towards the mountain resort Panitsite, and instead fork left. A couple of minutes later there is another junction, where this time you ignore a dirt track left, and instead keep straight on along the asphalt lane.

The lane leads on and on between fields, with **Botev** (2376m), the Stara Planina's highest peak, rising up directly ahead. After 15mins fork left on the old asphalt lane, ignoring the dirt road right. Less than 10mins later you reach another junction, where it is simplest to keep following the asphalt lane as it loops down left, passing above a water source that lies just below the road.

After about 5mins the asphalt temporarily ends and turns into a dirt road; however, it is very probable that this section too will actually be asphalted by the time this book is published. Some 15mins later, ignore a fork left and keep straight on along the main lane. Another left fork is ignored 5mins further on. Keeping straight on along the asphalt road, you cross a bridge and then wind up to the next junction. Here, ignore the fork right to *kafé* Sv. Panteleimon and keep straight on along the asphalt, following the road to arrive after 1hr 30mins from Kalofer at the **Nativity of the Virgin Monastery**.

View towards Botev (2376m) from the Nativity of the Virgin Monastery

The original **monastery**, founded in 1640, was destroyed at an unknown date. It was eventually rebuilt in 1819, only to be destroyed again in 1877 during the ransack of Kalofer. A couple of years later it was resurrected once more, and then given a thorough renovation in the early 1980s. Although originally founded as – and still known as – a monastery, this beautiful tranquil place is actually now home to a small community of nuns. It is possible to stay the night here in one of the guest rooms (0884-596417), but there is no food available.

To continue, follow the asphalt lane, which runs on along the right side of the monastery. This peters out after 5mins and you drop down to reach the **Byala Reka river**, at the edge of the Central Balkan National Park. ▶ Keeping straight on along the true right bank of the river for another 5mins, you then reach the start of the **Byala Reka eco-trail**.

Here, tucked away on the right, is an official camping spot called *bivak* Byala Reka.

If you have the time and energy, it is well worth making a circular loop around the Byala Reka eco-trail. With the aid of specially constructed wooden ladders and bridges, you can explore an otherwise inaccessible part of the **valley**. At certain points along the route there are information boards giving details of the flora and fauna of the national park. The path is well signed and maintained, and the full loop can easily be walked in 1hr 30mins. However, climbing up and down the succession of wooden ladders can be quite tiring if you are carrying a full pack.

For hizha Ray, continue on the green-blazed trail, which begins near the start of the eco-trail crossing a suspension footbridge over the Byala Reka. Beyond the lovely riverside meadow, you cross a gully and join up with an old track, following it on beside a shed and smallholding. Then, having passed through a wooden gate, fork right onto a path and begin a steep climb through scrubby woodland. Keep a close eye on the green blazes, as there are several animal tracks fanning out here that could lead you astray.

Eventually, after about 25mins, you emerge at a meadow. Continue straight on up, but be careful, for after a couple of minutes the line of the trail temporarily disappears. Ignore the most obvious path, which bends right across a small gully, and simply keep straight on up the grassy ridge. Although there is often little sign of a path underfoot, faint blazes reappear and help you thread your way up the hillside between a patchwork of wild rose bushes – which are used as larders and look-out posts by red-backed shrike.

After about 15mins the blazed trail begins to bend gradually right, and then 5mins later turns into a clearer grassy path. This leads in another 5mins to a water source near some old shepherds' huts (*kolibi*). This is a good place to take a break and watch the sousliks, a type of ground squirrel that has a small colony here, which can be seen scampering over the pasture and poking their heads out of the entrances to their burrows. However, the water here seems of dubious quality, so I don't recommend you drink it. There is a much cleaner source 5mins further up the hillside, just down to the left of the path. From there, it then takes another 5mins to join up with a clear track close to an old isolated stone building on the Paradzhika ridge.

After the long ascent, the next section of the walk offers a welcome, if somewhat brief, respite. Follow the track on left, passing through a barrier to enter the Dzhendema Reserve.

View over the Dzhendema Reserve along the trail to hizha Ray

After 15mins you come to a wonderful viewpoint that overlooks the deeply cut valley of the Bazovitsa. The trail, now blazed in blue, continues along the track for a short time, but then suddenly forks off left on a path that brings you down after 10mins to **Kamenlivitsa**. ▸

Here, beautifully sited on a small rocky spur, are a table and benches.

Continue by looping round the spur, then drop down to cross a wooden bridge over the **Malka Bazovitsa** before arriving after 10mins at Mechata Glava, a drinking fountain that has been decorated with a small bas-relief of a bear's head. Beyond the fountain you enter beech forest, where after 5mins you start the final climb. This is long and steep, and quite a sting in the tail at the end of the day. Having passed another water source, Cheshma Edelvaysa, you zigzag up to reach a concrete bridge over the **Golyama Bazovitsa** after 25mins.

Climbing ever on, up through another steep section of forest known as Rogacheva Gora, you eventually emerge after 30mins on a ridge col beside a marker post and bench. The spur is a lovely viewpoint, and it is worth the effort to detour up to the top of nearby **Malkiya Kupen** (1479m). From there you can survey the entire western part of the Dzhendema Reserve, before finally dropping down in about 10mins to **hizha Ray** (1430m).

The hut can accommodate about 100 people, and usually you will be served with a simple evening meal on request.

The surrounds of hizha Ray are truly wonderful, the hut being located directly beneath the **Rayski Skali** ('paradise rocks'), a bristling wall of granite crags down which thunders Rayskoto Praskalo, the highest waterfall in Bulgaria. Birdwatchers will want to scan the crags for wallcreeper, as well as enjoy observing the large colony of alpine chough that usually roosts low down and close to the hut. The Rayski Skali are also renowned for their flora. The rocks are covered in *Geranium macrorrhizum* and *Potentilla rupestris*, but with a more careful search you may also find the beautiful yellow-flowered lily *Lilium jankae*, the local endemic primrose *Primula frondosa* and the beautiful *Iris reicenbachii*.

DAY 2
Hizha Ray to Hizha Vasil Levski

Time	3hrs 15mins
Distance	8.5km
Ascent	540m
Descent	635m
Highest point	1870m (Dyuza locality)

Several steep undulations make this short stage somewhat more tiring than a cursory glance at the map may suggest, but in general it is a straightforward and highly enjoyable walk. Much of it is out in the open, and there are some fine views as you skirt along the rocky northwestern edge of the Dzhendema Reserve. There are plenty of interesting butterflies to look out for along the trail, including Balkan copper, Arran brown, large ringlet, Bulgarian ringlet, woodland ringlet, almond-eyed ringlet, common brassy ringlet, Ottoman brassy ringlet, black ringlet and bog fritillary.

From **hizha Ray** (1430m) set off northwest on the blue-blazed trail, with **Rayskoto Praskalo** directly ahead. Below the water-fall, bend left across the Praskalska Reka, ignoring the red-blazed path that climbs on upstream. Then just beyond, about 10mins from the hut, you reach a second junction beside an avalanche warning sign. Here, ignore the green-blazed path that forks off right – this is the so-called Tarzanska Pateka ('Tarzan path'), which ascends to the meteorological sta-tion on the summit of Botev. Instead, keep straight on along the blue-blazed trail, which climbs up to reach a ridge spur marked with a metal pole. The path then undulates steadily on along the southern flank of the ridge to arrive after 35mins at the so-called Spasitelna Skala ('life-saving rock'), which as well as being bedecked with several memorial plaques, also offers a water source and rudimentary shelter.

Continue on along the mountainside, crossing a strong stream below several small cascades and an impressive backcloth of jagged peaks. After about 15mins you enter a short stretch of forest, crossing a stream before emerging again after less than 10mins beside an information board about the Dzhendema Reserve. Then, 10mins further on, you cross another stream and start a very steep climb straight up onto a small spur clad with nettles and docks. Drop over the spur, then cross another stream before climbing once more past the extensive stone ruins of Bashmandra (1765m) after 15mins. ▸

Bashmandra is the site of what was once one of the biggest dairies in the Stara Planina.

After about 10mins you reach the top of the next spur, the watershed between the Byala Reka to the east and the Derindere to the west, and then dip down in another 10mins to cross the Derindere itself. A steady 15mins ascent then brings you to the important junction of trails at **Dyuza** (1870m), a small shallow saddle on the back of a side spur that connects the Ravnets massif to the south with the main ridge of the Stara Planina to the north.

Ignore the path northeast, which leads to zaslon Botev, as well as that southwest to hizha Ravnets, and keep straight on west along the blue-blazed trail. This starts a steep and occasionally rocky descent, crossing a succession of side streams, tributaries of the **Golyama Reka**. Eventually, after

The Rayski Skali and Raysko Praskalo waterfall

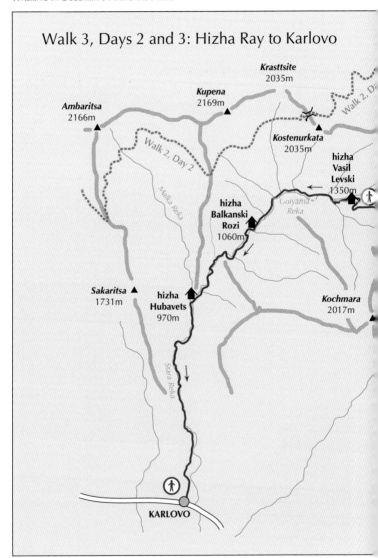

Walk 3, Days 2 and 3: Hizha Ray to Karlovo

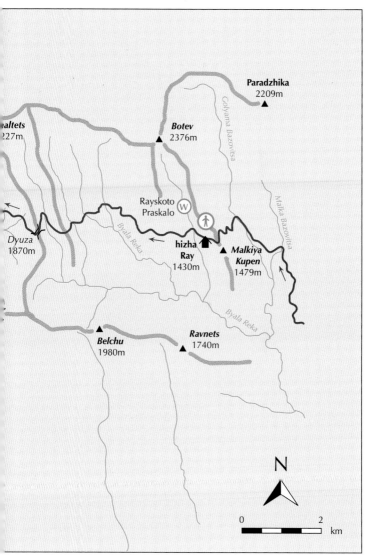

Stara Reka Reserve

about 40mins, a pole-marked winter trail breaks off right towards the main ridge, then just beyond you reach some ruined cattle-sheds at Govedarnika. The trail winds on down, soon reaching the upper edge of the treeline, then dropping steeply through the beech forest to emerge again after about 25mins at **hizha Vasil Levski** (1350m).

Hizha Vasil Levski is one of the oldest huts in the Stara Planina. It stands in a small forest glade and can accommodate about 50 people. There is water available, but it's best to bring your own supplies of food.

DAY 3
Hizha Vasil Levski to Karlovo
(via Hizha Balkanski Rozi and Hizha Hubavets)

Time	3hrs
Distance	13km
Ascent	15m
Descent	930m
Highest point	1350m (hizha Vasil Levski)

This, the final day of the walk, is a long, straightforward descent through the heart of the Stara Reka Reserve. Almost the entire stage is through forest, much of the time in immediate proximity to the river. Mammals such as brown bear, wild cat, pine marten, beech marten, roe deer and red deer roam the forest, but are rarely seen. As for birds, dipper and grey wagtail are common along the streams, and black woodpeckers are present here in very good numbers. Also, in wet weather keep an eye open for the fire salamander, as it is common in the leaf litter.

From **hizha Vasil Levski** (1350m) set off straight down into the forest below the hut. After 5mins you reach the first of many footbridges. The trail leads on and on down through the Stara Reka Reserve, crossing a succession of small forest streams. Eventually, after about 45mins, you arrive at **hizha Balkanski Rozi** (1060m), a cluster of old buildings situated on both banks of the river.

Hizha Balkanski Rozi can accommodate about 50 people, but is not always open. It was originally established in 1923 as a mountain retreat for tuberculosis and cancer sufferers.

Resuming the descent, the trail continues to switch back and forth from one riverbank to the other, passing a table and benches after about 15mins, then 5mins later the grave of a bear, which is dated 1950. Eventually, after 25mins, you reach **hizha Hubavets** (970m).

Hizha Hubavets is a large three-storey hut that can accommodate about 60 people. It is attractively located at the point where the Golyama Reka and Malka Reka unite to form the Stara Reka. Meals are sometimes available on request.

From the hut a green-blazed path climbs steeply up along the valley of the Malka Reka towards the main ridge. However, for Karlovo you continue the long descent beside the Stara Reka. After a little under 20mins you pass a water source and boulder slope, and then about 20mins further on, reach a junction where you ignore a yellow-blazed trail that forks left for hizha Ravnets.

Just beyond the junction, and having crossed over to the right bank of the **Stara Reka**, ignore the clear track that drops left towards a building, and instead follow a path that climbs up right. Having run on above the building, the path becomes clearer again, soon dropping down over rocks. After 10mins you cross a bridge to the left bank of the river, which here cascades between a chaos of giant boulders, then 5mins later cross back to the right bank once more. Soon afterwards, having passed through a rock cleft, a view opens up over Karlovo below.

The trail drops steeply down over rocks, and then makes a final short climb to surmount a rocky spur after 15mins. Continuing the descent, the path leads on down through a burnt patch of forest, then passes under a large pipe and reaches a small water source. Eventually, after 15mins, you exit the national park and keep straight on down a sandy gully path. Then, a few minutes later, having passed some villas, you reach the edge of town. Keep on down *ulitsa* Buzludzha, then fork left along *ulitsa* Parchevich. After a couple of minutes this unites with *ulitsa* Vodopad, and you go right to arrive after 20mins at *ploshtad* 20 Yuli in the heart of **Karlovo** (440m).

KARLOVO

Like Kalofer, where the walk began, Karlovo is a historic town with several sights of interest. It was the birthplace of the revolutionary hero Vasil Levski, one of the leading figures in the struggle against the Ottoman yoke. The old part of town contains several picturesque houses, as well as a couple of interesting churches, the striking, pink-coloured St Nicholas church, dating from 1847, and the Holy Virgin church, dating from 1859. There is also a very old mosque, known as the Kurşum Mosque, which dates from 1485, but unfortunately it is currently closed to visitors.

GETTING BACK

Should you wish to stay the night, there are a number of hotels and guest-houses to choose from, but for those wanting to move straight on, then Karlovo's bus and train stations lie at the southern edge of town, about 15mins walk from the centre. To reach Plovdiv, there are at least hourly buses throughout the day from the avtogara (0335-93155), while for Sofia, trains are the most convenient option, with six services per day, currently departing at 3.20am, 3.51am, 5.00am, 9.17am, 4.30pm and 6.48pm.

WALK 4

The Peeshtite Skali and Sokolna Reserves

33km/3 days

View into the valley of the Kurudere and the heart of the Sokolna Reserve (Day 2)

This beautiful walk explores the eastern part of the Central Balkan National Park, and offers a short section along the main ridge of the Stara Planina, as well as a wonderful wild traverse of the mighty Triglav massif. Not only does the walk include some of the most spectacular and rugged scenery that the national park has to offer, it also leads along the fringes of two of its most remote and fascinating nature reserves. During the first half of Day 2, you cross an array of jagged Jurassic limestone outcrops known as 'the singing rocks', which have given their name to the neighbouring Peeshtite Skali Reserve. Later in the day, while

threading your way through the southeastern part of the Triglav massif, you will enter the Sokolna Reserve. This lies on the southern flank of the Stara Planina, encompassing the dramatically craggy gorges of the rivers Kuru Dere (Sokolna) and Kyui Dere (Selska Reka).

GETTING TO THE START

The starting point for this walk is the locality Lagat, which lies tucked into the northern folds of the Stara Planina some 36km south of Sevlievo. This is the site of the Rositsa State Game Breeding Centre, not only an internationally renowned hunting reserve, but also the source of game meat for many high-class restaurants around the country. For hikers, the only place to stay is *pochiven dom* Rositsa (067305-335), but be aware that this is often fully booked at weekends. Currently there are buses from the avtogara in Sevlievo (0675-33627) to Lagat at 6.50am and 3.30pm, but only on Tuesdays, Fridays and Sundays. Alternatively, you can easily find a taxi to drive you there instead. Sevlievo itself is served by nine buses each day from the tsentralna avtogara in Sofia.

DAY 1
Lagat to Hizha Mazalat

Time	2hrs 15mins
Distance	8.5km
Ascent	1075m
Descent	75m
Highest point	1525m (hizha Mazalat)

This is a straightforward day that involves a long ascent up the northern flank of the Stara Planina. The trail starts along a dirt road, and then follows a zigzag path that climbs up through lovely beech forests before emerging into the open on the main ridge close to hizha Mazalat. Although the path is steep in places, it is mostly well graded, and not as demanding as one might expect.

From the front of *pochiven dom* Rositsa in **Lagat** (530m), set off south-southwest upstream along the main dirt road. Be aware that although marked as green on most maps, this trail has in fact been blazed in red! After 5mins, when the track splits, branch uphill left, climbing on upstream along the valley of the Rositsa into a water protection zone – just ignore the barrier and the sign telling you that entrance is forbidden!

Eventually, after less than 25mins, you reach the confluence of the **Rositsa** and **Malka Bihalshtitsa**. Here, ignore the minor track that heads straight on up the latter valley, and instead fork right along the main dirt road, still following the valley of the Rositsa at the very edge of the national park.

After 10mins the track hairpins left, but you break off right on a marked path that climbs directly up through the trees to cut off the bend. On rejoining the road a few minutes later, follow it on right until the point when, after a little over 10mins, it makes another big bend left. Here leave the forestry road behind, and head straight on along an older track marked with red/white/red blazes. This leads on upstream along the true right bank, before narrowing into a path after about 5mins. Some 5mins later, the trail then reaches the confluence of two streams. Here, fork

Walk 4: The Peeshtite Skali and Sokolna Reserves

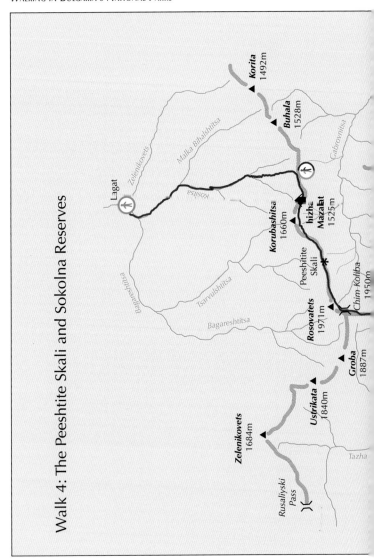

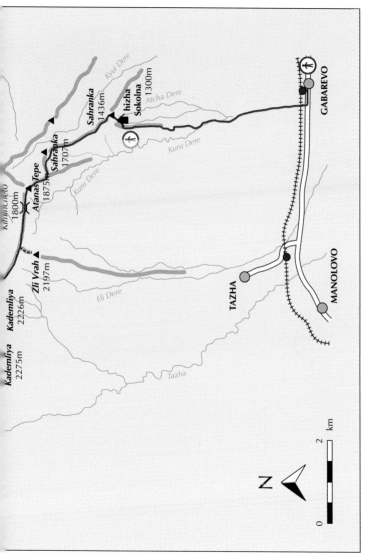

Hizha Mazalat and Korubashitsa (1660m)

right, crossing a broken wooden footbridge to reach some benches. This is a good place to pause before starting the steepest part of the climb.

Beyond the benches, the trail finally enters the national park, the path zigzagging southeast up a beech-clad spur. As you climb, you should keep a careful eye out for the blazes, as the path underfoot is not always clear, due to a thick covering of leaf litter. However, on the whole, given the altitude gained, the ascent is not difficult or unpleasant, and within 1hr you should emerge from the forest on a small grassy top situated on the main ridge of the Stara Planina to the southwest of Buhala (1528m). The hut is now close at hand to the west, so if the weather is good, this makes a lovely spot to lie back and enjoy the views and the tranquillity of the mountains.

To continue, drop gently down west-southwest from the peak to Lokvata where, having skirted a small pool, you join a track and follow it on right through the top edge of the beech forest to emerge after 15mins at **hizha Mazalat** (1525m).

Although hizha Mazalat is only a small hut, accommodating just over 30 people, it is very clean and comfortable, and a pleasant place to stay. You should, however, bring your own food.

Having secured a bed, it is well worth venturing out again to climb onto **Korubashitsa** (1660m; Valcha Glava), the rocky peak that rises up directly west of the hut. From the ridge crest there are expansive views west-northwest across the Peeshtite Skali Reserve, as well as an even more stunning panorama south across the deep defile of the Gabrovnitsa valley towards the mighty Triglav massif, your goal for the following day. While you are exploring, keep an eye open for butterflies such as Arran brown, large ringlet, Scotch argus, woodland ringlet and black ringlet.

DAY 2
Hizha Mazalat to Hizha Sokolna

Time	5hrs 10mins
Distance	16.5km
Ascent	1000m
Descent	1250m
Highest point	2226m (Malak Kademliya)

Today's stage is long and demanding, and the traverse of the Triglav massif should only be undertaken in fine, settled weather, as the terrain there is very exposed to the elements, and the path on the ground difficult to follow if visibility turns poor. However, in good weather it is a real delight, a perfect combination of expansive mountain landscapes, wonderful views and some great opportunities to observe interesting wildlife. The day begins by skirting the southern edge of the Peeshtite Skali Reserve, after which you climb over several of the highest peaks in the Triglav massif. Eventually, having crossed Zli Vrah (2197m), the trail drops down towards the Sokolna Reserve, where the limestone outcrops are home to a rich flora as well as the rare saker falcon. Make certain you carry plenty of water, as there are no reliable sources directly along the route, and sometimes the taps at hizha Sokolna run dry.

Immediately beyond **hizha Mazalat** (1525m), fork left on the red-blazed summer trail that heads west through the top edge of the beech forest on the southern flank of **Korubashitsa** (1660m; Valcha Glava). Cross a small stream and then make a steady looping climb on a narrow path to join, after about 35mins, with the pole-marked ridge route. This is then followed southwest, the path running gently on before dipping slightly into a shallow saddle after 15mins.

You now climb up and over **Peeshtite Skali**, crossing the highpoint of these dramatic crags after about 15mins. As well as enjoying the stunning view south towards the imposing northern face of the mighty Triglav massif, keep an eye open for Balkan chamois and peregrine falcon as you thread your way over the so-called Singing Rocks, which do indeed moan and whistle in strong winds.

Continue west-southwest up an expansive grassy slope, before breaking away left from the poles to follow the red-blazed summer path as it skirts across the southern flank of **Rosovatets** (1971m), high above the headstreams of the River Gabrovnitsa. Finally, after about 25mins, you reach an important junction at the plateau-like ridge saddle **Chim Koliba** (1950m).

Malak Kademliya (2226m) and Golyam Kademliya (2275m)

Saying goodbye to the main red-blazed ridge route, which continues south-southwest, bound for hizha Tazha, break off south on a grassy track marked with winter-poles and faint blue blazes. After just under 10mins you intersect a dirt road near a small pool, but keep on climbing south just to the left of the road.

Some 10mins later you meet the dirt road again at a big bend, but immediately break off and continue very steeply south following the pole-markers. The path and blue summer blazes are very faint, and in places missing, so the simplest thing is just to keep straight on up the ridge, ascending along the line of winter-poles to arrive after 20mins on the summit of **Malak Kademliya** (2226m). ▸

Resuming east-southeast, drop down to a small col, then climb to reach the summit of the next peak, **Pirgos** (2195m), after about 15mins. You then make a long, grassy 15mins drop to the Gyola saddle, before beginning a steep climb up and over the northern shoulder of **Zli Vrah** (2197m; Mazalat). The actual summit of Zli Vrah lies about 10mins south, so it is worth making a short detour to the top.

From the shoulder, drop east, following the pole-markers and enjoying the wonderful view that opens up southeast into the head of the **Kuru Dere**, towered over by a dramatic array of bristling pinnacles and crags. The path levels off temporarily as it skirts Belite Kladentsi, a region usually frequented by a large herd of semi-wild horses. ▸ Undulating on along a narrowing ridge studded with outcrops, and having skirted across the southern flank of a pair of rocky peaks, you then arrive after about 35mins from Zli Vrah at the saddle **Kimincheto** (1800m).

The saddle is an important junction. The green-blazed trail that breaks off left leads back to hizha Mazalat via the narrow side spur Tankata Ratlina and the deep valley of the Gabrovnitsa. As well as ignoring this, I also suggest you now temporarily abandon the blue-blazed summer trail for hizha Sokolna. This loops down right from the col, before skirting on southeast along the southern flank of the ridge. The problem is that almost no one uses this route, so there is little or no sign of a path on the ground, and the few blazes there are have almost faded away. Much simpler, therefore, is to keep straight on east, climbing steeply along the ridge following the line of pole-markers. The ascent is not as steep

Directly across the Groba saddle to the southwest is Golyam Kademliya (2275m; Triglav), the second highest peak in the Stara Planina.

The horses are a rare primitive autochthonic breed known as the Karakachan horse (*Karakachanski kon*).

Hiking through the Sokolna Reserve

as it first looks, and it only takes about 10mins to reach the old metal rain gauge on the summit of **Atanas Tepe** (1875m; Tanastepe).

Bending south-southeast, you run on along the ridge-back, which for a short time becomes broader again, and after less than 10mins reach a small saddle, where you will see the blue blazes of the summer path cutting away diagonally left to contour across the northern flank of the ridge. However, once again it is just as easy to keep on along the crest, so simply follow the pole-markers over the next small top. Finally, after 10mins, you drop down towards an expansive plateau-like saddle area where you can pick up the summer trail once again.

Follow this blue-blazed summer trail as it runs on across the southwestern flank of the crest, skirting below **Sahranka** (1707m). After about 10mins you loop up to the ridge crest, before switching back and forth between both flanks. It is a spectacular route, but you will need to use your hands in places, as the trail starts to drop steeply, threading its way round and over a succession of limestone rocks and crags.

Eventually, after about 15mins, you reach Portata, where you squeeze through a narrow cleft in a rock. Then, after another steep and rocky 10mins descent, you arrive at the raspberry-clad saddle Praznoto Myasto ('the empty space').

Keep straight on, crossing to the western flank of the ridge for a short time, before switching back to the eastern flank and running on through the top edge of the beech forest. After 15mins you reach the next saddle, where you ignore a path coming in on the left. Instead, keep straight on south-southeast, first along the grassy ridgeback, then along the eastern flank on a broad soft path through the beech forest.

After about 15mins you leave the trees, and passing through another large patch of raspberries, emerge on a wide, open pasture known as Paraardan. Then, picking up pole-markers once again, follow them on as they bend south, dropping steadily on and on down the back of the grassy spur to arrive after 20mins at **hizha Sokolna** (1300m).

Hizha Sokolna can accommodate about 40 people, and is beautifully situated on the southern flank of the mountains, gazing out across the Valley of Roses towards the Sredna Gora range, with the dark outline of the Rodopi Mountains rising up on the far horizon. Directly below to the southeast, the shimmering waters of the Koprinka reservoir catch the eye, occupying the valley between the towns of Pavel Banya and Kazanlak. Be aware that the hut's water supply is unreliable, so make certain you still have some with you just in case. You will also need to bring your own food.

DAY 3
Hizha Sokolna to Gabarevo

Time	2hrs 30mins
Distance	8km
Ascent	Negligible
Descent	840m
Highest point	1300m (hizha Sokolna)

A straightforward stage that takes you steadily down from the mountains into the Valley of Roses. Although quite steep, the path is comfortable and easy to follow, running down a forest-clad spur at the edge of the Sokolna Reserve. From time to time there are rocky viewpoints from where you can get a glimpse back up the Kuru Dere valley towards the higher peaks. Finally, on reaching the foot of the mountains, you have an interesting and highly contrasting finale, as you thread your way between orchards and plantations to reach the village of Gabarevo.

From **hizha Sokolna** (1300m), set off south down the steep meadow below the hut following the pole-markers. At the second pole, bend right, entering the forest and, having crossed a small gully, resume directly south down the narrow ridge spur. The path is broad, clearly marked with blue blazes, and not too steep. After 15mins you reach a viewpoint and bench, then 25mins later a second bench and memorial plaque at an open rocky area.

The path continues on down the ridge, becoming somewhat rougher, here and there bordered by lilac bushes. In less than 10mins you reach more rock outcrops and another viewpoint, after which the path begins to get steeper, making a series of zigzags. Then, 10mins later, and having passed a final viewpoint, you bend sharp left to arrive after 5mins at a table and bench in the forest.

Here a signed path breaks off left, heading for a water source known as Dyadogachovo Kladenche. However, the main blue-blazed trail keeps straight on down the spur, becoming somewhat eroded and slippery in places. After 10mins you pass a water pipe set into the trunk of a tree,

beyond which the forest floor becomes divided by several dry gullies. However, the line of the path is well marked, and after 10mins you emerge at the foot of the mountains.

Following a clear path right, pass some information boards about the Sokolna Reserve, and then set off southeast following a track across the Valley of Roses, with the Sredna Gora range rising on the horizon directly ahead. The track soon becomes a broad dirt road, passing through a patch of stunted hornbeam scrub, and after 20mins crosses an irrigation channel. A few minutes beyond there is an old pole-marker standing at a point where a track cuts back on the right; however, you keep straight on along the dirt road, bending left past a small water-pumping station after about 5mins.

The track leads on through a lavender plantation, then between a large raspberry plantation on the right and an old cherry orchard on the left. After 15mins you reach a junction by a powerful drinking fountain. Here, keep straight on south via an orchard of cherry and walnut, until after 15mins you cross a railway line and reach the main highway at the southern foot of the Stara Planina. Heading left along the road for

Forest water source on trail from Hizha Sokolna to Gabarevo

5mins brings you to a junction where a lane leads left to the small yellow building of *gara* **Gabarevo** (Gabarevo station).

GETTING BACK

Currently there are three trains each day to Karlovo, at 6.05am, 12.13pm and 8.32pm, and three to Kazanlak at 6.51am, 8.25am and 6.17pm. Alternatively, you can catch a bus to Kazanlak. To do so, keep on along the highway for a few more minutes to the next junction. Here, where a lane breaks off right to enter Gabarevo village, is the place where buses stop, currently at 7.20am, 12.15pm, 2.15pm and 4.50pm. From Kazanlak station there are three trains per day to Sofia, at 2.51am, 0.22am and 5.35pm. From Kazanlak bus station (0431-62383), currently six buses per day to the capital, at 5.30am, 6.30am, 7.00am, 8.00am, 1.00pm and 4.00pm.

PART 2
THE RILA NATIONAL PARK

Entrance to Rila National Park and Malyovitsa (2729m)

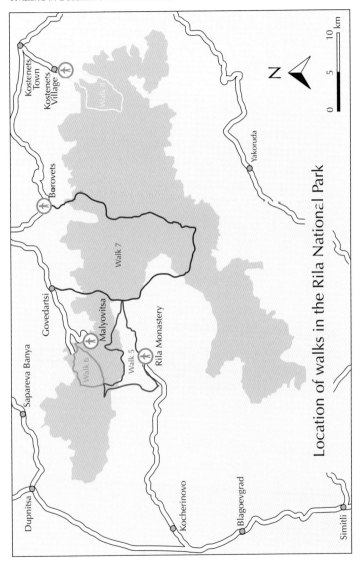

Location of walks in the Rila National Park

INTRODUCTION

Truly, Rila is the most splendid of Bulgaria's mountains. It is a large piece
of the Alps cast in the middle of the Balkan Peninsula…
Ivan Vazov, *The Great Rila Wilderness* (1892)

TOPOGRAPHY

Situated some 100km south of the Bulgarian capital Sofia, the Rila Mountains are the highest range not only in Bulgaria, but on the entire Balkan Peninsula. Their loftiest peak, Musala (2925m), rises eight metres higher than Mitikas in Greece's Olympos range, and according to some, the name Musala literally means 'nearer to God', an apt title for a peak that towers closer to the heavens than even the throne of the Olympian gods.

The Rila Mountains are bordered by the Struma valley to the west and the valley of the River Mesta to the southeast. To the north they connect with the Verila range through the Klisura saddle (1024m), to the northeast with the Sredna Gora by means of the Borovets saddle (1307m), to the west with the Rodopi Mountains via the Yundola saddle (1375m) and Avramova saddle (1295m), and to the south with the Pirin Mountains by means of the Predel pass (1142m). Within these boundaries, the Rila encompass a total

Sedemte Ezera and Haramiyata (2465m) (Walk 6, Day 2)

area of 2393.6km², and have 140 main peaks above 2000m.

The Rila can be sub-divided into four distinct massifs. The Northwestern Rila accounts for about a quarter of the range, with 34 peaks over 2000m; the Central Rila covers eight per cent and has 29 peaks over 2000m; the Eastern Rila is almost 38 per cent, with 53 peaks over 2000m; and the Southwestern Rila some 30 per cent, with just 24 peaks over 2000m.

Founded in 1992, the Rila National Park encompasses almost a third of the Rila Mountains, and extends over parts of all four massifs. With an area of 81,046ha, it is Bulgaria's largest protected territory. About two-thirds of the national park is forested, with the remaining third made up of rocky peaks and ridges, high-mountain pastures and meadows. Within the boundaries of the national park are four nature reserves – the Parangalitsa, Skakavitsa, Ibar and Central Rila – accounting for a fifth of the territory of the national park. In 2005, the Rila National Park became the seventh national park in Europe to be awarded the prestigious title of PAN park, recognising it as the best of Europe's wilderness. A PAN park offers real wilderness with outstanding nature and high-quality tourism facilities, well balanced with wilderness protection and sustainable local development. See www.panparks.org.

GEOLOGY

Part of the so-called Macedonian–Thracian Massif, the core of the Rila Mountains is composed of ancient highly crystalline metamorphic rocks, such as gneiss, schist and amphibolites, the latter with some serpentine. Later, during the Palaeozoic Era, these metamorphosed rocks were uplifted and intruded by granites. Today it is these coarse-grained granites that are the dominant rocks encountered in higher parts of the Rila Mountains, forming almost two-thirds of the area of the national park.

The uplifting of the Rila Mountains continued over a very long time scale, and at different intensities, and it was also interspersed by periods of relative calm. This alternating succession of uplift then lull is clearly seen today in four characteristic plateau-like terraces that are found at altitudes of 2600m, 2200m, 1600m and 1200m. However, it is the effects of Pleistocene glaciation that have had the most dramatic impact on the Rila's contemporary appearance and relief, forming typical relict glacial features such as pyramidal peaks, deep trough valleys, moraines, terraced cirques, and numerous shimmering lakes.

HYDROLOGY

The Rila Mountains are thought to derive their name from the ancient Thracian word *roula*, meaning 'rich in water'. It is a fitting title, for this range is one of the most important water catchment areas on the whole of the Balkan Peninsula, and also forms part of the main Balkan watershed between the Aegean Sea and the Black Sea. Two of the greatest rivers in the region, the Mesta and Maritsa, have their source here, while a third, the Struma, receives many of its major tributaries from the western part of the

On the trail above Mineralno Ezero (Walk 5, Day 3)

national park. All three of these rivers eventually flow out into the Aegean Sea. However, the Rila also give rise to the River Iskar, which at 368km is the longest river in Bulgaria. This eventually feeds north into the Danube and thence into the Black Sea. In total, some 78 per cent of the water from the national park flows into the Aegean Sea, while the rest flows into the Black Sea.

One of the most striking features of the Rila Mountains is the large number of glacial lakes that lie scattered throughout higher parts of the range. There is some disagreement about the exact number, but it is generally accepted that there are approximately 140 permanent and 30 temporary lakes. The majority of the lakes are located in a zone between 2100m and 2500m, with 28 lakes situated between 2300m and 2350m, 23 between 2350m and 2400m, and 19 between 2400m to 2450m. The highest situated is Ledenoto Ezero, at 2709m.

In general the lakes vary in length between 20m and 800m, with widths between 10m and 375m, and areas measuring between 0.1ha and 21ha. Most lakes have maximum depths of between 2m and 10m, but there are four lakes deeper than 20m, with Okoto Ezero, at 37.5m, being the deepest mountain lake in Bulgaria.

CLIMATE

The Rila National Park lies on the boundary between moderate continental and transitional Mediterranean climates. However, the actual microclimate of any

109

given part of the national park is directly influenced by altitude and terrain, in particular the exposure of slopes and the orientation of dissecting valleys.

In terms of stable weather, August is the ideal month for long-distance walking in the Rila National Park, when the region enjoys some 248 hours of sunshine. By contrast, December, January and May tend to be the cloudiest. Naturally, the amount of cloud cover experienced in the mountains has a direct impact on the temperature. The average annual temperature in the national park is fairly low, varying from 5°C to 0°C at altitudes between 1500m and 2500m. Above 2500m the average annual temperature remains below zero, and on Musala (2925m) it is only -3°C. Not surprisingly, the coldest temperature ever registered in the national park, -31.2°C, was recorded on Musala – this was during the month of February, when the average monthly temperature on the summit is a mere -11.6°C. In fact, the average monthly temperature on Musala remains below 0°C for eight months a year (from early October to late May), and typically the temperature on the peak remains below 0°C for about 270 days per year.

For most of the territory of the Rila National Park, average daily temperatures are above 0°C between mid-April and the beginning of November, and from early June to early September they usually top 10°C, with August being the warmest month. Typically, during these summer months there are about five to ten days on which the average temperature climbs above 15°C.

Altitude and slope exposition both have a marked impact on precipitation patterns within the national park. The average annual precipitation varies between 700mm and 800mm in the lowest parts of the national park, and up to almost 1200mm on Musala. On northern and western slopes, June or occasionally May tend to be the wettest months, with a secondary maximum in October, while on eastern slopes maximum precipitation tends to fall in winter. In general, the heart of the national park, being more sheltered, usually experiences less precipitation than peripheral regions. Driest months, throughout the range, are normally late summer (August and September) and mid-winter (February).

Naturally, the higher the altitude, the greater the possibility that any precipitation will fall as snow. In Borovets, at the northern foot of the Rila Mountains, snow falls on average 130 days per year, while on Musala the total is 250 days – indeed, 80 per cent of all precipitation on the peak falls as snow. In general, at altitudes between 1500m and 2500m the first snows come in mid-November, and the last falls are sometime between mid-April and mid-May. In the highest parts of the national park, above 2500m, the first flurries are usually seen in October, and the last late into June and occasionally even early July. Typically, stable snow cover lasts for between 70 and 80 days in the lowest regions of the national park, but more than 200 days at altitudes above 2000m. The covering of snow normally reaches its maximum thickness sometime towards the end of March, when in higher parts of the national park it can reach a depth of between 100cm to 240cm.

Avalanches are an ever-present danger in the Rila Mountains during winter, and are typically caused by sudden changes in temperature, and in particular by the influx of warm Mediterranean air masses from the nearby Aegean Sea. It must be remembered that the walks described in this book are only safe to be followed in snow-free summer conditions, as they lead through regions that are subject to a very high avalanche risk in winter.

Wind speeds and directions in the Rila National Park tend to be quite variable, because of the terrain, but a number of generalisations can be made. In spring, winds are often from the south, as a result of changes in the atmospheric circulation above southeastern Europe, while in summer northwesterly winds seem to be predominant. Autumn winds tend to be more unpredictable, but usually they are from the northeast or southeast. In winter, western parts of the Rila tend to experience northwesterly or southwesterly winds, while those in eastern parts are predominantly from the northeast. Autumn winds are usually lightest, with average speeds of between 1m/s to 5m/s, while winter winds are usually strongest, averaging between 3m/s to 10m/s. Typically, the strongest winter winds come from the southwest, often reaching maximums of between 25m/s to 40m/s.

Up-to-date weather information and forecasts for the Rila Mountains can be found at http://vremeto.v.bg, and then follow the link for Peak Mousala.

PLANT LIFE

Approximately 1400 species of vascular plant have been recorded in the Rila National Park, which represents some 38 per cent of Bulgaria's higher flora. The coniferous forest and sub-alpine scrub zones are the richest in species, while the alpine treeless zone has fewest. The flora of the national park is composed of typical Eurasian and Central European species, along with an interesting assortment of relict and endemic plants.

There are 31 species classed as Tertiary or pre-glacial relicts, and 104 species that are glacial relicts. The latter group contains a whole host of typical alpine flowers that are so beloved by walkers. These include: the rock-jasmine (*Androsace villosa*), narcissus-flowered anemone (*Anemone narcissiflora*), catsfoot (*Antennaria dioica*), alpine rockcress (*Arabis alpina*), two-flowered sandwort (*Arenaria biflora*), mountain thrift (*Armeria alpina*), alpine bartsia (*Bartsia*

The local endemic Rila primrose (Primula deorum)

Clockwise from top left: Dianthus microlepis; Lilium jankae; *the snowbell (*Soldanella *sp.) and crenate buttercup (*Ranunculus crenatus*)*

alpina), snow gentian (*Gentiana nivalis*), spring gentian (*Gentiana verna*), small white orchid (*Gymnadenia albida*), mountain sorrel (*Oxyria digyna*), grass of Parnassus (*Parnassia palustris*), crimson-tipped lousewort (*Pedicularis oederi*), verticillate lousewort (*Pedicularis verticillata*), birdseye primrose (*Primula farinosa*), least primrose (*Primula minima*), dwarf snowbell (*Soldanella pusilla*), tozzia (*Tozzia alpina*) and alpine speedwell (*Veronica alpina*). There are also several saxifrages: mossy saxifrage (*Saxifraga bryoides*), purple saxifrage (*Saxifraga oppositifolia*), livelong saxifrage (*Saxifraga paniculata*), retuse-leaved saxifrage (*Saxifraga retusa*) and starry saxifrage (*Saxifraga stellaris*).

The flora of the Rila National Park comprises 51 endemic species. These include 36 Balkan endemics, species that occur only on the Balkan Peninsula. Some of the most striking of these are yellow columbine (*Aquilegia aurea*), Balkan spike-heath (*Bruckenthalia spiculifolia*), Bulgarian gentian (*Gentianella bulgarica*), Bulgarian avens (*Geum bulgaricum*), and the beautiful lilac-coloured *Crocus veluchensis*, which is so typical of spring and early summer as it pushes up through melting snow patches. Another interesting plant is the Balkan butterwort (*Pinguicula balcanica*), an unusual insectivorous species whose striking violet-blue flowers have a long distinctive spur. Within the national park there are also 18 Bulgarian endemics – species that do not grow outside the borders of Bulgaria – and three local endemic species that are unique to the Rila Mountains. The latter species are the lady's mantle *Alchemilla pawlowskii*, the so-called Rila rhubarb (*Rheum rhaponticum*) and the beautiful Rila primrose (*Primula deorum*).

While walking in the Rila National Park you will encounter four distinct vegetation zones. Between about 900m and 1600m, forests of European beech (*Fagus sylvatica*) tend to predominate, often in pure stands, but occasionally mixed with Balkan durmast oak (*Quercus dalechampii*), hornbeam (*Carpinus betulus*) and aspen (*Populus tremula*) at lower altitudes, or with silver fir (*Abies alba*), Norway spruce (*Picea abies*) and black pine (*Pinus nigra*) towards the upper border of the belt. Hazel (*Coryllus avellana*) and spindle tree (*Euonymus verrucosa*) are the must typical shrubs. The ground layer of the beech forests tends to be quite limited, due to the amount of shade and the acidity of the leaf litter. The most typical plants to be seen are species such as sanicle (*Sanicula europaea*), wood-sorrel (*Oxalis acetosella*), woodruff (*Galium odoratum*), coralroot (*Cardamine bulbifera*), herb paris (*Paris quadrifolia*), ramsons (*Allium ursinum*) and rock cranesbill (*Geranium macrorrhizum*).

Between about 1600m and 2000m, the national park is covered in a thick belt of coniferous forest, just under a third of which is aged over 100 years. Norway spruce (*Picea abies*) is the dominant coniferous species, followed by Scots pine (*Pinus sylvestris*) and Macedonian pine (*Pinus peuce*), the latter tending to predominate at higher altitudes, as it tends to cope better with a harsher climate. The typical under-storey of these coniferous forests includes species such as whortleberry (*Vaccinium myrtillus*), cowberry (*Vaccinium vitis-idaea*), wood-sorrel (*Oxalis acetosella*), small cow-wheat (*Melampyrum sylvaticum*), wood spurge (*Euphorbia amygdaloides*) and rock cranesbill (*Geranium macrorrhizum*).

In places where the coniferous forests have been damaged by avalanche, silver birch (*Betula pendula*) and aspen (*Populus tremula*) are quick to establish themselves, along with flowering plants such as wood ragwort (*Senecio nemorensis*), perforate St John's wort (*Hypericum perforatum*) and rosebay willowherb (*Epilobium angustifolium*). Elsewhere, alongside brooks and rivers, green alder (*Alnus viridis*) is frequently found growing, as well as typical streamside plants such as large yellow ox-eye (*Telekia speciosa*), the Balkan endemic thistle *Cirsium appendiculatum*, the hogweed *Heracleum verticillatum*, and *Angelica pancicii*.

Between about 2000m and 2500m is the sub-alpine zone, dominated by dwarf mountain pine (*Pinus mugo*) and Siberian juniper (*Juniperus sibirica*). Here too one finds bog whortleberry (*Vaccinium uliginosum*), whortleberry (*Vaccinium myrtillus*), cowberry (*Vaccinium vitis-idaea*) and the Balkan broom (*Chamaecytisus absinthioideş*), The myrtle leaf rhododendron (*Rhododendron myrtifolium*) also occurs, but only in the Rila's eastern massif.

As mentioned earlier, the sub-alpine scrub zone is where the majority of the Rila's glacial lakes are found.

Because of the short vegetation period, low temperatures and rocky lake bottoms, most lakes in the Rila Mountains have poorly developed vegetation. However you can see the pretty white flowers of common water crowfoot (*Ranunculus aquatilis*) on some of the lakes, and both awlwort (*Subularia aquatica*) and floating bur-reed (*Sparganium angustifolium*) also occur, the latter occasionally covering large areas of the water surface.

At altitudes over 2500m you finally enter the alpine zone proper, the realm of typical arctic-alpine species. The vegetation here is dominated by grasses and sedges, although also found are dwarf shrubs such as least willow (*Salix herbacea*), bog whortleberry (*Vaccinium uliginosum*) and occasionally crowberry

(*Empetrum nigrum*). Here grow characteristic species such as mountain avens (*Dryas octopetala*), alpine avens (*Geum montanum*), crenate buttercup (*Ranunculus crenatus*) and spotted gentian (*Gentiana punctata*).

WILDLIFE

Dragonflies
So far, 16 species of dragonfly have been recorded in and around the Rila National Park: migrant spreadwing (*Lestes barbarus*), robust spreadwing (*Lestes dryas*), common spreadwing (*Lestes sponsa*), common winter damsel (*Sympecna fusca*), common bluet (*Enallagma cythigerum*), azure bluet (*Coenagrion puella*), large red damsel

Moorland hawker (Aeshna juncea)

114

(*Pyrrhosoma nymphula*), blue-eyed hawker (*Aeschna affinis*), moorland hawker (*Aeschna juncea*), bog hawker (*Aeschna subarctica*), brilliant emerald (*Somatochlora metalica*), yellow-winged darter (*Sympetrum flaveolum*), southern darter (*Sympetrum meridionale*), common darter (*Sympetrum striolatum*), moustached darter (*Sympetrum vulgatum*) and, the most recent addition to the list, small whiteface (*Leucorrhinia dubia*).

Butterflies

The Rila National Park is host to a wealth of butterflies, and has recently been recognised as a Prime Butterfly Area. Important species include: Apollo (*Parnassius apollo*), clouded Apollo (*Parnassius mnemosyne*), clouded yellow (*Colias crocea*), Berger's clouded yellow (*Colias alfacariensis*), Balkan clouded yellow (*Colias caucasica*), Balkan copper (*Lycaena candens*), sooty copper (*Lycaena tityrus*), false Eros blue (*Polyommatus eroides*), purple emperor (*Apatura iris*), Balkan fritillary (*Boloria graeca*), shepherd's fritillary (*Boloria pales*), small pearl-bordered fritillary (*Boloria selene*), lesser spotted fritillary (*Melitaea trivia*) and eastern large heath (*Coenonympha rhodopensis*). There are also a bewildering variety of ringlets, including: common brassy ringlet (*Erebia cassioides*), silky ringlet (*Erebia gorge*), black ringlet (*Erebia melas*), bright-eyed ringlet (*Erebia ocme*), dewy ringlet (*Erebia pandrose*), water ringlet (*Erebia pronoe*), Ottoman brassy ringlet (*Erebia ottomana*), Nicholl's ringlet (*Erebia rhodopensis*) and Bulgarian ringlet (*Erebia orientalis*).

Scarce swallowtail (*Iphiclides podalirius*)

Fish

Historically, a total of 12 fish species have been established in the national park, but during recent studies only five of these were recorded. The two main species occurring in the park's rivers and lakes are the brown trout (*Salmo trutta fario*) and the minnow (*Phoxinus phoxinus*). Rainbow trout (*Oncorhynchus mykiss*) and brook trout (*Salvelinus fontinalis*) have also both been introduced. The miller's thumb (*Cottus gobio*) is rare, only reported from the River Cherni Iskar.

Amphibians

The park has ten species of amphibians. The most likely species to be encountered by walkers is the grass frog (*Rana temporaria*), which lives in and around many of the glacial lakes. There is also the marsh frog (*Pelophylax ridibundus*) and European tree frog (*Hyla arborea*), as well as the yellow-bellied toad (*Bombina variegata*), common toad (*Bufo bufo*) and green toad (*Epidalea viridis*). The fire salamander (*Salamandra*

salamandra) is often encountered in forests, particularly early in the morning on wet days. Newts are harder to find, but if you are lucky, you can sometimes catch a glimpse of the rare Alpine newt (*Ichthyosaura alpestris*) in one of the glacial lakes. The southern crested newt (*Triturus karelinii*) and smooth newt (*Lissotriton vulgaris*) are also present at a number of sites in and around the park.

Reptiles

There are 10 species of reptile in the national park. The slow worm (*Anguis fragilis*) and viviparous lizard (*Zootoca vivipara*) are both frequently seen in higher parts of the range. Other lizards include sand lizard (*Lacerta agilis*), green lizard (*Lacerta viridis*), Erhard's wall lizard (*Podarcis erhardii*) and common wall lizard (*Podarcis muralis*). There are also four species of snake: smooth snake (*Coronella austriaca*), Aesculapian snake (*Zamenis longissimus*), grass snake (*Natrix natrix*) and common viper (*Vipera berus*).

Birds

Around 112 species of bird have been recorded in the Rila National Park, of which about 100 are known to have nested, although several of these are no longer present in the mountains. As you climb up through the extensive coniferous forests, birds such as chaffinch (*Fringilla coelebs*), coal tit (*Parus ater*), willow tit (*Parus montanus*), crested tit (*Parus cristatus*), goldcrest (*Regulus regulus*), firecrest (*Regulus ignicapillus*), treecreeper (*Certhia familiaris*), great spotted woodpecker (*Denrocopos major*), middle spotted

woodpecker (*Dendrocopos medius*), black woodpecker (*Dryocopus martius*), wren (*Troglodytes troglodytes*), song thrush (*Turdus philomelos*), nutcracker (*Nucifraga caryocatactes*), chaffinch (*Fringilla coelebs*), bullfinch (*Pyrrhula pyrrhula*) and common crossbill (*Loxia curvirostra*) are typically encountered. These forests also harbour rarer and more elusive species such as capercaillie (*Tetrao urogallus*), hazel grouse (*Bonasa bonasia*), white-backed woodpecker (*Dendrocopos leucotos* ssp. *lilfordi*), three-toed woodpecker (*Picoides trydactylus* ssp. *alpinus*), Tengmalm's owl (*Aegolius funereus*) and pygmy owl (*Glaucidium passerinum*).

Emerging into the sub-alpine scrub zone, you pass through often dense thickets of dwarf mountain pine inhabited by dunnock (*Prunella modularis*), ring ouzel (*Turdus torquatus*), mistle thrush (*Turdus viscivorus*), whinchat (*Saxicola rubetra*), chiffchaff (*Phylloscopus collybita*) and linnet (*Carduelis cannabina*). Here too, in more open rocky habitats, you can see black redstart (*Phoenicurus ochrurus*), rock thrush (*Monticola saxatilis*) and rock partridge (*Alectoris graeca*), while along the streams there are dippers (*Cinclus cinclus*) and grey wagtails (*Motacilla cinerea*).

Finally you reach the rugged alpine zone, where climbing amongst the highest peaks you can find Balkan horned lark (*Eremophila alpestris* ssp. *balcanica*), water pipit (*Anthus spinoletta*), alpine accentor (*Prunella collaris* ssp. *subalpina*), wallcreeper (*Tichodroma muraria*), raven (*Corvus corax*) and alpine chough (*Pyrrhocorax graculus*), as well as raptors such as the kestrel (*Falco*

*Common mole (*Talpa europaea*)*

tinnunculus) and the majestic golden eagle (*Aquila chrysaetos*).

Mammals

There are 49 species of mammal within the park, including 10 of bat. Of the 16 large mammals in the national park, 10 are carnivores. Surveys undertaken in 2000 showed that there were then about 48 brown bears (*Ursus arctos*) and 49 wolves (*Canis lupus*) in the region, as well as some 288 Balkan chamois (*Rupicapra rupicapra* ssp. *balcanica*), 262 roe deer (*Capreolus capreolus*), 50 red deer (*Cervus elaphus*) and 153 wild boar (*Sus scrofa*).

WALKING OPPORTUNITIES

The Rila National Park has a good network of well-maintained hiking trails, including sections of the E4 and E8 European long-distance walking paths. There are also a number of special botanical routes and eco-trails. For accommodation inside the national park, walkers have at their disposal 17 mountain huts and four refuges, not to mention the numerous hotels and guesthouses that are found in settlements around the periphery of the region.

For the purposes of this guidebook, I have described four walks with durations of between two and four days (22.5 to 61km). Three of these walks overlap in places and could be combined to make a variety of longer tours. The walks themselves not only lead through some of the most spectacular parts of the Rila, but have also been chosen specifically for their natural history interest, offering a perfect opportunity to discover more about the rich flora and fauna of the region.

MAPS

- Rila (1:50 000) – published by Domino
- Rila Mountains (1:55 000) – published by Kartografiya EOOD

WALK 5

*The Rila Monastery Nature Park
and Forest Reserve*

44.5km/4 days

Rila Monastery (Day 1)

This wonderful circular walk explores the northwestern fringes of the Rila National Park, focusing on the Malyovitsa massif, one of the most spectacular parts of the Rila Mountains. As well as leading through stunning mountain scenery, the walk is also rich in both cultural and natural history highlights. The trail starts and finishes at the breathtaking Rila Monastery, the largest monastery on the Balkan Peninsula and a UNESCO World Heritage Site. Lying tucked away in the depths of the Rilska Reka valley, the origins of the monastery date back to the beginning of the 10th century, when a hermit named Ivan set up home in the forests thereabouts. Gradually, a small monastic community grew up around him, and this eventually relocated to the present site in the early 14th century,

when the feudal lord Hrelyo Dragovola funded the construction of a new monastic complex. Unfortunately, the monastery was subsequently destroyed several times, the last disaster occurring in 1833, when it was burnt to the ground.

The only surviving original building is a five-storey fortified stone tower known as Hrelyo's Tower, which was built in 1335 and houses the Transfiguration of the Lord chapel, with fragments of rare 14th-century frescoes. Standing next to this is the Nativity of the Holy Virgin church, which was built in 1834–37 and then decorated in 1840–48 with an outstanding array of frescoes. Inside, beside the main iconostasis gate, is a casket containing the relics of St John of Rila, the hermit who founded the monastery and Bulgaria's patron saint.

The church and tower stand in a large cobbled courtyard, which is enclosed by four-storey wings, severe and fortress-like on the outside, gracefully arched and colonnaded within. They are pierced by two impressive gateways, the Dupnitsa Gate to the west and Samokov Gate to the northeast. Built above the latter gateway is the St John the Theologian chapel, and above that the St Simeon and St

Sabas chapel. Meanwhile, one above the other over the Dupnitsa Gate, are the St John the Precursor chapel and Archangels Michael and Gabriel chapel. Unfortunately, Hrelyo's Tower and these other smaller chapels are usually closed to visitors, but what is always open and well worth a look is the old monastic kitchen (*magarnitsa*), located on the ground floor of the northern wing.

The Rila Monastery lies at the very centre of the so-called Rilski Manastir Nature Park, a large protected territory that was established in the year 2000 when the Bulgarian government agreed to return a large core region of the Rila Mountains to its original owners, the Bulgarian Orthodox Church. It was decided that this part of the mountains, comprising ancient forests, high sub-alpine pastures and a ring of rugged peaks, be withdrawn from the Rila National Park and instead re-classified as a nature park. The flora of this region is exceptionally rich. Some 1400 species of plant have been recorded in the nature park, including six local Rila endemics, 27 Bulgarian endemics and 90 Balkan endemics. The fauna is also interesting, particularly the avifauna. So far 122 species of bird have been recorded within the boundaries of the nature park, which, remarkably, is more species than occur in the entire Rila National Park. Of these 122 species, 97 are known to have bred. The nature park is also home to 54 species of mammal, including 12 of carnivore and 15 of bat.

Located within the northern part of the Rila Monastery Nature Park, on both slopes of the Rilska Reka valley, is the Rila Monastery Forest Reserve. About half of the reserve is forested, with oak, hornbeam and beech dominating the northwestern slope of the valley, and silver fir, Norway spruce and Macedonian pine predominant on the southeastern slope. Above the treeline there are large areas of sub-alpine pasture, particularly in the northern part of the reserve, where they are towered over by a rugged, avalanche-scarred backcloth of peaks.

GETTING TO THE START

Currently there is one bus each day direct to the Rila Monastery from Sofia's western bus station avtogara Ovcha Kupel (02-9555362). This departs Sofia at 10.20am and is scheduled to arrive at the monastery about 1.00pm. There are also two direct buses a day from the avtogara in Dupnitsa (0701-51780) to the monastery, at 6.40am and 2.15pm. Most likely you will want – and/or need – to stay the night somewhere in the region before setting off on the first stage of the walk. It is possible to get a bed at the Rila Monastery (07054-2208) in one of its guest rooms, which offer simple but atmospheric accommodation, but be aware that these can fill up fast. A short walk northeast of the monastery is the refurbished hotel Tsarev Vrah (07054-2280). A little further upstream are *kamping* Bor (07054-2106) and *kamping* Zodiak (07054-2291), where you can pitch a tent or rent a wooden bungalow.

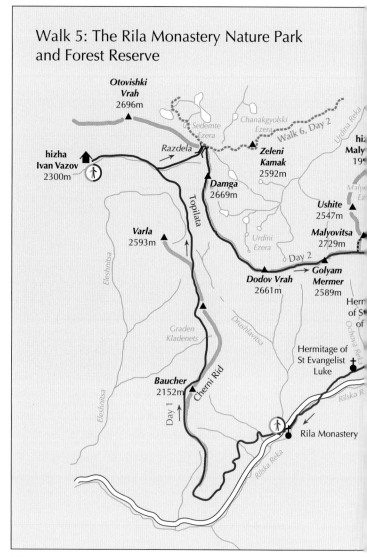

Walk 5: The Rila Monastery Nature Park and Forest Reserve

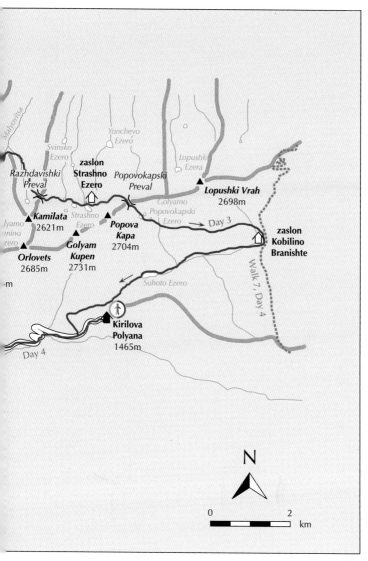

DAY 1
Rila Monastery to Hizha Ivan Vazov

Time	4hrs
Distance	12.5km
Ascent	1360m
Descent	205m
Highest point	2465m (Koncheto)

Climbing out of the Rilska Reka valley, the trail snakes its way up via the Rila Monastery Forest Reserve, passing through ancient beech forests as well as a stand of the unique local endemic Rila oak (*Quercus protoroburoides*). Emerging from the forest, there then follows a prolonged climb up the open pastures of Cherni Rid, being rewarded for your efforts with far-reaching views and the chance of seeing some interesting butterflies, such as the large grizzled skipper, clouded yellow, eastern large heath, Nicholl's ringlet, common brassy ringlet, Ottoman brassy ringlet and Balkan fritillary. You may also catch sight of the pair of golden eagles that inhabit this region.

From the car park in front of the western gate of the **Rila Monastery** (1147m), set off on the clearly signed path.

After less than 100m you can make a short detour right to visit the grave of **James Bourchier** (1850–1920). Working as the main Balkan correspondent for *The Times*, he wrote powerfully in support of the Bulgarian cause at a time when the future of Bulgaria was being decided by other international powers.

The main trail winds pleasantly on through ancient beech forests, part of the Rila Monastery Forest Reserve. After about 20mins you cross a small stream known as the Kalugerska Reka, and a short distance beyond, fork up right. Some 10mins later the path becomes rather overgrown with nettles and shrubs, but after 5mins you are through this patch. Climbing on steadily through the forest for another 15mins, you then reach an old oak tree. This is situated on the back of a spur from which there is a fine view into the valley below.

Climbing steeply on up the spur, after 15mins you emerge from the forest at the first winter pole-marker. There now begins a prolonged and fairly steep climb up the open ridge of **Cherni Rid** (Karabunar), through lush grass and thick dwarf shrubs of Balkan broom (*Chamaecytisus absinthioides*).

> The Balkan broom is the larval host plant for the distinct Bulgarian sub-species of the beautiful little butterfly known as **Idas blue**, so it well worth keeping an eye open in case you can pick one out from the numerous other butterflies seen flying along this section of the trail. The butterflies, coupled with the lovely views, help to take the mind off what is, in summer, a very hot and tiring climb.

Eventually, after 25mins, the spreading branches of a small stand of old Scots pine make a good shady place to pause and take in the fine panorama. Resuming the climb, after about 10mins the summer trail slants away to the left-hand flank of the ridge, skirting across the western slope of **Baucher** (2152m), a peak named after James Bourchier. About 20mins later you pass through a belt of Norway spruce marking the very upper limit of the treeline, and then arrive 5mins further on at an open ridge terrace on which is the traditional summer hut (*koliba*) for a family of livestock herders.

Continue straight on up the eroded ridge above the hut, once more following the line of winter-pole markers, but after a couple of poles, break off left on the summer path, heading on across the western flank of the ridge. After 20mins you then reach the water source known as **Graden Kladenets**, although unfortunately this usually dries up in August.

Continue steadily on up the flank of the ridge for another 30mins, then cross over the narrow rocky crest at a small col sometimes referred to as Koncheto (2465m). ▸ Having crossed the ridge, the path drops slightly before leading on through a grassy plateau-like region in the upper valley of the Drushlavitsa, to arrive after 10mins at **Topilata** (2440m).

Koncheto is another great place to pause and take in the views and topography of the region.

Also known as **Konopishte** ('the hemp field'), Topilata is a broad boggy saddle between Varla to the southwest and Damga (Vazov Vrah) to the northeast, and gives rise to the rivers Eleshnitsa and Drushlyavitsa. It is also a crucial junction of trails.

Ignore the yellow-blazed path that slants off north-northeast towards the **Razdela** saddle, as well as a blue-blazed trail that climbs directly east to join the main ridge at the southern foot of **Damga** (Vazov Vrah). Instead, keep straight on north-northwest along the red-blazed trail. This leads gently on into the upper end of the Malko Pazardere (Malka Mokritsa) cirque. Here, bend northwest, crossing almost imperceptibly over the Pazarderenski (Mokrishki) Rid, a short low spur that connects Damga (Vazov Vrah) to the east with Golyam Kalin to west-southwest. Then, bending gently west-northwest, you drop into a broad grassy trough of Golyamo Pazardere (Golyama Mokritsa).

Joining up with the pole-marked winter route that comes in south from Varla, you now arch west, and having also picked up the green-blazed route that descends from the saddle Razdela, continue on across boggy ground to arrive at **hizha Ivan Vazov** (2300m) after just under 1hr from Topilata.

Hizha Ivan Vazov, which can accommodate about 70 people, lies on the right bank of the Dupnishka Bistritsa at the southeastern foot of Seymenski Kamak (2666m; Skalitsa).

DAY 2
Hizha Ivan Vazov to Hizha Malyovitsa

Time	4hrs 40mins
Distance	12.5km
Ascent	715m
Descent	1025m
Highest point	2729m (Malyovitsa)

For those who enjoy ridge-walking, this stage is a delight. The trail undulates along the main crest of the Malyovitsa massif, taking in many of the highest peaks. Having ascended Malyovitsa (2729m) itself, you then make a steep rocky descent past a beautiful glacial lake into the valley of the River Malyovitsa. During the walk it is possible to see rock partridge, alpine chough, alpine accentor, Balkan horned lark, golden eagle, peregrine falcon and, if you are lucky, the rare lanner falcon. This region is also good for the wallcreeper, and in some years a pair nests on the walls of hizha Malyovitsa. There are also plenty of butterflies, including Balkan clouded yellow, Bulgarian ringlet, Nicholl's ringlet, Ottoman brassy ringlet, dewy ringlet, Cynthia's fritillary and Balkan fritillary.

From **hizha Ivan Vazov** (2300m), set off east across the bogs of Golyamo Pazardere (Golyama Mokritsa). The red-blazed trail for Rilski Manastir, by which you arrived at the hut on the previous day, soon breaks off right, but you keep straight on east, following the green-blazed trail as it climbs steadily up, to arrive after 50mins at the expansive plateau-like saddle **Razdela** (2610m). The saddle is a key junction of trails (and is marked by a strange-looking metal contraption with two bells).

From the saddle, a red-blazed trail runs north-northwest towards the Sedemte Ezera cirque (Walk 6, Day 2), while a blue-blazed path heads northeast down Zeleni Rid (also Walk 6, Day 2). However, you resume east-southeast, following the pole-marked trail that climbs steeply up a grassy slope for 15mins to the summit of **Damga** (2669m; Vazov Vrah).

Beyond the summit, drop south for 15mins to a small memorial and water source. Here too is a junction, where a blue-blazed trail comes in on the right from Topilata – a path that you saw the previous day. Continuing along the ridge on the main trail, you now bend southeast, climbing fairly gently up the western flank of **Dodov Vrah** (2661m) to reach the memorial plaque near its summit after 30mins. ◄

The memorial, and indeed the name of the peak, honour Nikola Dodov, the man responsible for the construction of the first hikers' hut in Bulgaria, and for producing the first relief map of the Rila Mountains.

Resume steeply down the peak's narrow, rocky eastern shoulder to reach the col at its foot. Then bend gently east-northeast, and having skirted a minor rocky top known as Malak Mermer (2562m; Malak Mramorets), you arrive after 25mins at the next col. Here, a green-blazed path cuts off right, dropping steeply south down Dalgiya Rid towards the Rila Monastery, but you keep on along the main ridge trail, climbing slightly as you skirt across the northwestern flank of **Golyam Mermer** (2589m; Golyam Mramorets), before running on east-northeast to arrive after 10mins at the broad grassy saddle Mermerski (Mramoretski) Preslap.

A steep 15mins climb from the saddle brings you to the shoulder of **Malyovitsa** (2729m). From the shoulder of Malyovitsa it is an easy 5mins detour north along the broad grassy spur to the summit. Returning to the main trail, continue east-southeast along the rocky crest. After just over 5mins you pass the point where the winter poles drop away on the left – however, you keep straight on along the rocky crest, following the red-blazed summer trail.

After less than 10mins, just before reaching **Eleni Vrah** (2654m), the path bends away left and starts to drop steeply northeast down the slippery, badly eroded northern flank of the peak. Eventually the path becomes more pleasant and, bending north, you drop down after 25mins to the southeastern corner of **Golyamo Elenino Ezero** (2472m).

Golyamo Elenino Ezero is a beautiful **kidney-shaped lake** that takes its name from Eleni Vrah, which rises directly to the south. It is a picturesque spot, and a great place to have an extended rest before continuing the long steep descent.

Resuming on the summer trail from the lake's outflow, drop steeply over rocky terrain on the eastern flank of Malka Malyovitsa (2640m). In a few places the exact line of the path is not always obvious, but in general it is reasonably well marked with blazes and cairns. Eventually, after 30mins, there is a respite as you reach the head of the

Malyovitsa valley. The trail runs on north, downstream along the left bank, and after 5mins brings you to a rock covered in memorial plaques at the end of the so-called Vtora (Gorna) Terasa ('second upper terrace'). ▶

From the rock a blue-blazed trail cuts off east-southeast, leading to zaslon Orlovets, a popular base for climbers attempting routes on the surrounding peaks. However, for hizha Malyovitsa continue on the main trail downstream, descending a valley threshold and crossing the river to its right bank. Eventually the gradient eases again, and the path levels off as it crosses the Parva (Dolna) Terasa ('first lower terrace'), at the northern end of which, after 20mins, is a small spring. Descending again, and crossing back over the river to its left bank, you finally pass through a belt of dwarf pine to emerge after 15mins at **hizha Malyovitsa** (1992m).

Hizha Malyovitsa actually comprises two buildings plus a collection of wooden bungalows, and can accommodate over 100 people. It is usually possible to order a meal.

Golyamo Elenino Ezero

The memorials honour a host of Bulgarian climbers and alpinists who have lost their lives, not just here, but in mountains around the world.

DAY 3
*Hizha Malyovitsa to Kirilova Polyana (via Zaslon
Strashno Ezero and Zaslon Kobilino Branishte)*

Time	5hrs 30mins
Distance	13.5km
Ascent	560m
Descent	1150m
Highest point	2525m (Popovokapski Preval)

This day of the walk is long but very enjoyable, and a true delight for botanists
and butterfly enthusiasts. After beginning with a very steep climb, the ascent
becomes more gradual, leading past one of the most dramatically sited lakes in
the Rila Mountains. There then follows a short rocky scramble before reaching
the highpoint of the day. The trail then begins what is a prolonged descent, first
dropping steeply to the Popovokapski Ezera, before gently slanting down towards
the Kobilino Branishte saddle. The descent continues past Suhoto Ezero, before
finally plunging down into valley the Rilska Reka.

From **hizha Malyovitsa** (1992m) set off east on the red-blazed
trail that drops down directly behind the hut to cross the river.
The path slants diagonally northeast, crossing some large awkward boulders. After about 15mins you are over these and,
changing direction, begin to climb very steeply southeast
beside a small stream, the Malka Malyovitsa. The path follows
an open strip that was specially cut through the dwarf pine in
2000 to prevent the spread of a major forest fire.

Eventually, after about 20mins, you reach the first winter pole-marker, after which the gradient eases. Continue on
upstream, winding your way across soft grassy swards, over
a scattering of rocks and boulders, and between clumps of
dwarf mountain pine, until finally after 35mins you cross the
small dwarf-pine-clad col known as the **Razhdavishki Preval**
(2360m). ◄

*The Razhdavishki
Preval is a good place
to pause, as there is
a fine view southeast
towards **Golyam
Kupen** (2731m), the
highest peak in the
North West Rila.*

From the col, drop slightly into the Prekorechki cirque,
then begin to climb again, threading your way east to arrive
after about 10mins at a small shallow lake. From here it is

128

just over a 10mins climb to reach a second, larger lake, known as Mineralno Ezero (2395m). Finally, after another 10mins ascent, you arrive at **zaslon Strashno Ezero** (2465m).

> This small refuge, accommodating about 15 people, is located just above **Strashno Ezero** ('the terrifying lake'). Towering above, to the south, is a wall of bristling peaks and pinnacles, formed by the jagged crest connecting Golyam Kupen (2731m) to the west with Popova Kapa (2704m) to the east.

From the refuge, drop down to cross the outflow at the northern end of Strashnoto Ezero, then ascend a rock ledge above the northeastern bank of the lake to reach an open grassy area scattered with rocks. Climbing gently on up this, you then bend slightly northeast and begin to make your way across the northern flank of **Popova Kapa** (2704m). After about 10mins things start to get a little more difficult, as you find yourself scrambling across a section of large fractured rocks. These can be slippery when wet, so a rusty cable is attached to the rocks for assistance. It is only a short scramble, and beyond, the path becomes easy again, leading out after 15mins onto the spur at the northeastern foot of Popova Kapa.

An old pole-marked route breaks off north, bound for **Yonchevo Ezero**, but you bend gently east-southeast, following the main red-blazed trail, passing through a damp hollow that appears to have been the bed of a shallow former lake. ▸ Eventually, after a little less than 10mins, you reach an important junction at **Popovokapski Preval** (2525m), the saddle that separates Popova Kapa to the southwest from Lopushki Vrah (2698m) to the northeast.

Ignoring the green-blazed trail that forks off north-northwest towards Yonchevo Ezero, and the yellow-blazed trail that heads on along the main ridge east-northeast towards Lopushki Vrah, you keep to the red-blazed path. This soon starts a steep drop, threading its way down beside a stream to arrive after a little less than 15mins at **Golyamo Popovokapsko Ezero** (2352m). ▸

The next section of the walk is gentle and very pleasant, the path running on southeast through the cirque past

The large flat flagstone-like slabs have earned this place the name Rimskiya Drum ('the Roman road').

This is a beautiful spot, and the perfect place for a pause.

Sub-alpine pastures above Kobilino Branishte

a second smaller lake. After 15mins you reach a small water source and junction, where an almost unused and indiscernible path breaks off right, heading directly south via Malka Popova Kapa (2180m) to Suhoto Ezero. However, you keep straight on southeast along the main red-blazed trail, slanting down across the lush mountain pastures on the southern flank of **Lopushki Vrah** (2698m).

There are a number of **orchids** to be seen along this section of the route, including *Dactylorhiza cordigera*, *Orchis ustulata*, *Gymnadenia frivaldii* and *Gymnadenia rhellicani*. Also, if you look up to the left, you will see that the mountainside above is strikingly marked with strips of stones. This is a good example of 'patterned ground', an interesting periglacial formation from the end of the ice age.

After about 35mins you cross a deeply eroded stream gully, and then carry on down to arrive 5mins later at **zaslon Kobilino Branishte** (2145m).

Zaslon Kobilino Branishte, located on the expansive Kobilino Branishte saddle, can accommodate about 20 people, but is in fairly poor condition, and there is no good source of drinking water. It is sometimes used for shelter by the livestock herders who graze their horses and cattle on the surrounding pastures. Occasionally these animals fall prey to the wolves and brown bears that also frequent this region.

At the saddle you say goodbye to the red-blazed trail, which starts a long steady climb up the northern flank of Vodni Rid (Walk 7, Day 4), and instead set off west-southwest from the refuge on a green-blazed path. This leads through a large patch of dock, and having passed the herders' shack (*koliba*), after 5mins crosses to the right bank of the river. Heading gently on and on downstream, you pass through a boggy area after less than 20mins, and then, some 20mins later, arrive at the northern end of **Suhoto Ezero** ('the dry lake'), which in summer often resembles a large brown bowl of semi-dry mud.

A small tempting path leads down left towards the lake-bed, but in fact the actual line of the trail, not immediately apparent, continues straight on through the trees, and through thick, ankle-scratching dwarf juniper higher up on the northern bank of the lake.

As you follow this path, keep an eye open for the beautiful **yellow lily** *Lilium jankae*, which can be seen growing on the mountainside to your right. The region around Suhoto Ezero is also an excellent spot for butterflies, such as southern festoon, clouded yellow, Balkan clouded yellow, southern small white, sooty copper, mountain argus, geranium argus, mazarine blue, false Eros blue, large ringlet, Bulgarian ringlet, dewy ringlet, poplar admiral, silver-washed fritillary and Balkan fritillary

It takes about 15mins to skirt round the lake and arrive at its western end. Shortly afterwards you reach the upper edge of the treeline and begin descending through beautiful ancient

Rila Monastery Forest Reserve

pine forest, but a little later the pines are replaced by silver birch when you enter a zone that is subject to frequent avalanche damage. After about 30mins a wonderful view opens up, down the valley of the Rilska Reka towards the Rila Monastery.

Then, returning again to thicker forest, another 35mins descent finally brings you to **Kirilova Polyana** (1465m), a large sunny meadow that lies some 6km northeast of the Rila Monastery, at the end of an asphalt lane. Not surprisingly, this is a popular picnic spot, as there are fine views north-northeast towards some of the most spectacular crags and pinnacles in the Rila Mountains, notably Iglata ('the needle'), Dvuglav ('two headed') and Zliya Zab ('the evil tooth').

For somewhere to stay, turn left up the valley along the asphalt lane, and after a few minutes you reach the motel Pri Chicho Kiro (048-860560). This offers small chalets containing very comfortable en-suite rooms.

DAY 4
Kirilova Polyana to Rila Monastery

Time	1hr 35mins
Distance	6km
Ascent	50m
Descent	350m
Highest point	1465m (Kirilova Polyana)

The final day of the walk is delightful. You return to the Rila Monastery following a traditional pilgrimage route that leads past several sacred sites connected with the life story of St John of Rila. Before setting off on the walk, butterfly enthusiasts may like to spend some time on and around Kirilova Polyana. This is a renowned butterfly hot-spot, frequented by a host of interesting species such as small skipper, silver-spotted skipper, dingy skipper, mallow skipper, safflower skipper, grizzled skipper, large grizzled skipper, wood white, eastern pale clouded yellow, orange tip, black-veined white, Duke of Burgundy fritillary, sloe hairstreak, Lang's short-tailed blue, green-underside blue, blue argus, brown argus, common blue, large wall brown, woodland ringlet, Glanville fritillary, heath fritillary, cardinal fritillary and Niobe fritillary.

From **Kirilova Polyana** (1465m), set off west-southwest down the valley following the asphalt lane. After less than 10mins fork left from the road into the forest, following a track marked with yellow and green blazes. The track soon curves left, but the marked path forks right, cutting off a bend. Then, having crossed a dry stony gully, you rejoin the asphalt after about 10mins.

Continue straight on down the road, but shortly cut off left on a marked path into the woods, which then rejoins the road less than 5mins later. The important thing now is to keep on the road itself, and not to be tempted off left again at the next marked trail junction. Instead, you are looking for the start of the traditional pilgrimage path, which breaks off on the right some 10mins further down the road. The start of the path is clearly marked with an enormous painting of St John of Rila. Climbing gently through ancient beech forest, the path winds over boulders and roots and emerges after about 10mins at the **Hermitage of St John of Rila**.

> At the Hermitage of St John of Rila is the **Assumption of St John of Rila church**. This was constructed in 1746 on the site of an earlier 15th-century chapel, but then rebuilt in 1820. It was then that the beautiful frescoes depicting scenes from the saint's life were painted inside. Directly behind, and overhanging the church, is a large rock that contains a cave used by St John of Rila in his early years as a hermit. It was also where his body was initially placed after his death. The entrance to the cave is directly behind the back wall of the church, and tradition dictates that pilgrims, having made their way inside, should then exit via a narrow hole in the roof. You will need to leave your pack outside before attempting this. On emerging, and before going back down to the church, it is worth climbing a few more steps to the holy well (*ayazmo*) and then, just beyond that, the Rock of Prayer, where the saint is said to have sat and meditated.

To continue the walk, return to the front of the church and resume on the clear path that descends southwest. After 10mins the trail crosses a footbridge over the **Ochova Reka**, and then passes through a broad scrubby area where the original beech forest was swept away by an enormous avalanche some years ago. After about 5mins, on the far side of the avalanche gully the path re-enters the forest proper

Hermitage of St John of Rila

and immediately forks. Ignore the path down left and keep
straight on through more ancient beech forest, to arrive after
less than 10mins at the **Hermitage of St Evangelist Luke**.

> According to tradition, the Hermitage of St Evangelist
> Luke was the place where St John of Rila's young nephew
> Luke was fatally bitten by a snake. A chapel was built on
> the spot and later, in 1799, this was incorporated into
> the present **St Evangelist Luke church**. Later, during the
> 19th century, a cell-school was added to the western
> end of the church by Neophyt of Rila. On a small terrace
> directly above to the north is the Holy Virgin's Shroud
> church. This was built in 1805 and decorated by the
> renowned painter Toma Vishanov in 1811.

Continuing southwest, you emerge from the ancient forest
after 5mins to cross a meadow. Then, having passed through
a thin belt of hazel, you need to fork down left on a boggy
path across a second elongated meadow. ▶ At the far side of
the meadow fork left again, and following the line of electricity wires, drop down to arrive after 10mins on the asphalt
road. If you want to stay at *kamping* Zodiak, this lies less than
10mins up the road to the left.

As you cross the
meadow, take a look
back as there is a
fine view towards the
majestic peaks of the
Malyovitsa massif.

  To continue the walk, follow the road right, but after only
20m you then fork left over a bridge to the left bank of the
Rilska Reka. Here the lane splits. The left-hand branch leads in
about 5mins to *kamping* Bor; however, to reach the monastery
you go right. After about 5mins you pass below the currently
non-functioning Hotel Rilets, and fork right along a stony
track beside the river. Less than 5mins later you then fork right
again, crossing a wooden bridge over the river. The trail leads
on past Hotel Tsarev Vrah, and then arrives after 10mins at the
eastern gate of the **Rila Monastery** (1147m).

GETTING BACK

There is one direct bus each day from the monastery to
Sofia, currently departing at 3.00pm and arriving back
at the capital's avtogara Ovcha Kupel about 6.00pm.
There are also three daily buses from the monastery to
Dupnitsa, at 9.00am, 1.30pm and 5.00pm, from where
you can get a connection to Sofia.

WALK 6

Sedemte Ezera and Zeleni Rid

22.5km/2 days

The main focus of this circular walk is the region known as Sedemte Ezera ('the seven lakes'). These beautiful lakes lie high up in the northwestern corner of the Rila National Park, and are situated in a series of small terraced cirques that rise one above the other in an altitudinal belt between 2095m and 2535m. But it is not just the lakes themselves that are so appealing – the surrounding mountain landscape is stunning. It comprises a dramatic ring of rugged peaks and cliffs that form a huge natural rock amphitheatre, which gapes open to the north, and is scattered by fractured outcrops, glacial moraines and thresholds, and a patchwork of soft grassy swards.

The region of Sedemte Ezera is not only a favourite place for walkers and naturalists, it is also a place of pilgrimage for Danovisti. Sometimes referred to as Byaloto Bratstvo ('the white brotherhood'), the Danovisti follow the spiritual teachings of the Bulgarian mystic Petar

Views towards the Malyovitsa ridge from Zeleni Rid (Day 2)

Danov (1864–1944), better known to his followers as Beinsa Duno. These teachings encompass various Christian, eastern and pagan features, and provide advice on how to live in harmony with oneself, with others, with the natural world and with the divine. During the month of August, and in particular the period 19–21 August, the followers of Beinsa Duno come to Sedemte Ezera in large numbers, camping out here high in the mountains. For them, mountains in general, and the Rila Mountains in particular, offer a special place where they can temporarily rid themselves of the restrictions of the material world and get close to nature.

By observing and participating in nature, the Danovisti believe they can gain a better understanding of the nature of life itself. Beinsa Duno used to say that nature was his library and his source of knowledge for the school of life. Furthermore, for him, mountains were one of the most important elements of nature. He believed that it is on the highest peaks that cosmic energy hits the earth and can be utilised for the benefit of the world. According to Danovist philosophy, the means by which this energy can be tapped is through a combination of meditation, prayer and paneurhythmy.

Paneurhythmy is a fundamental part of Danovist ritual, and takes the form of a sacred dance that involves what can be best likened to a mix of Tai Chi type exercises, music and words. Come to Sedemte Ezera in August, and you can watch the dancers, dressed in white, as they circle slowly, flowing gently across the soft alpine turf on the broad

back of the ridge known as Suhi Chal. The ritual as a whole is supposedly symbolic of the wheel of life and the steady evolution of the soul towards perfection, but the individual exercises are said to improve physical and psychological health, as well as emotional and spiritual wellbeing.

GETTING TO THE START

The starting point for this walk is *komplex* Malyovitsa, which stands on the northwestern slopes of the Rila Mountains, some 13km from the village of Govedartsi and 26km southwest of Samokov. From the avtogara (0722-66540) in Samokov there are a couple of mini-buses each day that make the journey up to the complex, currently departing at 8.15am and 4.15pm. Samokov itself is easily reached from Sofia's avtogara Yug (02-8722345), with a half-hourly service operating throughout the day between 7.00am and 8.00pm. The tourist complex comprises several buildings, including the hotel Malyovitsa (07125-2222). Directly below this is the Tsentralna Planinska Shkola (Central Mountain School), usually simply referred to by its Bulgarian initials ЦПШ (pronounced *tsay pay shay*). This was founded in 1952 as an instructional centre to train alpinists and mountain guides, as well as cave and mountain rescue personnel.

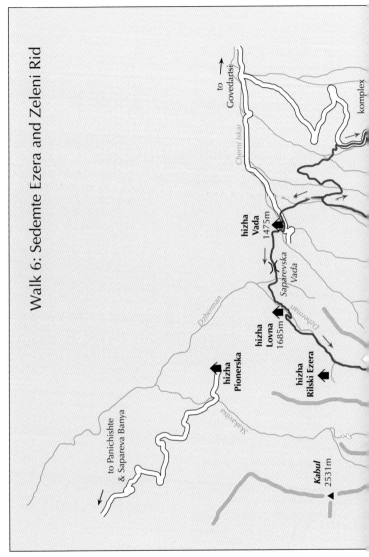

Walk 6: Sedemte Ezera and Zeleni Rid

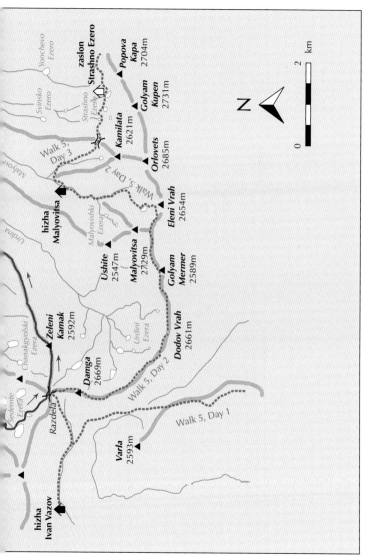

DAY 1
*Komplex Malyovitsa to Hizha Sedemte Ezera
(via Hizha Vada and Hizha Lovna)*

Time	3hrs 50mins
Distance	9.5km
Ascent	+790m
Descent	330m
Highest point	2196m (hizha Sedemte Ezera)

A fairly straightforward and non-demanding stage, which steadily wends its way up through forest before emerging into the sub-alpine zone and finally entering the Sedemte Ezera cirque. I have, on a couple of occasions, caught a fleeting glimpse of a wolf while walking this route, but the mammal you are most likely to see is the red squirrel. Birds are more in evidence – typical forest species including coal tit, willow tit, nuthatch, nutcracker, ring ouzel, common crossbill, serin, bullfinch, black woodpecker and, if you are lucky, hazel grouse. Another interesting species to look out for before you set off is the pallid swift, which can be seen flying around *komplex* Malyovitsa.

The Tsarska Pateka was established in the 19th century to allow royal hunting parties easier access to the valley of the Urdina Reka.

From the main car park beside the Tsentralna Planinska Shkola (1725m), set off north-northeast back down the asphalt lane towards Govedartsi. After 5mins fork left on a path marked with both red and blue blazes. This trail gradually winds its way down a steep forested slope towards the **Malyovitsa** river, where, after about 15mins, you join up with a broad track, the so-called Tsarska Pateka ('tsar's path'). ◄

Having crossed the river on a solid log bridge, continue along the track, contouring gently north-northwest through the forest round the lower end of the Kalbura ridge. Ignore a faint track that drops down right after about 15mins, and then a second path that cuts back right some 5mins later. The trail bends sharply southwest, and after a little under 10mins you pass through a forest clearing known as Yavorova Polyana, then about 5mins later arrive at a bridge over the **Urdina Reka**.

Just beyond the bridge is an important junction. Ignore the special botanic trail that branches left upstream, and instead keep right on the main track, following the red-blazed trail north as it heads on downstream along the left bank of the river. However, after less than 5mins the trail leaves the track and breaks off left, climbing north-northwest to surmount the highpoint of a little spur some 10mins later. Having done so, you then dip down again, and after 5mins cross a small stream known as Studenata Voda ('the cold water'), where there is another important junction.

Ignore the blue-blazed trail that forks left here, up Zeleni Rid towards the Razdela saddle (Walk 6, Day 2), and instead keep straight on along the main red-blazed path. This eventually drops northwest to reach an asphalt lane after 10mins. Here, turn left and follow the road west-southwest for another 5mins to arrive at **hizha Vada** (1475m).

Hizha Vada is situated in the valley of the Cherni Iskar, some 14km southwest of Govedartsi village. It is a small single-storey building that can accommodate about 35 people.

Follow the asphalt lane past the hut, but just round the next bend fork right on a rough track, and then 5mins later cross the **Cherni Iskar river** on a makeshift bridge. Beyond, the trail starts to zigzag its way steeply up the forested spur that connects the Malyovitsa massif to an outlying massif known as the Lakatishka Rila.

There are several paths to choose from, all deeply furrowed by feet, hooves and rain. Crisscrossing each other as they climb, they are all heading the same way, but for reassurance it is probably best to try and follow the red and blue blazes of the 'official' trail. Eventually, after 20mins, you reach the top of the climb at **Saparevska Vada**, a small, elongated saddle at the southwestern foot of Zekritisa (1734m), the highest peak of the Lakatishka Rila.

Running through the saddle is a narrow **irrigation channel** – *vada* – which gives Saparevska Vada its name. The channel is 15km long and was constructed in 1862 by the people of the village Saparevo, to transfer water from the Cherni Iskar river across the Balkan watershed and down towards their village.

At the saddle a blue-blazed trail breaks off left, leading directly to hizha Sedemte Ezera. However, in my opinion the somewhat longer, more looping route via hizha Lovna is more pleasant. To follow this, step over the *vada* and follow the red-blazed path that drops down diagonally left through the trees. This emerges after 5mins at Barzanska Polyana, an area of lush boggy meadows crossed by a dirt road.

Continue straight along the track for a couple of minutes, then, at a well-signed junction, fork left onto a pleasant path that climbs gently into the coniferous forest. After about 10mins you cross a small wooden footbridge over the **river Dzherman**, then climb on upstream through the forest to arrive some 10mins later at **hizha Lovna** (1685m).

Hizha Lovna is a small hut accommodating about 50 people, situated on the left bank of the river at the northeastern end of a large flowery glade know as Parlyako. Apart from a small stream running through the meadow in front of the building, there is no other source of water.

From the hut set off on the green- and red-blazed trail. This crosses the little brook that runs through the centre of the meadow, and then enters the forest. The path climbs west, and after 5mins reaches a junction at a place known as Voynishka Baraka ('soldiers' barrack'). ◄

The name recalls the fact that there used to be a guardhouse here that was used by soldiers to protect the local capercaillie population in what was then a royal hunting reserve.

At the junction, the path splits into three. The main red-blazed trail that keeps straight on northwest eventually leads to hizha Rilski Ezera, a large modern hut that is situated directly north of Sedemte Ezera. Another red-blazed path forks right, leading to hizha Pionerska. You, however, branch left, following the green blazes, and begin a very steep zig-zag climb southwest through attractive ancient coniferous forest.

After about 20mins ignore a path that cuts back right, and keep straight on along the main trail. Approaching the upper edge of the forest, the gradient gradually eases, and after about 10mins you emerge at a place sometimes referred to as Dvata Smarcha ('the two spruces') – an open glade

surrounded by dwarf pine and overlooked by a couple of old spruce trees.

Here, from the second of the winter pole-markers, which you have now picked up since exiting the forest, a yellow-marked trail forks off right, bound for Zla Bara. However, you keep straight on along the green-blazed trail, continuing southwest through patches of dwarf juniper and dwarf pine.

Having crossed a number of brooks, passed beside a couple of small cascades, and skirted several clumps of dwarf mountain pine and small boggy pools, the path leads on south-southwest along the true left bank of the river, and after 15mins reaches a junction. Ignore the pole-marked trail that breaks off right and climbs northwest through thick dwarf pine to hizha **Rilski Ezera**, and instead keep straight on south, just to the east of Dolnoto Ezero (2090m), the lowest of the seven lakes in the Sedemte Ezera cirque.

Finally, having skirted the lake, you meet up after 25mins with the heavily used and badly eroded red- and yellow-blazed trail that joins hizha Rilski Ezera to hizha Sedemte

Crossing the Dzherman river near hizha Lovna

Ezera. Following this left, and zigzagging up southeast through dwarf pine, you surmount a rocky cirque threshold to arrive after 10mins at the outflow of Ribnoto Ezero (2184m), the shallowest of the seven lakes. From here, it takes just a couple of minutes to reach **hizha Sedemte Ezera** (2196m), which is situated on the cirque threshold just above the lake.

Hizha Sedemte Ezera can accommodate about 90 people, and is very popular; however, facilities are fairly basic. The best place to get drinking water is from a special fountain, constructed by the Danovisti, about 10mins walk away on the eastern bank of the lake.

DAY 2
Hizha Sedemte Ezera to Komplex Malyovitsa

Time	4hrs 10mins
Distance	13km
Ascent	590m
Descent	1050m
Highest point	2610m (Razdela)

Although tiring, this is a beautiful and rewarding walk. The trail climbs steadily up past the remaining lakes of the Sedemte Ezera group, before eventually reaching the high ridge saddle Razdela. During the climb, keep your eyes open for alpine chough, raven, kestrel, wallcreeper, black redstart and alpine accentor. There then follows a panoramic ridge-walk along the back of Zeleni Rid, where Balkan horned lark, water pipit and whinchat are usually in evidence, before descending into the forest and returning to *komplex* Malyovitsa. The views during this walk are some of the best that the Rila National Park has to offer – stunning mountain landscapes dominated by craggy peaks and ridges.

From **hizha Sedemte Ezera** (2196m), return to the junction by the outflow at the northern end of Ribnoto Ezero, then set off south along the western bank of the lake, following the yellow- and green-blazed trail that steadily winds up through the **Sedemte Ezera** cirque. The path crosses the stream flowing from the eastern side of Trilistnikovo Ezero (2216m), and passes a small stone building sometimes referred to as zaslon Ribarnika ('fish farm refuge'). ▸

Running on southwest, you soon reach the northern end of Ezero Bliznaka (2243m), an elongated lake that lies dramatically tucked in beneath a rugged curtain of cliffs at the western foot of Haramiyata (2465m; Hayduta). From here, a short sharp climb then brings you up after 45mins to the pole-marked junction above the southern end of Ezero Babreka (2282m). This is one of the most striking lakes in the Sedemte Ezera cirque, its name deriving from its distinctly kidney-shaped form; it is also the third largest mountain lake in Bulgaria.

A red-blazed trail breaks off north from the junction, running on along the open grassy back of Suhiya Chal towards hizha Skakavitsa. However, you continue zigzagging up south on a steep eroded path, to arrive after 5mins at the water source Tsartsorko. Then, climbing steeply on

The building is used by regional forestry officials responsible for restocking the lakes with trout.

View over Sedmete Ezera from Zelen Kamak

In the past, monks regularly maintained the paths that led across the mountains to the Rila Monastery, ensuring they were safe for pilgrims.

up the next cirque threshold, you pass a memorial plaque honouring Dimitar Sevdin, a monk from the Rila Monastery whose duty it was to maintain this section of the trail. ◄ Just beyond, some 5mins later, you reach the outflow from Okoto Ezero (2440m). With a maximum depth of 37.5m, this is the deepest mountain lake in Bulgaria.

From the outflow of Okoto Ezero, a blue-blazed trail heads off west, ultimately bound for hizha Otovitsa. However, you stick with the main trail, following it on along the eastern bank of the lake before climbing steeply again to reach a small col. This lies on the rocky spur that connects Otovishki Rid to a seemingly insignificant outlying top often referred to by hikers as Ezerniya Vrah (2555m).

The name **Ezerniya Vrah** literally means 'the lake peak', and although nothing special in itself, it is well worth a few minutes detour to the large summit cairn for the view, since this is the only place from which all seven lakes can be seen simultaneously.

From the col, dip down to the outflow of Ezero Salzata (2535m), the highest and smallest of the seven lakes in the Sedemte Ezera cirque. Then, having skirted its northern bank, climb once more, to arrive after about 20mins at the large metal marker post that rises up in the middle of the expansive plateau-like saddle **Razdela** (2610m).

From the saddle the red-blazed trail continues east-southeast, following a line of pole-markers towards the summit of **Damga** (2669m; Vazov Vrah), and ultimately hizha Malyovitsa (Walk 5, Day 2). Another path, blazed in yellow, leads west-southwest, descending Cherni Rid to the Rila Monastery (Walk 5, Day 1), while the green-blazed path which drops west leads to hizha Ivan Vazov (Walk 5, Day 2). You, however, cut off left, following the blue-blazed trail west towards the mighty side spur known as Zeleni Rid (Green Ridge), so-called because of the lush pastures that are draped across its back. ◄

Some of the locals refer to the ridge by another name, Chernata Maka ('the black agony'), a reference to the prolonged slog involved when you have to ascend it in the opposite direction.

Although marked with blue blazes, in poor visibility the winter-poles and cairns are the vital guides here, for after about 5mins the ridge bends northeast and suddenly narrows into a short rocky crest that drops away precipitously on the left towards the **Chanakgyolski Ezera** cirque. A memorial plaque reminds you of the potential danger of straying too far north, particularly during winter, when massive cornices often form here, overhanging the abyss.

The ridge begins to broaden again, and after 15mins you reach **Zeleni Kamak** (2592m), the highest peak on the ridge, although it is quite hard to distinguish the actual summit, as the ridgeback here is scattered with several strangely shaped rock formations. A pole-marked winter trail comes in on the left here from hizha Sedemte Ezera via the Chanakgyol cirque. However, you continue straight on down the ridgeback, a delightful walk that on a clear day offers fantastic views southeast towards the rocky main ridge of the Malyovitsa massif.

Eventually, after about 45mins, you near a wooden shack where it is important to ignore a tempting path that bends away left. Instead, keep straight on northeast down the ridge – following the pole-markers, and trying to spot the almost indiscernible line of the path through a patch overgrown with dock, dwarf juniper and dwarf pine.

After 10mins you reach the upper edge of the treeline, where the blazed trail becomes clearer again, beginning a long steep drop down a narrow spur covered in ancient

Views towards the Malyovitsa ridge from Zeleni Rid

pines. Eventually, after about 30mins, you reach a junction where the blue-blazed trail splits in two. I suggest you ignore the right-hand branch and instead keep straight on down the main ridge trail. Some 10mins later, this intersects the red-blazed path you used the previous day when walking to hizha Vada. By going right and simply retracing your steps along this for 1hr, you will arrive back at the Tsentralna Planinska Shkola and **komplex Malyovitsa** (1725m).

GETTING BACK

From Tsentralna Planinska Shkola there are daily minibuses back to Samokov at 9.00am and 5.00pm.

WALK 7
The Central Rila Reserve

61km/4 days

Trail across Vodni Chal (2683m) (Day 4)

This is an outstanding mountain trek, much of it ridge-walking, which takes you over Musala (2925m), the highest summit on the Balkan Peninsula, as well as a succession of other rugged peaks. Most of the time you will be walking at altitudes of well over 2000m, and not surprisingly the trail is undulating and often rocky. However, given good weather the trek is not unduly difficult or challenging.

The route forms a giant horseshoe around the fringes of the Central Rila Reserve, the largest nature reserve in Bulgaria. This was established in the heart of the Rila Mountains to protect a large swathe of typical alpine and sub-alpine eco-systems that are home to a wealth of rare animals and plants. Only a small part of the reserve

is forested – mainly ancient mixed forests of Macedonian pine and Norway spruce. The rest of the region comprises extensive areas of dwarf mountain pine, sub-alpine pastures, and vast swathes of scree and rocks. Here, one not only finds the highest peaks of the Rila Mountains, but also the most striking alpine-type terrain and classic post-glacial relief.

GETTING TO THE START

The starting point for this walk is Borovets, one of the main ski resorts in Bulgaria. Formerly known as Chamkoriya, it became established as a winter resort in the 1890s, when the Bulgarian royal family created a palace here, as well as a number of hunting lodges in the mountains above. To reach Borovets you first need to take one of the half-hourly buses that shuttle back and forth between Sofia's avtogara Yug (02-8722345) and Samokov. Then from the avtogara in Samokov (0722-66540) there are half-hourly buses to and from the resort. If you need to stay in Borovets, there are countless hotels from which to choose – although prices, quality of service and the overall atmosphere of the resort may tempt you to set straight off on the walk.

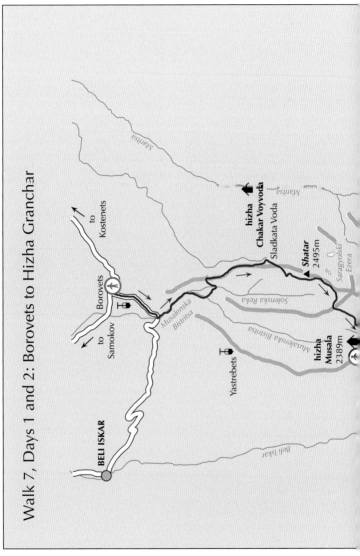

Walk 7, Days 1 and 2: Borovets to Hizha Granchar

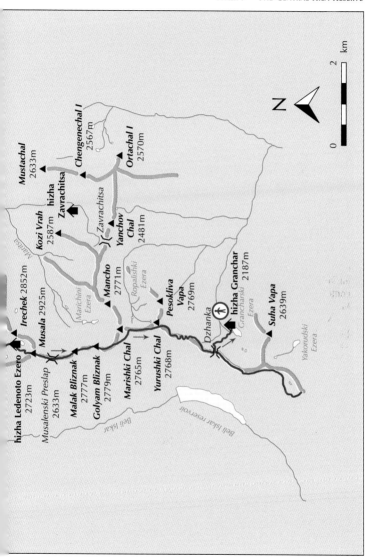

DAY 1
Borovets to Hizha Musala

Time	4hrs 15mins
Distance	12km
Ascent	1230m
Descent	150m
Highest point	2525m (Sredniya Chukar)

This stage involves a prolonged ascent. You begin by climbing steadily through coniferous forest, then continue tunnelling your way up through a dense thicket of dwarf mountain pine. Finally, having skirted Shatar (2495m), the path contours round the flank of Deno (2790m) and drops gently down into the Musalenski cirque.

Warning Be aware that the last section of the trail is often impassable until the beginning of July because of a large, late-lying snow patch. Trying to cross it can be extremely dangerous, as the slope is very steep, and a single slip would see you hurtling down into the valley below.

From the old centre of **Borovets** (1310m) set off south through the resort, passing the giant Samokov hotel and then the lower station of the gondola-lift. The road leads on between the Flora hotel and the headquarters of the local mountain rescue service, and then starts to bend gently southwest. After about 25mins you reach the entrance to the Bistritsa Royal Palace, just beyond which is the start of the trail.

Here, beside a drinking fountain, break off left from the road, following a track upstream through the forest. After about 25mins the red-blazed trail bends right, crossing a bridge over the river, beside which are some picnic tables and benches. The trail now climbs steadily on through the forest, a section of route that is currently subject to felling and bulldozing, so keep a careful eye on the red blazes. However, the general direction is clear enough – southwest upstream.

Eventually, after about 15mins, you reach a junction in the forest, where you leave the red-blazed trail to continue its climb southwest along the newly blasted ski-track. Instead, fork left, following a green-blazed trail that leads southeast, crossing the **Musalenska Bistritsa** after 5mins, and then the **Solenska Reka** a little less than 15mins later. Finally, bending northeast, you climb steadily for 15mins to arrive at a small saddle glade known as Markov Grob. ▶

From the saddle, set off directly south on the green-blazed trail and begin a prolonged climb up the ridge through forest and glades. At one such glade, after about 20mins, you can see a strangely twisted spruce, a form sometimes referred to as the Snake-branched Spruce (*Picea abies* var. *virgata*). You now begin to tunnel on through dwarf pine, after 15mins emerging at a small glade. Here, look carefully for the true line of the path, which bends up left, and don't be tempted straight on

It's worth making a couple of minutes detour north from Markov Grob to the rocky viewpoint known as Sitnyakovska Skala, a good place to take a pause.

Musalenski cirque

153

into the more open area ahead. Some 30mins later you reach a pole-marker, and about 5mins beyond, arrive at an important junction known as **Sladkata Voda**.

Continuing straight across the meadow is a path that winds down to the Saragyolska Polyana and **hizha Chakar Voyvoda**; however, you fork right, still climbing south along the green-blazed trail. This once again tunnels through thick dwarf pine, which in places squeezes in so tightly that you will be forced to crawl forwards on your hands and knees. Eventually, after about 25mins, the dwarf pine thins and you emerge onto the more open, boulder-strewn western flank of **Shatar** (2495m), with fine views northwest towards the Markudzhik ridge, and the gondola-lift dropping down from Yastrebets towards Borovets. Then finally, after another 15mins, you arrive at a large cairn located directly at the southern foot of the peak.

From the cairn a path breaks off left, snaking down towards **Saragyolski** (Zhalti) **Ezera**; however, you keep straight on south-southeast across the saddle. After 5mins there is a rock outcrop on the left from which there is a fine view down east over the three Saragyolski (Zhalti) Ezera. The trail now bends west, crossing the northern flank of **Deno** (2790m), and after about 10mins reaches the start of Sredniya Chukar, a rocky crest that breaks off north between the valleys of the Musalens Bistritsa to the west and Solenska Reka to the east. ◄

Keep an eye open for Balkan chamois here, as this seems to be one of their favourite haunts.

Having crossed the spur, the trail starts to slant down southwest, passing a water source after about 10mins, before dropping down into the Musalenski cirque. Here, after about 15mins, you cross the Musalenska Bistritsa, and 5mins later arrive at **hizha Musala** (2389m).

Hizha Musala, a small wooden hut accommodating about 60 people, stands close to the stone ruins of what was once the main building, tragically burnt down in 1988. Meanwhile, towering over it is the forlorn, empty shell of a monstrous third construction. This was begun in 1986 but never completed, and is itself now little more than a ruin.

DAY 2
Hizha Musala to Hizha Granchar

Time	3hrs 45mins
Distance	10.5km
Ascent	765m
Descent	960m
Highest point	2925m (Musala)

This outstanding mountain trek starts with a very enjoyable, non-technical ascent of Musala (2925m), the highest peak on the Balkan Peninsula. There then follows a spectacular panoramic ridge-walk, before descending into the Grancharski cirque. From a natural history point of view, the highlights of the day are undoubtedly the plants and butterflies. In particular, while ascending Musala look out for beautiful alpine flowers such as Bulgarian sheepsbit (*Jasione bulgarica*), Pyrenean gentian (*Gentiana pyrenaica*), spotted gentian (*Gentiana punctata*), Rila hawkbit (*Leontodon riloensis*), alpine thrift (*Armeria maritama* ssp. *alpina*), Bulgarian avens (*Geum bulgaricum*), least primrose (*Primula minima*), Rila primrose (*Primula deorum*), Balkan butterwort (*Pinguicula balcanica*), alpine coltsfoot (*Homogyne alpina*), alpine bellflower (*Campanula alpina*), alpine bartsia (*Bartsia alpina*), heart-leaved leopardsbane (*Doronicum columnae*), yellow aquilegia (*Aquilegia aurea*), narcissus-flowered anemone (*Anemone narcissiflora*), crenate buttercup (*Ranunculus crenatus*), Piedmont saxifrage (*Saxifraga pedemontana* ssp. *cymosa*) and purple saxifrage (*Saxifraga oppositifolia*).

From **hizha Musala** (2389m) set off following the red-blazed summer trail along the northern bank of the Sedmo (Dolno) Musalensko Ezero (2385m), the lowest of the seven Musalenski Ezera. The trail bends west-southwest, zig-zagging steeply up to arrive after 15mins at the Chetvarto Musalensko Ezero. Having continued south along its eastern bank, you climb again, and after 10mins reach Tretoto (Alekovo) Musalensko Ezero (2545m). ▶

Having skirted the lake, you then reach a junction where, beneath a small rocky top known as Paletsa (2603m), the winter-pole-marked route from the hut comes in on the left. For a time, both winter and summer routes now continue more or less together, making their way

This is considered by many to be the most beautiful of the lakes, with a reflection of Musala shimmering on its surface.

155

View across Alekovo Ezero towards Musala (2925m)

surprisingly gently across the rocky boulder-strewn western flank of **Irechek** (2852m). Finally, after about 35mins, you pass a water fountain and climb up to arrive at **hizha Ledenoto Ezero** (2723m).

> Erected here in 1986 to replace an older, smaller refuge, the hut (sometimes called zaslon Everest) has a permanent warden and is maintained in excellent condition, offering accommodation for about 30 people, as well as providing hot drinks and meals.

From the refuge, skirt round above Parvoto (Ledenoto) Ezero (2709m) and start to climb the northeastern edge of **Musala**. If there are still late-lying snow patches on the peak, then you should continue up the rocky crest following the poles and cable of the winter route, but if the mountain is snow free, you can follow the red-blazed summer path, which zigzags its way across the eastern flank. After about 25mins the two routes reunite at a rocky outcrop, from where you get a fantastic view north over the Musalesnki cirque and its beautiful blue lakes.

Finally, having switched to the western flank, the gradient eases, and you emerge after less than 15mins on the summit of **Musala** (2925m), the highest peak not only in Bulgaria, but on the whole of the Balkan Peninsula.

> To the irritation of many Greeks, Musala just beats Mitikas (2917m), in the Olympus range, to the honour of **highest peak on the Balkan peninsula** by a mere eight metres! Not surprisingly the peak offers fine views in every direction, but the summit itself is pretty scruffy, with a meteorological station located here, as well as a special ecological observatory set up by the Bulgarian Academy of Sciences. If caught on the summit in bad weather, the meteorological station can offer emergency accommodation.

From the summit keep on past the ecological observatory and begin a steep zigzag drop down the southern flank of the peak. After about 10mins, and having passed a metal cross marking the grave of the renowned Bulgarian climber Georgi Stoimenov, who died near here in an avalanche in January 1941, you reach a junction. Ignore the faint green-blazed path that drops away east towards the Marichini (Marishki) Ezera and hizha Zavrachitsa, and continue zigzagging steeply south to arrive at the saddle **Musalenski Preslap** (2633m) after about 15mins.

Continuing south, you now begin zigzagging up the northern flank of **Malak Bliznak** (2777m), before skirting round its western flank just beneath the summit. Then, having switched over to the eastern side of the crest, dip down into a small col, before continuing south across the eastern flank of craggy **Golyam Bliznak** (2779m).

After 35mins you descend to another saddle, where a green-blazed trail breaks off east via Marishki Chal towards hizha Zavrachitsa. Ignoring this, continue southeast along the main ridge, following the red-blazed trail that cuts across the southwestern flank of **Marishki Chal** (2765m; Marishki Vrah). The path then drops down to the next saddle, beyond which the ridge narrows once again into a rocky crest.

Continuing south, ascend gently across the western flank of the ridge high above the valley of the Beli Iskar and the shimmering waters of the Beli Iskar reservoir. Having skirted below the highest top of **Yurushki Chal** (2768m; Ovcharets), you then cross a small col and, bending southwest, run on across the eastern flank of the rocky crest. Finally the terrain suddenly mellows, and you drop steadily down a grassy slope through clumps of dwarf pine and dwarf juniper to arrive after about 50mins at the saddle **Dzhanka** (2335m; Dolni Kuki).

From the saddle, a once important but now disused track snakes its way down west towards the Beli Iskar reservoir. The region is now a water protection zone, and off-limits to walkers, so instead break off east from the main ridge, zigzagging steeply down through dwarf pine into the Grancharski cirque. There, after about 15mins, you will reach **hizha Granchar** (2187m).

The hut is situated on the northern bank of Grancharsko Ezero (2185m) and can accommodate about 140 people.

The region around hizha Granchar is well known for **butterflies**, so if you have the time and energy to do any exploration here during the latter part of the afternoon, keep an eye open for dusky grizzled skipper, common blue, false Eros blue, eastern large heath, Bulgarian ringlet, common brassy ringlet, Ottoman brassy ringlet, black ringlet, bright-eyed ringlet and dewy ringlet, as well as more familiar species such as red admiral, painted lady and peacock butterfly.

DAY 3
Hizha Granchar to Hizha Ribni Ezera

Time	3hrs 50mins
Distance	14.5km
Ascent	640m
Descent	600m
Highest point	2600m (shoulder of Kovach)

Apart from a couple of steeper climbs, and a final sharp descent into the Ribni Ezera cirque at the end of the day, the majority of this walk is surprisingly gentle. There is plenty of opportunity to stride out along the ridge while enjoying some fine panoramic views. However, be aware that if visibility is poor, navigation can be difficult along the stretch between Nalbant and Kanarata.

From **hizha Granchar** (2187m) retrace your steps out of the Grancharski cirque by climbing steeply back up for 20mins through the dwarf pine to the **Dzhanka** (2335m) saddle. Rejoining the main ridge trail, follow it southwest along the ridge. Having skirted high above the Grancharsko Ezero, the trail bends south-southeast, climbing gently on to the point where a side spur breaks off east towards **Suha Vapa** (2639m). The trail now realigns itself, bending steadily west across a grassy plateau-like area, before skirting past some small shallow pools after about 45mins.

A steep zigzag climb now brings you up and over the shoulder of **Nalbant** (2634m; Kovach), passing just northwest of the actual summit. Having dropped down the southern flank of the peak, you then arrive after 20mins near a rock outcrop on which there is a memorial honouring those from the village of Yakoruda who lost their lives during the 1903 Ilindensko-Preobrazhensko Rising.

Beyond Nalbant, head on across the grassy saddle, where a side spur breaks off east towards **Kurdzhilak** (2469m; Strazhnik). The path now bends sharply west along the main ridge, before slanting gently west-southwest across the northern shoulder of **Lopatishki Vrah** (2530m), and dipping down to a water source after about 30mins. Then, skirting north

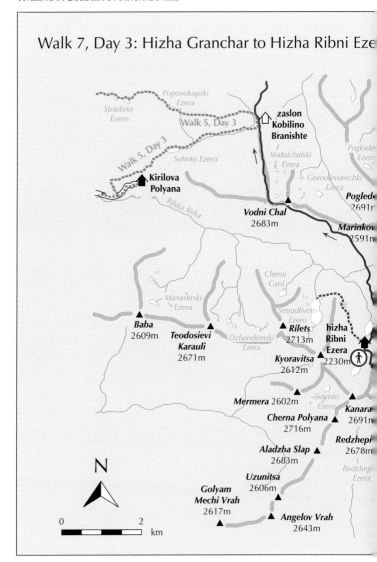

Walk 7, Day 3: Hizha Granchar to Hizha Ribni Eze

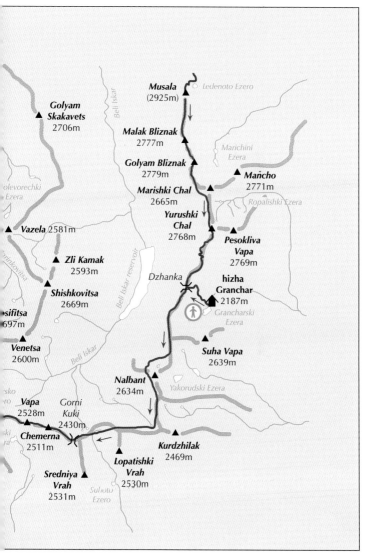

of **Sredniya Vrah** (2531m), you arrive after another 10mins at the saddle **Gorni Kuki** (2430m), where a blue-blazed trail forks off south via the valley of the Stankova Reka towards hizha Semkovo.

Continuing on the red-blazed trail, which realigns itself once again, you follow it undulating gently on northwest, then west along the broad back of the main ridge. Then, having crossed the almost indiscernible top of **Chemerna** (2511m), you arrive after about 15mins near the summit cairns of **Vapa** (2528m). Beyond the peak, the ridge narrows dramatically, forming a rocky crest along which you carefully thread your way, high above the **Vapski Ezera**. Eventually, after 15mins, you reach a small col where the pole-marked winter trail breaks off north from the main ridge and drops down towards **Kanarsko Ezero**.

Continue on the red-blazed summer trail west along the main ridge, which now broadens out again as you run on gently across the northern flank of **Redzhepitsa** (2678m; Skalets). Here, after about 10mins you cross a brook, passing close to a small water source, which unfortunately usually dries up in summer. Then, having passed through the grassy col that separates Redzhepitsa from Kanarata, you arrive after

View over Vapski Ezera

Hizha Ribni Ezera and Yosifitsa (2696m)

10mins at a junction where a pole-marked path breaks off west for hizha Makedoniya.

Resuming north-northwest on the red-blazed summer trail, zigzag down the rocky eastern flank of **Kanarata** (2691m), crossing a chaos of fractured rock blocks, slabs and boulders before climbing again to arrive after 30mins at the saddle Kanarski Preslap. ▸

Crossing over the saddle, you now begin a very steep zigzag drop down towards the Ribnoezeren cirque. Eventually, having passed a weak water source, you arrive after about 15mins at a small slope terrace on which there is a boggy pool, a dry fountain, and a memorial to three mountaineers killed by an avalanche in December 1954. From there it is just a short descent to reach the cirque bottom, where you cross a broken footbridge over the outflow from Gorno Ribno Ezero (2225m), and so arrive after 10mins at **hizha Ribni Ezera** (2230m).

Here there is an information board about the Rilski Manastir Nature Park, as well as a small memorial to a dead mountaineer.

Hizha Ribni Ezera is an old hut beautifully located in the dramatic Ribnoezeren cirque. The main building accommodates about 60 people, but there is room for many more in the surrounding rather dilapidated shacks and bungalows.

If the weather is good and you arrive early enough at the hut, it is well worth making an afternoon excursion to nearby **Smradlivoto Ezero** ('the stinking lake'). Don't be put off by the name – it is the largest glacial lake in Bulgaria, and a very pleasant spot to while away an hour or two, especially if you are interested in dragonflies, as there are species such as moorland hawker, brilliant emerald and small whiteface to be seen in this region. To reach the lake, set off northwest from the hut on a path that is distinctly etched into the peaty turf. To start with it is unmarked, but having passed above some small shallow pools known as the Kyoravishki Ezera, yellow blazes start to appear. Finally, having skirted the northern end of the Kyoravitsa crest, wind on down through dwarf pine to arrive at the lake. It takes a little under an hour to walk there from the hut.

DAY 4
Hizha Ribni Ezera to Govedartsi
(via Zaslon Kobilino Branishte and Hizha Mechit)

Time	7hrs 40mins
Distance	24km
Ascent	945m
Descent	2015m
Highest point	2650m (eastern flank of Vodni Chal)

This day is very long, and although not difficult, it is physically demanding, particularly the prolonged final descent. The stage starts with the trail running gently down from the Ribni Ezera cirque towards the valley of the Marinkovitsa. Having crossed the river, a long steep climb then follows over Vodni Rid, before dropping sharply down to the refuge at Kobilino Branishte. From the saddle, a panoramic track leads gently up and over Golyam Mechit (2568m). Then, having finally crossed the ridge, an extremely long descent awaits, as the trail plunges ever down towards the village of Govedartsi.

From the back of **hizha Ribni Ezera** (2230m), set off diagonally right under the washing lines. The trail crosses a stream

and then runs on north beside the eastern bank of Dolno Ribno Ezero (2210m). Eventually you start to drop, and having crossed a boggy area, enter the dwarf pine zone. Here, about 20mins from the hut, you reach a junction.

Trail across Vodni Chal (2683m)

Ignore the most tempting path, which forks down left, as this leads into the valley of the **Rilska Reka**, and instead keep straight on, following a red-blazed pole-marked trail. This leads on through the dwarf pine to arrive after another 20mins at the Goren Govedarnik, a picturesque spot where the river **Marinkovitsa** meanders peacefully through sunny meadows and small clumps of dwarf pine.

Having forded the shallow waters of the river, you pass a water source, and then climb steeply on through more dwarf pine thickets. As you gain height, take a look behind you, for a fine view opens out back over the valley of the Marinkovitsa. Eventually, after 40mins, the winter-poles bend right, climbing directly north towards the crest of the Marinkovitsa ridge; however, you keep straight on along the red-blazed summer trail, steadily ascending the southern flank of the ridge, crossing a small stubby spur. Then, having dropped slightly, you contour gently on to arrive after about 15mins at a small water source.

Resuming your ascent, you arrive after about 20mins on the main ridge, from where there are fine views north over the **Gornolevorechki Ezera**, and south across the valley of

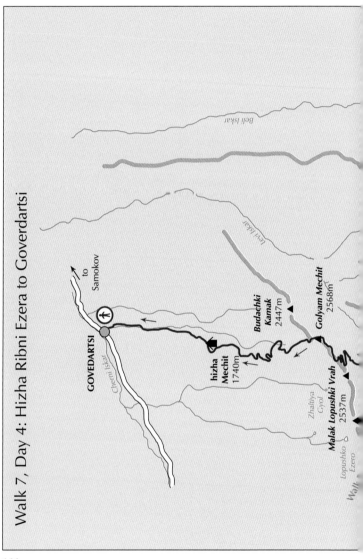

Walk 7, Day 4: Hizha Ribni Ezera to Goverdartsi

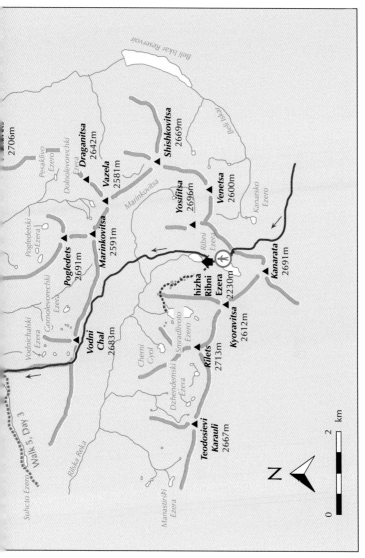

167

the Rilska Reka towards Smradlivoto Ezero and neighbouring Chernoto Ezero. Continue west along the grassy col, before climbing again to cut across the southern flank of **Vodni Chal** (2683m; Vodni Vrah). Beyond the peak you join the ridge-back once more, and thread your way on along a rocky crest, until after about 40mins you reach the final top.

Bending sharply north-northwest, you now begin a very steep, stony drop. It takes about 20mins to reach the bottom of this jarring section, after which you climb straight on over a rock into a thick belt of dwarf pine. Descending steadily through this, you then arrive after 35mins at **zaslon Kobilino Branishte** (2145m).

Climbing from Kobilino Branishte along the king's track

The refugo, which is located on the expansive Kobilino Branishte saddle, can accommodate about 20 people, but is in fairly poor condition, and there is no good source of drinking water.

From the refuge a green-blazed trail breaks off west-south-west, heading down towards **Kirilova Polyana** in the Rilska Reka valley (Walk 5, Day 3), while a red-blazed route climbs steadily west-northwest towards the Popovokapsi Preval en route to zaslon Strashno Ezero and hizha Malyovitsa (Walk 5, Day 3). You, however, continue north, following a green-blazed pole-marked trail that climbs gently up the southern flank of the ridge, crossing a succession of small brooks.

After about 25mins you join the line of an old grassy track-way known as Tsarskiya Pat ('the king's track'). ▶ With a succession of large hairpins, the track steadily gains height, and after about 20mins brings you up to a ridgeback col at the eastern foot of **Malak Lopushki Vrah** (2537m), where a yellow-blazed path comes in on the left from the saddle Popovokapski Preval.

The official trail continues northeast along the crest of the ridge, but it is actually easier and more enjoyable simply to stick with the track as it threads its away round the next couple of minor tops. After about 30mins, having passed a memorial plaque and a section of dry-stone wall, cut off a bend by dropping straight down the crest to a saddle. Then, rejoining the track, follow it on across the eastern flank of **Golyam Mechit** (2568m; Golyam Medarnik) to reach Malak Mechit (2535m; Malak Medarnik).

Beyond the peaks, the track switches back and forth from one side of the ridge to another, before dropping down into the broad grassy saddle at the western foot of **Budachki Kamak** (2447m) after about 40mins. From here, the long descent towards Govedartsi now begins, the track snaking its way down a watershed spur between the valley of the Golyama Lopushnitsa to the west and that of the Yurushka Reka to the east. While it is worthwhile cutting off the first big hairpin of the track on a pole-marked, green- and yellow-blazed trail, the subsequent short-cuts can be ignored, since they are awkward to follow through the thick dwarf pine and save very little time.

After about 20mins you reach a meadow and keep straight on across, with a rock outcrop rising up just over to the left. Eventually, some 40mins later, you come to a junction where you ignore a little-used path that breaks off left towards Zhaltiya Gyol. Some 5mins beyond, you exit the national park and bend left. Then, having crossed the meadow Govedarnika, you arrive after 15mins at **hizha Mechit** (1740m).

Tsarskiya Pat was built in 1916 to provide Tsar Ferdinand with direct access through the mountains between Samokov and the Rila Monastery.

Hizha Mechit comprises two buildings, and can accommodate about 90 people. The new part has a restaurant where it is usually possible to get a meal.

Resume straight on along the track between the two huts, descending through spruce forest. When the track splits after 5mins, fork down left, and then left again 5mins later when it splits again. Another 5mins walk brings you under the line of a chairlift, where you keep straight on following a grassy track. Then, a couple of minutes later, fork left onto a steep path into the woods. This rejoins the track a few minutes later, but you then quickly fork again, right on a grassy forest track. After about 10mins you reach a ski-piste and cut off right, winding down into the forest. The path soon becomes very steep, before finally arriving after about 10mins at the back end of an old summer camp.

Following a stony dirt road north, you reach the main entrance, and then just beyond, fork right along a dusty farm track, before forking left via an old stand of conifers. The trail then crosses right over a stream, before running on along its bank. Finally, you reach an asphalt lane and follow it down to arrive at the edge of the village. The easiest thing then is to take the street that leads on down the right bank of the stream to arrive after 20mins at the final bus stop in the village of **Govedartsi** (1160m).

If you decide to stay in the village there are several good family-run hotels and guesthouses, including the Dzhambazki (07125-2361) and Kalina (07125-2643) hotels.

GETTING BACK

To leave Govedartsi, there are currently 11 buses each day – at 6.40am, 7.05am, 8.20am, 9.15am, 11.00am, 11.15am, 12.30pm, 2.00pm, 4.30pm, 5.15pm and 6.30pm – to the avtogara in the nearby town of Samokov (0722-66540), from where there are half-hourly connections to Sofia.

WALK 8
The Ibar Reserve

26km/2 days

The Roman road between Pomochena Polyana and Kostenets (Day 2)

This interesting circular walk is located in the far northeastern corner of the Rila National Park, above the town of Kostenets. The walk is fairly demanding, and involves an ascent of Belmeken (2626m), one of the highest peaks in the region. As well as some steep sections, there are also places where route-finding can be difficult, especially in poor weather. For much of the way, the trail skirts round the fringes of the Ibar Reserve. This was established to preserve typical sub-alpine biotopes, characterised by thickets of dwarf pine, extensive areas of high mountain pasture, and in several places, cliffs and rock outcrops. There are also some patches of ancient coniferous forest. Although only a relatively small reserve, it has a rich flora and fauna, with over 400 species of higher plant, and more than 50 breeding species of bird. The reserve also provides an important refuge for rare mammals such as the brown bear, wolf and Balkan chamois.

GETTING TO THE START

The starting point for this walk is the Kostenets resort at the northeastern foot of the Rila Mountains. Be aware that there is a town, a village and a villa zone all bearing the same name! To get to the trail-head you first need to travel to the town of Kostenets. This is currently served by 13 trains each day from the sentralna gara in Sofia, the first departing at 6.38am and the last 11.40pm. On arrival at Kostenets town, the easiest way to reach the actual starting point of the walk is to take one of the taxis that congregate outside the front of the station. Ask the driver to take you to *vili* Kostenets, the resort district where the walk begins. It is about 9km up the road beyond the village of Kostenets. You need to be set down in the centre of the resort, by a large drinking fountain decorated with a statue of a chamois.

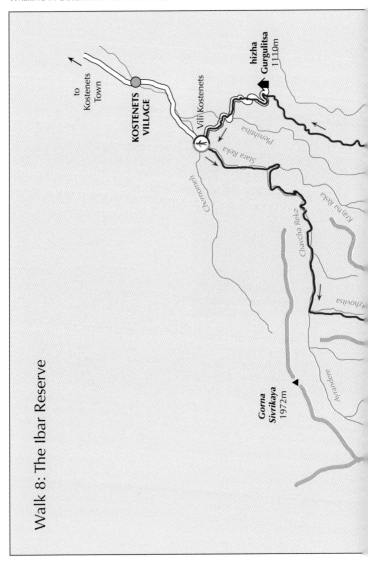

Walk 8: The Ibar Reserve

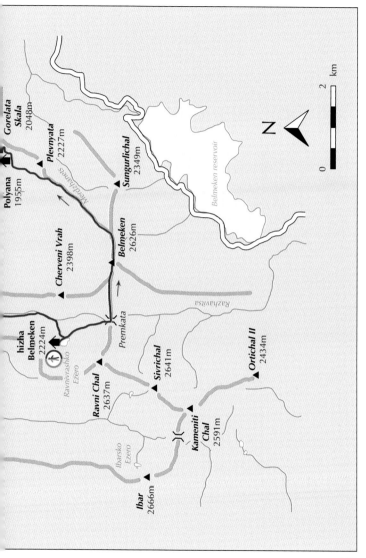

DAY 1
Kostenets to Hizha Belmeken

Time	3hrs 30mins
Distance	11.5km
Ascent	1385m
Descent	Negligible
Highest point	2224m (hizha Belmeken)

Before setting off on the walk proper, it is worth making a short detour upstream from the centre of the resort to see the 7m high Kostenski Vodopad (Kostenets waterfall). This is a popular local tourist attraction, despite the strong 'rotten-egg' smell coming from the hot sulphurous mineral water which bubbles up from the ground here. The trail proper leaves Kostenets along a rocky defile, following a track upstream beside a sparkling river. You pass a succession of small cascades and pools that are a favourite haunt of birds such as dipper and grey wagtail. Eventually you leave the gorge and start climbing steeply, first threading your way up through old coniferous forest, then dwarf pine, before finally arriving at hizha Belmeken.

From the 'chamois fountain' in the centre of **vili Kostenets** (840m), set off along the asphalt lane just to the right of a yellow-painted forestry building. There is a sign indicating that this is the starting point for a red-blazed trail to hizha Gerginitsa and hizha Venetitsa. After a few minutes, leave the latter trail and fork left over a bridge on a stony forestry track. This curls up and passes above the waterfall, before running on steadily upstream along the rocky, gorge-like valley of the **Stara Reka**.

The track crosses back and forth between both banks of the river, and after about 30mins brings you to some buildings at the entrance to the national park. Then, 5mins beyond, you arrive at an important junction at Dvete Reki ('the two rivers'). Here, ignore the track straight on south up the valley of the **Krayna Reka**, and instead keep on the main track, which cuts back right upstream along the rocky valley of the **Chavcha Reka**.

The chamois fountain in the Kostenets resort at the start of the trail to hizha Belmeken

After about 15mins you pass some benches and a place for making open fires, as the track makes a big hairpin left. Then, less than 10mins later, you reach another junction. Ignore the newly blasted track that drops down towards the river, and instead fork up left on the main track, which runs on through a rock cutting and past a little cascade. After about 20mins you pass a ruined building and enter the boundaries of the Ibar Reserve, then 25mins later reach another key point at Adzhivalitsa, the confluence of the **Odzhovitsa** (Ravnivrashka Reka) with the river Chavcha.

Here, just before the track bends across a bridge, is a small glade where you break off left, climbing into the trees on a green-blazed path. After 5mins the path splits and you bend left, then 10mins later it splits again, and this time you fork right, following both green and yellow blazes as you climb steeply up a stony, hollowed-out path. Eventually the trail starts to level off slightly, and after 20mins you emerge at **Pochivaloto**, where there is a large glade and a junction with an old grassy forestry track, along which is blazed a trail to hizha Venetitsa.

Continue straight on up the right-hand side of the glade, and when the path splits on re-entering the trees, fork right, although both branches do in fact quickly re-unite. A few minutes later, ignore the faint path that breaks off right past a small memorial, and keep straight on along the main trail. The forest now starts to thin, and you pass through a succession of pretty glades studded with clumps of whortleberry before entering the dwarf pine zone. Eventually, after about 30mins, you reach Golyamoto (Dalgoto) Torishte, where you meet up with the first of the pole-markers leading to the mountain hut.

About 5mins beyond the first pole, just before the trail crosses a brook, you will see a rock bearing just the stump of a metal pole. This is an almost indistinguishable junction where a faint red-blazed path comes in on the left from Kostenets via the valley of the **Krayna Reka**. However, for hizha Belmeken it is not a critical point, for the main trail is obvious, climbing steadily on up through the dwarf pine.

Eventually you catch a first glimpse of the hut's metal roof, poking up straight ahead above the tops of the dwarf pine. The path snakes on up towards it, crossing a stream, and then passing a pretty cascade formed by the Odzhovitsa. Finally, having passed a small memorial, you emerge after 35mins onto the retaining wall at the outflow of **Ravnivrashko Ezero** (2222m). ◄ Our goal, **hizha Belmeken** (2224m), lies just a short distance away to the right.

The original hut was burnt down some years ago, but its replacement, accommodating about 40 people, is now operational.

Tucked in at the northern foot of Ravni Chal (2637m; Ravni Vrah), this is the most easterly glacial lake in the Rila Mountains.

DAY 2
*Hizha Belmeken to Kostenets
(via Belmeken and Zaslon Pomochena Polyana)*

Time	4hrs 10mins
Distance	14.5km
Ascent	400m
Descent	1785m
Highest point	2626m (Belmeken)

The day begins with an ascent of Belmeken (2626m), a pleasant and undemanding walk. There are several interesting butterflies to be seen on and around the peak, including large ringlet, Bulgarian ringlet, Nicholl's ringlet, Ottoman brassy ringlet, bright-eyed ringlet, dewy ringlet, Cynthia's fritillary, small pearl-bordered fritillary, shepherd's fritillary and Balkan fritillary. Golden eagle is quite common hereabouts, and occasionally it is even possible to catch site of an imperial eagle. The region holds a large and very important colony of souslik, and these small ground squirrels are a key source of food for the raptors.

Beyond the summit the walk becomes a little more challenging. Trail blazes along the open ridgeback are faint and sparse, and in general there is no obvious path. The walk should, therefore, not be undertaken in bad visibility, as there is a great danger of going astray in this open, featureless terrain. Eventually, a prolonged and at times steep descent begins, first through the dwarf-pine zone, then into coniferous forest proper, where, on my last visit, I was fortunate enough to get a wonderful sighting of a young brown bear.

From **hizha Belmeken** (2224m) return to the retaining wall at the outflow of Ravnivrashko Ezero, and keep straight on east along the trail marked with red, yellow and blue blazes. The path begins a zigzag climb up a steep rocky slope that

View back towards hizha Belmeken and Ravnivrashko Ezero

is known as Stapalata ('the stairs'). Then, after 15mins, and having passed a small memorial, it starts to level off on the grassy terrace Sedloto. Climbing gently on, and crossing a stream, you then arrive 15mins later at the important saddle junction **Premkata** (2365m), which separates Belmeken to the east from Ravni Chal (2637m; Ravni Vrah) to the west.

Ignore the pole-markers that break off right for Ravni Chal, as well as those straight on bound for komplex Belmeken, and instead fork left, following poles and yellow blazes directly east up the grassy slope, to reach the summit of **Belmeken** (2626m) after a steady 30mins ascent. ◄

The summit, marked with a cairn and several upright stones, can be a forbidding place in foul weather, and the continuation of the trail along the ridge is not advisable in poor visibility.

On a fine clear day, the **views from the summit** of Belmeken are far-reaching, stretching west across much of the Rila, east into the rippling folds of the Rodopi, and south towards the highest peaks of the Pirin. Meanwhile, away to the northeast, you can see the outline of the Sredna Gora, with the Stara Planina rising up faintly on the far horizon.

From the summit set off east along the ridge, the path and blazes both almost indiscernible on the ground. After about 10mins the main ridgeback starts to realign itself northeast and you follow on along it. Your best guide is the small dark cone-shaped peak of Plevnyata, which should now be standing out clearly straight ahead of you to the northeast, beyond a broad shallow saddle.

After about another 20mins of descent you reach the start of the saddle, passing through a dense, maze-like thicket of dwarf pine. Again care is needed to keep on the proper trail. The key is to look for the path at the right-hand edge of the saddle, just at the lip of the steep slope that drops down towards the valley of the **Merdzhanets**.

The path gradually bends north, and after 5mins suddenly becomes clearer, having thankfully been recently cleared and remarked. Then, 5mins further on, you emerge in the centre of the saddle. Heading straight on north across it, the path then becomes rockier, and begins to drop steeply down through more dwarf pine thickets on the western flank of **Plevnyata** (2227m).

Eventually, after about 20mins, you emerge at a glade, where you keep straight on past a small stunted pine. Then, a few minutes later, fork down left, and then left again a couple of minutes after that, to arrive after less than 10mins at the small but well-maintained refuge known as **zaslon Pomochena Polyana** (1955m).

> The refuge stands beside a track that links the valley of the Krayna Reka to the west with the Belmeken reservoir to the southeast.

A green-blazed trail follows the track in the latter direction, bound for komplex Belmeken. However, you cut straight across the track into the forest, picking up the line of an ancient Roman trackway (*kaldarama*), the flagstones of which are still clearly visible in several places. After about 15mins, the trail passes some boulders in the forest and levels off, becoming pleasantly soft and gentle.

Some 5mins later it skirts a spur, passing an information board at the edge of the national park, and then after another 5mins crosses over a small rise near some rock outcrops. The descent now gets steeper again, and a couple of minutes later fork left from the main track on a marked path that drops down through bushes to cut off a bend. You can then cut straight across it again a couple of minutes later. Finally, after about 15mins, you rejoin the main track and follow it on down.

After another 5mins, and having passed a small water source, you reach a junction where it is best to fork left straight on down the steeper track, although both do in fact quickly reunite. Some 5mins further on, you reach a glade where timber is collected, and once again keep straight on along the main track. Then, 5mins later, ignore the red-blazed trail left towards Stariya Bachiya, and instead keep right along the yellow-blazed route for hizha Gurgulitsa.

After a little over 10mins, this brings you to a viewpoint corner, where you fork diagonally right off the track on a steep path. This rejoins the track after 5mins, and you follow it on right, but less than 10mins later you can break off right once again, cutting off a couple more bends. Finally, after 5mins, you emerge into the open at the popular local picnic spot known as Milikini Nivi. Here, by detouring right along the asphalt lane for 5mins, you can reach **hizha Gurgulitsa** (1110m).

Hizha Gurgulitsa is a pretty mountain hut offering accommodation for about 80 people.

However, to reach Kostenets you need to go in the opposite direction, following the asphalt lane left. After 10mins along the road you can cut off a bend by using a path on the right, which then rejoins it a few minutes later beside a drinking fountain, table and benches. Resuming right along the road you can then cut off bends three more times by forking off on paths to the left. The last of these short cuts leads on down beneath a power-line.

Eventually, after 15mins you rejoin the road again for a final time and follow it on down, ignoring the small asphalt lane that breaks off left after about 5mins. Finally, 5mins later you arrive back in the centre of **vili Kostenets** (840m), directly opposite the 'chamois fountain' where the walk began.

If you would like to stay the night here and recuperate at the end of the walk, there is a pleasant spa hotel nearby called Ezeroto (07144-5000), where you can enjoy a relaxing swim or massage.

GETTING BACK

Leaving the villa zone is slightly more awkward than getting there. If you are very lucky you may find a taxi hanging about, but most likely you will need to walk some 3km down the road to the village of Kostenets. Finding a taxi there should be a lot easier, as they provide regular runs shuttling people to and from the station and centre of Kostenets town. Currently there are 14 trains each day back to Sofia from gara Kostenets, the earliest departing at 4.13am and the last at 5.29pm.

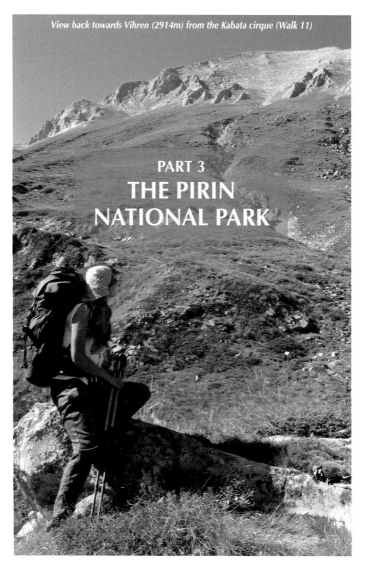

View back towards Vihren (2914m) from the Kabata cirque (Walk 11)

PART 3
THE PIRIN NATIONAL PARK

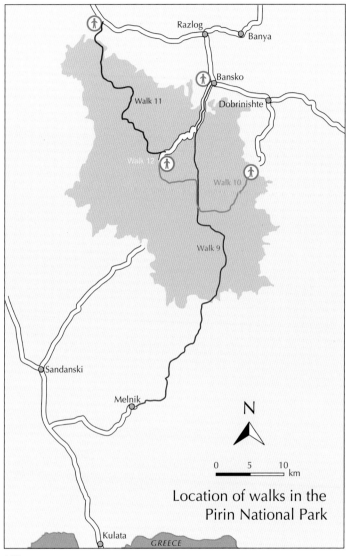

Location of walks in the
Pirin National Park

INTRODUCTION

*Yet for all her beauty, it is a feeling of awe rather than
admiration that Pirin awakens in the heart of man.*
Mercia MacDermott, *For Freedom and Perfection* (1988)

TOPOGRAPHY

The Pirin Mountains are the most imposing and unforgiving mountain range in Bulgaria – a wild realm of jagged peaks and ridges ruled over by the fearsome Slavic storm god Perun. His traditional throne was said to be on Vihren (2914m), the mightiest peak of the range and the second highest in Bulgaria.

Located in the far southwestern corner of the country, the Pirin are separated from the Rila Mountains to the north by the Predel pass (1142m), and from the Slavyanka Mountains to the south by the Paril saddle (1170m). The range has a distinct main ridge, which runs northwest to southeast for a distance of about 80km, bordered to the west by the Struma valley and to the east by the valley of the River Mesta. Within these boundaries the Pirin cover a total area of 2585km^2 and boast numerous peaks over 2000m, including 40 summits over 2500m and three which top 2900m.

Geographically, the Pirin Mountains comprise three distinct parts. The Northern Pirin is the largest, accounting for almost three-quarters of the entire range and with all but one of the 2000m peaks. Between the saddles Todorova Polyana (1883m) and Popovi Livadi (1430m) lie the Central Pirin,

*Looking in to the heart of the Pirin
National Park from Todorina Porta*

topped by Orelyak (2099m); then follows the Southern Pirin, but this fails to gain 2000m, its highest summit being Sveshtnik (1973m).

The origins of the Pirin National Park go back to 1962, but during the ensuing years its boundaries have been enlarged and altered several times. Today the national park occupies a total area of 40,332ha, and covers about 15 per cent of the Pirin Mountains, its entire territory falling within the Northern Pirin. Almost 60 per cent of the national park is located above 2000m. Not surprisingly, therefore, most of the region has a wild and rugged alpine character. Within the boundaries of the national park are two nature reserves – Bayuvi Dupki–Dzhindzhiritsa and Yulen – accounting for almost 15 per cent of its territory. In 1983 the national park as a whole was designated a UNESCO World Heritage Site.

GEOLOGY

Like the neighbouring Rila range, the Pirin Mountains belong to the Macedonian–Thracian Massif, and have a varied geological structure. The core of the mountains is formed from ancient Proterozoic metamorphic rocks such as marbles, gneiss, crystalline schist and amphibolites. These were later intruded by granites, mainly during the Late Cretaceous and Early Oligocene.

The narrow crest-like ridges, pointed pyramidal peaks, long U-shaped valleys and deeply scooped-out cirques, which are all such characteristic features of the Pirin's contemporary relief, were mainly the result of Pleistocene glaciation. So too are the extensive boulder fields that you will frequently encounter while walking through the Pirin National Park. These are the remnants of glacial moraines, and are composed of large weathered granite, gneiss or marble blocks.

HYDROLOGY

The Pirin Mountains form the main watershed between the valleys of the rivers Struma and the Mesta, two of the largest and most important rivers in the country. Both of these eventually flow south through Greece, where they finally run out into the Aegean Sea. The main hydrological features of the Pirin National Park, however, are not the rivers and streams, but the numerous lakes.

Within the Pirin there are reckoned to be about 176 permanent lakes, with numerous smaller pools that tend to dry up during summer. Almost two thirds of the lakes are found on the northeastern side of the watershed and feed into the river Mesta, with the remaining third on the southwestern flank feeding into the Struma. The lakes are situated at altitudes between 1960m and 2710m. The highest lying is Gorno Polezhansko Ezero, which at 2710m is the highest glacial lake on the Balkan Peninsula. In general, the Pirin's lakes have lengths between 45m and 500m, widths between 20m and 336m, areas between 0.1ha and 12.5ha, and maximum depths between 0.5m and 23.5m. During the summer, the average water temperature varies between 10°C and 14°C, but can occasionally reach 18°C in the shallowest parts.

View across Ribno Vasilashko Ezero towards the Strazhite crest (Walk 10, Day 2)

CLIMATE

In general, the far southwestern corner of Bulgaria experiences strong Mediterranean climatic influences, with warmer southern air masses penetrating north via the valleys of the rivers Struma and Mesta. However, with the vast majority of the Pirin National Park located above 1000m, the actual local micro-climate in the mountains is significantly influenced by the altitude, general relief and slope exposition.

For walkers, the best time to visit the Pirin is from the start of July to the middle of October. July and August offer least cloud and most sunshine. At 2000m the average temperature for these months is about 13°C. The absolute maximum temperature ever recorded, at hizha Vihren (1975m), is 23°C. January, February and March are the coldest months, when the average temperature varies between -2°C and -5°C at 2000m. The absolute minimum temperature recorded at hizha Vihren (1975m) is -23.5°C.

The average annual precipitation varies between 600mm in the lowest parts of the national park, up to about 1200mm at higher altitudes. The wettest periods are winter (especially November) and spring (notably the month of June). Late summer and early autumn are the driest periods (in particular August and September).

In winter, between November and April, much of the precipitation in the park falls as snow, with February and March being the snowiest months. The average duration of a permanent snow-cover is about 20 to 30 days in the lowest parts of the national park, but 120 to 160 days in the highest zones. At about 1000m the average depth of snow reaches between 40cm and 60cm, with a maximum depth in February. However, at altitudes over 2000m snow depth can be anything from 150cm to 250cm, reaching its maximum depth by the end of March. In high treeless parts of the Pirin Mountains, above 1800m, avalanches are a serious danger, and can occur in the upper reaches of many trough valleys and in almost all cirques.

The prevailing wind direction in the Pirin Mountains is from the northwest, but southwesterly winds are also not uncommon, especially in winter. Typically, winds are strongest during February and March and weakest in August and September. Of course, within the mountains themselves, altitude and relief can have a major influence on the both the direction and strength of winds. Wind speeds on the highest peaks and ridges reach 14m/s or more on some 75 to 100 days per year, and it is not unknown for winds to exceed 35m/s on occasions.

Up-to-date weather information and forecasts for the Pirin Mountains can be found at http://vremeto.v.bg and then follow the link for Bansko.

Top: *Yellow columbine (*Aquilegia aurea*)*
Bottom: *Spotted gentian (*Gentiana punctata*)*

PLANT LIFE

Because of its southerly location, variation in altitude and mix of both siliceous and limestone rocks, the Pirin National Park has a varied flora, totalling some 1315 species of vascular plant. It comprises a mix of Central European, Boreal, Arctic–Alpine and Mediterranean species, along with an impressive number of relicts and endemics. Indeed the northern part of the Pirin Mountains, particularly the limestone part, is recognised as one of the most important centres of speciation in Bulgaria, a place where, over time, a significant number of unique new plant species have evolved.

So far 18 plants have been classified as local Pirin endemics: *Oxytropis urumovii, Oxytropis kozuharovii, Poa* pirinica, Brassica nivalis ssp. jordanoffii, Alchemilla bandericensis, Alchemilla pirinica, Asyneuma kellererianum, Arenaria pirinica, Carex pirinensis, Erigeron vichrensis, Verbascum davidofii, Festuca pirinica, Galium demissum ssp. stojanovii, Heracleum angustisectum, Rhinanthus javorkae, Thymus perinicus, Daphne kosaninii and Papaver degenii.

While walking through the Pirin National Park you will pass through three distinct vegetation zones. The first is the coniferous forest zone, which typically starts at about 1500–1600m and extends up until about 1900–2000m. There are two main types of forest in this zone. Mesophytic coniferous forests are dominated by Norway spruce (Picea abies) and silver fir (Abies alba), with an occasional mix of European beech (Fagus sylvatica), while xeromysophytic pine forests are dominated by Scots

The local endemic Pirin cabbage (Brassica nivalis ssp. jordanoffii)

pine (Pinus sylvestris), black pine (Pinus nigra), Macedonian pine (Pinus peuce) or Bosnian pine (Pinus heldreichii). The latter two species are very characteristic of the Pirin. At the eastern foot of Vihren there are some wonderful old specimens of Bosnian pine. The oldest tree, known as Baykushevata Mura, is reputed to be over 1300 years old, making it one of the oldest trees in Bulgaria.

Some of the most typical flowering plants associated with these coniferous forests are whortleberry (Vaccinium myrtillus), wood-sorrel (Oxalis acetosella), small cow-wheat (Melampyrum sylvaticum), wood spurge (Euphorbia amygdaloides), sanicle (Sanicula europaea), woodruff (Galium odoratum), wood stitchwort (Stelaria nemorum), rock cranesbill (Geranium macrorrhizum) and the bellflower Campanula sparsa. There are also a number of orchid species, such as large white helleborine (Cephalanthera damasonium), red helleborine (Cephalanthera rubra), sword-leaved helleborine (Cephalanthera longifolia), broad-leaved helleborine (Epipactis helleborine), and lesser twayblade (Listera cordata).

Eventually the coniferous forests start to thin out, and at around 1900–2000m finally give way to the sub-alpine zone, which is dominated by dwarf mountain pine (Pinus mugo) and Siberian juniper (Juniperus sibirica). This zone accounts for about 30 per cent of the total area of the national park. Here, amongst the stunted pines and junipers, you can find many striking plants, such as yellow columbine (Aquilegia aurea), yellow gentian (Gentiana lutea), spotted gentian (Gentiana punctata), and the tall, woolly-leaved mullein *Verbascum longifolium* ssp. *pannosum*. There are also several species of orchid, including heart-shaped orchid (*Dactylorhiza cordigera*), burnt orchid (*Orchis ustulata*), small white orchid (*Gymnadenia albida*) and the dark vanilla orchid *Gymnadenia rhellicani*.

Typical streamside plants are the Balkan thistle *Cirsium appendiculatum*, the hogweed *Heracleum verticillatum* and the leopardsbane *Doronicum hungaricum*, as well as grass of Parnassus (*Parnassia palustris*), starry saxifrage (*Saxifraga stellaris*) and the delicate little catchfly *Silene pusilla*. Typical for the glacial lakes are common water crow-foot (*Ranunculus aquatilis*), floating bur-reed (*Sparganium angustifolium*), awlwort (*Subularia aquatica*) and lake quillwort (*Isoetes lacustris*).

Above 2500m you enter the Pirin's alpine zone, where the harsh climate and short vegetation period have a great impact on what plants can survive. Here, while climbing over rocks and scree, you will notice beautiful little alpine plants, including a variety of saxifrages such as *Saxifraga sempervivum*, *Saxifraga pedemontana* ssp. *cymosa*, *Saxifraga ferdinandi-coburgii* and *Saxifraga oppositifolia*. There is also edelweiss (*Leontopodium alpinum*), mountain avens (*Dryas octopetala*) and creeping avens (*Geum reptans*), along with *Androsace villosa*, *Arabis ferdinandicoburgii*, *Aubrieta gracilis*, *Achillea ageratifolia*, *Alyssum cuneifolium*, *Centaurea achtarovii*, and the beautiful lilac pansy *Viola grisebachiana*.

Balkan marbled white
(*Melanargia larissa*)

WILDLIFE

Dragonflies

At least nine species of dragonfly occur within the territory of the Pirin National Park; however, this number is expected to rise significantly after more detailed research. Species that can be seen flying around high-lying glacial lakes include the moorland hawker (*Aeshna juncea*), blue hawker (*Aeshna cyanea*), small bluetail (*Ischnura pumilio*) and yellow-winged darter (*Sympetrum flaveolum*). Other species known from the lower peripheries of the national park are beautiful demoiselle (*Calopteryx virgo*), banded demoiselle (*Calopteryx splendens*), white-tailed skimmer (*Orthetrum albistylum*), southern skimmer (*Orthetrum brunneum*) and southern darter (*Sympetrum meridionale*).

Butterflies

The Pirin National Park forms part of a Prime Butterfly Area. Some 116 species of butterfly have been recorded here, including Apollo (*Parnassius apollo*), clouded Apollo (*Parnassius mnemosyne*), false Eros blue (*Polyommatus eroides*), mountain alcon blue (*Maculinea rebeli*), large blue (*Maculinea arion*), yellow-legged tortoiseshell (*Nymphalis xanthomelas*), Titania's fritillary (*Clossiana titania*), marsh fritillary (*Eurodryas aurinia*), Cynthia's fritillary (*Hypodryas cynthia*), woodland ringlet (*Erebia medusa*), eastern large heath (*Coenonympha rhodopensis*), Lulworth skipper (*Thymelicus action*) and dusky grizzled skipper (*Pyrgus cacaliae*). There are also several rare ringlets: Bulgarian ringlet (*Erebia orientalis*), silky ringlet (*Erebia gorge*), Nicholl's ringlet (*Erebia rhodopensis*), black ringlet (*Erebia melas*) and bright-eyed ringlet (*Erebia oeme*).

Fish

Six species of fish have been reported from the Pirin National Park's lakes and rivers. Most typical are the minnow (*Phoxinus phoxinus*), brown trout (*Salmo trutta fario*), rainbow trout (*Oncorhynchus mykiss*) and brook trout (*Salvelinus fontinalis*), the latter two species both introduced from America. The European eel (*Anguilla anguilla*) has also been found, but is now regarded as extinct. Most interesting is the discovery of the varione (*Leuciscus souffia*) in lake Dolno Kremensko Ezero. This is the only place where it has been recorded in Bulgaria, and its presence here suggests it is an isolated relict population.

Amphibians

There are eight species of amphibians within the Pirin National Park: fire salamander (*Salamandra salamandra*), yellow-bellied toad (*Bombina variegata*), green toad (*Epidalea viridis*), common toad (*Bufo bufo*), tree frog (*Hyla arborea*), grass frog (*Rana temporaria*), agile frog (*Rana dalmatina*) and marsh frog (*Pelophylax ridibundus*). Surprisingly, the alpine newt (*Ichthyosaura alpestris*) has yet to be discovered in any of the high-lying glacial lakes within the national park.

Reptiles

The Pirin National Park is home to 11 species of reptile. There are seven species of lizard: slow worm (*Anguis fragilis*), sand lizard (*Lacerta agilis*), viviparous lizard (*Zootoca vivipara*), green lizard (*Lacerta viridis*), Balkan green lizard (*Lacerta trilineata*), common wall lizard (*Podarcis muralis*) and Erhard's wall lizard (*Podarcis erhardii*). There are also three species of snake: smooth snake (*Coronella austriaca*), grass snake (*Natrix natrix*) and common viper (*Vipera berus*). In warmer and drier places at the lowest peripheries of the national park it is sometimes possible to find Hermann's tortoise (*Testudo hermanni*).

Spur-thighed tortoise (*Testudo graeca*)

Birds

The Pirin National Park forms part of an internationally recognised Important Bird Area. During recent studies 159 species of birds have been recorded within the boundaries of the national park, of which 110 are known to have bred during the last 15 years. These include raptors such as honey buzzard (*Pernis apivorus*), common buzzard (*Buteo buteo*), long-legged buzzard (*Buteo rufinus*), lesser spotted eagle (*Aquila pomarina*), golden eagle (*Aquila chrysaetos*), booted eagle (*Hieraaetus pennatus*), kestrel (*Falco tinnunculus*) and peregrine (*Falco peregrinus*), any of which could be seen flying over higher parts of the mountains.

Other typical birds associated with the high mountain treeless zone are skylark (*Alauda arvensis*), Balkan horned lark (*Eremophila alpestris* ssp. *balcanica*), whinchat (*Saxicola rubetra*), black redstart (*Phoenicurus ochrurus*), alpine accentor (*Prunella collaris* ssp. *subalpina*) and linnet (*Carduelis cannabina*). There are also ravens (*Corvus corax*) and alpine chough (*Pyrrhocorax graculus*) to be seen. Beside lakes and streams, dipper (*Cinclus cinclus*), water pipit (*Anthus spinoletta*), grey wagtail (*Motacilla cinerea*), white wagtail (*Motacilla alba*) and occasionally common sandpiper (*Actitis hypoleucos*) can all be found.

Forests harbour a complete collection of European woodpecker species, with black woodpecker (*Drycopus martius*), green woodpecker (*Picus viridis*), grey-headed woodpecker (*Picus canus*), lesser spotted woodpecker (*Dendrocopos minor*), white-backed woodpecker (*Dendrocopos leucotos* ssp. *lilfordi*), middle spotted woodpecker (*Dendrocopos medius*), great spotted woodpecker (*Dendrocopos major*), Syrian woodpecker (*Dendrocopos syriacus*) and three-toed woodpecker (*Picoides tridactylus* ssp. *alpinus*) all to be found in the national park. There are also hazel grouse (*Bonasa bonasia*), capercaillie (*Tetrao urogallus*) and several owls, including tawny owl (*Strix aluco*), long-eared owl (*Asio otus*) and Tengmalm's owl (*Aegolius funereus*). Other typical birds of the coniferous forests are goldcrest (*Regulus regulus*), coal tit (*Parus ater*), willow tit (*Parus montanus*), treecreeper (*Certhia familiaris*), mistle thrush (*Turdus viscivorus*), ring ouzel (*Turdus torquatus*), nutcracker (*Nucifraga caryocatactes*) and common crossbill (*Loxia curvirostra*).

Mammals

Within the Pirin National park 45 species of mammal have been recorded, including 16 species of bat. The region also provides a refuge for 13 species of large mammal, including nine species of carnivore. Surveys from 2002 reported that within the boundaries of the national park there were eight wild cats (*Felis silvestris*), 47 wolves (*Canis lupus*) and 55 brown bears (*Ursus arctos*), along with 10 red deer (*Cervus elaphus*), 266 roe deer (*Capreolus capreolus*), 208 wild boar (*Sus scrofa*) and 157 Balkan chamois (*Rupicapra rupicapra* ssp. *balcanica*).

WALKING OPPORTUNITIES

The Pirin National Park has an excellent network of well-marked hiking trails, including a section of the E4

Trail into the Golyam Kazan cirque (Walk 11)

trans-European long-distance walking path. For accommodation in and around the national park, walkers also have at their disposal 14 mountain huts and four refuges, not to mention the numerous hotels and guest-houses that are found in settlements at the foot of the mountains.

For this guidebook I have described three multi-stage walks of either two or three days duration (18 or 45km), as well as a circular single-day day ascent of Vihren, the highest peak. These four walks overlap in places and could be combined to make a variety of longer tours. The routes described are not only beautiful mountain walks in their own right, but also offer an ideal opportunity to discover more about the rich flora and fauna of the region, taking in both the

Bayuvi Dupki–Dzhindzhiritsa and Yulen reserves, as well as the stunningly beautiful Melnishki Piramidi protected territory, which lies at the southwestern foot of the Pirin Mountains.

MAPS

- Pirin (1:50 000) – published by Domino
- Pirin Mountains (1:55 000) – published by Kartografiya EOOD

WALK 9
The Pirin Wine Trail

45km/3 days

Wending its way right across the Pirin Mountains from northeast to southwest, the majority of this wonderful walk runs through the high mountainous terrain of the Pirin National Park. However, the final stage leads you out of the national park itself and down into a labyrinth of strangely shaped sandstone ridges and gorges, to visit the beautiful Rozhen Monastery before arriving in Melnik, Bulgaria's smallest and prettiest town.

In many sections the walk follows an old packhorse route, which was used during the summer months by caravans of horses and mules. Leaving Bansko laden with wooden kegs and barrels, the pack trains would make their way through the heart of the Pirin Mountains to the famous wine-producing town of Melnik. Having unloaded their cargo, they would then retrace their steps, this time carrying the precious wine itself, transporting it in special soft skin bags (*mehove*).

Bansko, the starting point for the walk, was once a quaintly traditional mountain town seemingly content in its role as the gateway to the Pirin. However, in the last few years it has ballooned in size as a result of frenzied property speculation and development, and the outskirts have been enveloped by an urban sprawl of apartments that has sadly disfigured the place. Unfortunately, Bansko's reckless desire to try and prove itself to be one of Europe's leading ski centres has seen the cancer of over-development spreading beyond the town itself and into the mountains, infecting the sanctity of the Pirin National Park and thus jeopardising its UNESCO World Heritage Site status.

The old part of Bansko, with its traditional architecture and quaint cobbled alleys, has retained some of its original charm, and it is certainly well worth scheduling a full day here before beginning the walk. There are plenty of good family-run hotels within and around the old part of town, including the Elinor hotel (0749-88152), which is owned by the director of the Pirin National Park.

GETTING TO THE START

Not surprisingly, considering its ever-growing popularity as a resort, getting to Bansko is easy. Train enthusiasts, and those with time to spare, may like to spend a day travelling there on the excruciatingly slow yet highly picturesque narrow-gauge line linking Septemvri to Bansko and Dobrinishte. There are four trains each day, currently departing at 2.45am, 9.00am, 1.10pm and 5.25pm. A far quicker, if less entertaining option, is to take a bus to Bansko. There are seven buses each day from Sofia's tsentralna avtogara, currently departing at 7.30am, 8.30am, 9.45am, 11.25am, 1.15pm, 2.00pm and 4.45pm.

DAY 1
Bansko to Hizha Demyanitsa

Time	3hrs
Distance	12km
Ascent	995m
Descent	0m
Highest point	1895m (hizha Demyanitsa)

This straightforward walk, much of it along the picturesque valley of the Demyanitsa, utilises a combination of asphalt road, stony track and forest path. The trail ascends steadily, but is not unduly demanding. Much of the route is now marked out with information boards, as it is a special interpretive trail highlighting the geology and ecology of the Demyanitsa valley. The region is particularly good for butterflies, including clouded Apollo, Apollo, Balkan copper, Idas blue, blue argus, mountain argus, mazarine blue, false Eros blue, chalk-hill blue, Meleager's blue, pearly heath, dusky meadow brown, large ringlet, Ottoman brassy ringlet, black ringlet, heath fritillary, dark green fritillary, queen of Spain fritillary and weaver's fritillary. Be aware that the valley can also harbour many mosquitoes in early summer!

View from Bansko towards the Pirin National Park

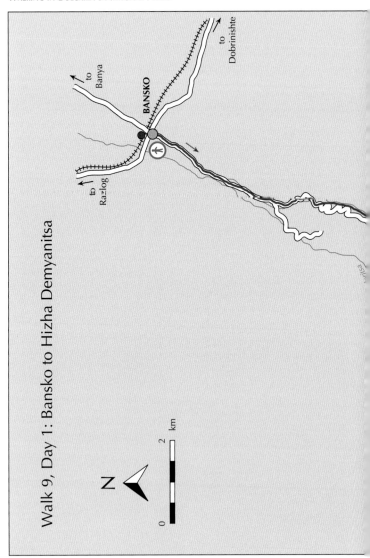

Walk 9, Day 1: Bansko to Hizha Demyanitsa

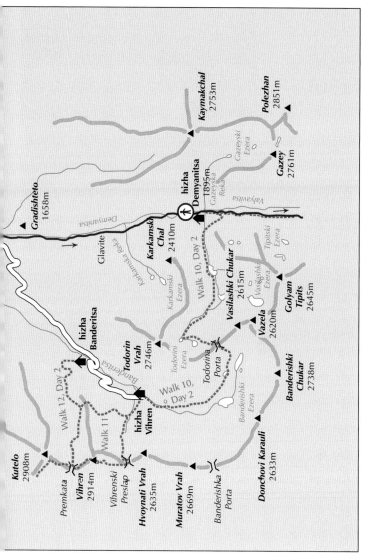

Lady spinning wool in the streets of Bansko

On leaving the *avtogara* (bus station) in **Bansko** (900m), cross the main road and go left. After a few strides, take the first street right, and make your way gently on up ulitsa Todor Aleksandrov (Todor Aleksandrov street) for about 10mins to reach the heart of the town at ploshtad Nikola Vaptsarov (Nikola Vaptsarov square).

> **Ploshtad Nikola Vaptsarov** is a bustling square overlooked by a memorial honouring Nikola Vaptsarov (1909–42), a poet and revolutionary who was executed for his communist tendencies. The building on the corner beside the statue was his family home, and is now a museum commemorating his life and work. If you need to stock up on provisions, there are several stores in the vicinity, as well as a daily fruit and vegetable market down the steps just below the square.

Continuing southwest up ulitsa Vaptsarov for 5mins, you arrive at a second square, ploshtad Vazrazhdane.

> **Ploshtad Vazrazhdane** is dominated by a giant memorial to Saint Paisius of Hilendar (1722–73). He was author of the *Slav–Bulgarian History*, a monumental work that helped rekindle national pride and a desire to throw off the Ottoman yoke.
>
> It is well worth a wander through the maze of small side streets that break off left from the square. They

thread into the heart of the old town, where you will see some of the best examples of traditional local architecture, with fortress-like stone houses hidden away in shady courtyards behind high, thick walls. Standing at the top end of the square is the Holy Trinity church, built in 1835. The neighbouring bell-tower dates from 1850 and is topped by a giant storks' nest. Just beyond the church, tucked away behind a high wall, is the Neofit Rilski Kashta, another museum house, which was the birthplace of Neophyt of Rila (1793–1881), one of the founding fathers of secular education in Bulgaria.

Outside the front gate of the church there are a couple of gushing fountains where you can, if necessary, fill your water bottles, before setting off southwest towards the mountains along ulitsa Pirin, passing the gondola terminal. The road climbs gently on, and after about 20mins reaches the headquarters of the local mountain rescue service, a large building set back on the left. Just beyond, the road enters the Pirin National Park, and the first blue blazes of the trail appear on roadside trees.

The road leads on, steadily gaining height, but as it does, you can, in places, find respite from the asphalt by paralleling it through the trees or by cutting off an occasional hairpin bend. Eventually, after about 10mins, the lane splits. Ignore the right-hand branch, along which runs a yellow-blazed trail for **hizha Banderitsa**, and instead keep left, following the main road, which 10mins later crosses a bridge known as Ilyov Most.

Some 5mins further on, the road makes a large bend right, passing in front of the Katerina hotel. However, you break off left at the bend, heading straight on into the trees on a blue-blazed path directly behind an electricity transformer box. The trail is stony, but fairly pleasant, climbing on upstream through the forest along the true left bank of the river **Demyanitsa**. After about 20mins you pass a water source, and then some 5mins later emerge on a track at a large clearing known as Todorova Ornitsa.

Keep straight on along the track into the forest. ▶ Eventually, after 20mins, you pass above Yulenski Skok, a 9m high waterfall, then a couple of minutes further on, reach a wooden bridge known as Yulenski Most. Ignore the trail that breaks off left across the bridge bound for the Yulen cirque, once a remote refuge for local partisans, and instead

Left through the trees you can see the scars of the old marble quarry that briefly functioned at the foot of Gradishteto (1658m, Kaleto), whose peak is capped by traces of a 4th-century fortress.

Trail along the Demnyanitsa valley

keep straight on along the main track, to arrive after another 10mins at Karamanitsa, where there is a water source in front of a small wooden villa.

Less than 10mins later, fork left off the dirt road onto a fainter and grassier track. This emerges after 5mins at **Glavite** ('the heads'), a small glade on which stands an enormous boulder.

The **glade** is so named because it was here, in 1810, that a small group of local freedom fighters, led by Terzi Nikola (c.1780–1845), successfully ambushed a band of renegade Ottoman soldiers who were terrorising the region. The commander of the Turkish band, Shaban Gega, and several of his followers were decapitated, and their heads placed triumphantly on the rock and surrounding trees as gruesome trophies.

The trail continues south, and after about 5mins crosses the stony bed of the **Karkamska** (Strizhishka) **Reka**. There then follows a short steep 10mins climb through Grozdeto, before you rejoin the track once more. However, within a couple of minutes you can cut off another section by climbing straight on south over an area of whortleberry and boulders, to meet up with the track once again after about 5mins.

Follow the track on left, but a few strides later there is choice. One option is simply to stay on the track, getting a good view down towards the 11m high waterfall Demyanishki Skok. Alternatively, the marked trail cuts off right, heading through a belt of trees, and then on south across an elongated meadow known as Demyanishka Polyana.

At the start of **Demyanishka Polyana** there are a couple of characteristic *roches moutonnées*, large, rounded rocks moulded by the glacier that once edged its way down the valley of the Demyanitsa. In winter the meadow is often subject to avalanches thundering down east from the outlying craggy peak Varlata Skala.

The two routes reunite after less than 10mins at the far end of the meadow, near a small building that is sometimes used as a refuge by both walkers and shepherds. Continuing upstream along the track, you arrive 10mins later at Roshkov

Grob. Here the trail crosses a sturdy log bridge to the true right bank of the river, before switching back to the left bank again over a small footbridge after about 150m. Climbing steadily on southwest up the valley for another 10mins, you then arrive at **hizha Demyanitsa** (1895m).

The hut stands on a small terrace above the confluence of three rivers, the Valyavitsa, Vasilashka Reka and Gazeyska Reka. It and the surrounding 14 wooden bungalows can accommodate a total of about 175 people. It is also usually possible to order a hot meal from the kitchen.

DAY 2
Hizha Demyanitsa to Hizha Pirin
(via Zaslon Tevno Ezero)

Time	5hrs 30mins
Distance	15km
Ascent	710m
Descent	965m
Highest point	2590m (Kralevdvorska Dyasna Porta)

This is a long, picturesque day that leads through the very heart of the Pirin Mountains. The first part of the route is fairly gentle, making its way upstream along the beautiful valley of the River Valyavitsa. It then climbs steeply over a high pass, before dropping easily down to Tevno Ezero. After a short climb up and over the highest col of the day, there then follows a sharp drop into the glacial trough-valley of the Demirkapiyska Reka. The remainder of the walk is a pure delight, running downstream alongside the sparkling river.

From **hizha Demyanitsa** (1895m) set off south on the blue-blazed trail upstream along the **Valyavitsa** river. Directly below the hut, you cross the Vasilashka Reka, and then begin climbing a stony track at the edge of the forest. After about 10mins you reach a junction where a green-blazed trail breaks off right, bound for hizha Vihren (Walk 10, Day 2); however, you keep straight on south and, after about 10mins, emerge from the upper edge of the treeline to ford the Tipitska Reka.

The next section of the walk is a joy, as you climb gently on up the broad trough-valley of the Valyavitsa through Dalgata Polyana ('the long meadow').

> The path underfoot mostly runs over soft springy turf, but occasionally there are scattered rocks and boulders. Most of these are a legacy of the former glacier that scooped out the valley, but some owe their origins to the frequent avalanches that come thundering down from the eastern flank of **Golyama Strana** (2644m).

Eventually you reach Tiyatsite, where the path runs gently on directly beside the Valyavitsa, crossing a flat, lush, and sometimes rather boggy, meadow area. ▸

At the far end of the meadow you come to an important junction, about 1hr 15mins from hizha Demyanitsa. Here, a yellow-blazed trail breaks off left for hizha Bezbog by way of the high pass Dzhengalska (Samodivska) Porta (Walk 10, Day 1). However you continue right, still following the blue-blazed trail, and begin a short sharp climb into the Prevalski cirque. Here, after about 20mins, you reach Chetvarto Prevalsko Ezero (2305m), the lowest of the four **Prevalski Ezera**.

This is a beautiful spot, so an ideal place to take a pause beside the meandering stream.

A green-blazed path forks off right, climbing past Tretoto Prevalsko Ezero (2310m) towards the saddle **Chairska** (Vinarska) **Porta** en route for hizha Yane Sandanski. However, you keep south on the blue-blazed trail, passing Vtoro Prevalsko Ezero (2312m), the largest of the group, and then Parvo Prevalsko Ezero (2394m), which lies over to the left. Finally, after another steep zigzag climb over boulders, you arrive at **Mozgovishka Porta** (2530m; Prevalska Porta), some 35mins from the junction near the lowest lake.

At the saddle you say goodbye to the blue-blazed trail, which continues straight on south, dropping down towards the meandering river Mozgovitsa en route for hizha Kamenitsa.

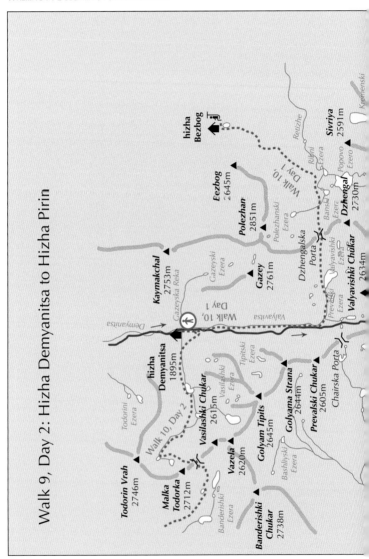

Walk 9, Day 2: Hizha Demyanitsa to Hizha Pirin

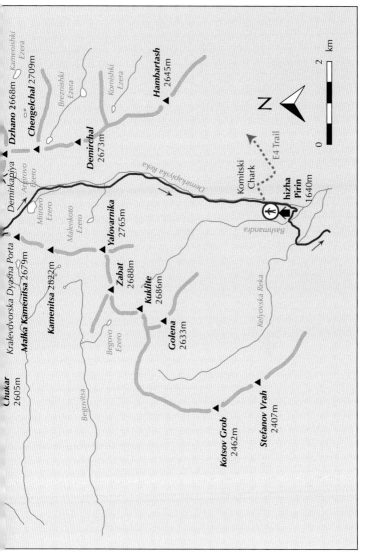

The head of the Valyavitsa valley and the high saddle Mozgovishka Porta (2530m)

Instead, you now pick up the red-blazed trail and follow it left as it skirts round the rocky un-named peak that rises directly east of the col. The trail leads on through the elongated Belemeto (Ezernik) cirque, which contains a group of lakes known as the Malkokamenishki Ezera. Most of these are quite small, but one, **Tevno Ezero** (2512m), is significantly larger. Here, on the bank of the latter lake, some 20mins from Mozgovishka Porta, you reach **zaslon Tevno Ezero** (2515m).

Zaslon Tevno Ezero is a small stone refuge that can accommodate about 30 people. It is usually manned, and very popular, especially during the main summer season, when it is often full. If this is the case, then camping or bivouacking is allowed in the immediate surroundings, but expect to pay for this privilege, and you must first ask permission from the refuge warden.

From the refuge, continue east through the cirque, then begin a steady climb up an eroded rubble path to arrive after 35mins at **Kralevdvorska Dyasna Porta** (2590m), a high col located between Kralev Dvor (2680m) to the north and Malka Kamenitsa (2679m) to the south. From the saddle, drop east-southeast, beginning a steep, stony and somewhat slippery descent into the Demirkapski (Zheleznishki) cirque, passing **Mitrovo Ezero** (2291m). ▶

Having passed the lake, continue southeast, descending beside the outflow to a junction of trails. Here, some 1hr 30mins from zaslon Tevno Ezero, you join a green-blazed trail coming in from hizha Bezbog. This latter path, another traditional wine route, descends from the saddle **Demirkapiya** (Zhelezni Vrata) past Argirovo Ezero.

The onwards walk down the valley of the **Demirkapiyska Reka** (Zheleznitsa) is wonderful, following a soft springy path that descends gently alongside the river. Flanking the valley to the east is Debeli Rid, part of the main ridge of the Pirin, along which rise **Chengelchal** (2709m; Krivets), **Demirchal** (2673m; Zheleznik) and **Hambartash** (2645m; Hleven), while to the west are mighty **Kamenitsa** (2822m) and **Yalovarnika** (2763m).

After about 30mins from the junction, you cross the outflow stream coming from **Malenkoto** (Manenkoto) **Ezero**, an isolated lake tucked away at the northeastern foot of Yalovarnika. The trail heads on and on down the valley, becoming somewhat steeper and more stony. Meanwhile the Demirkapiyska Reka begins to drop away to the left, becoming stronger and more deeply cut, as well as enlivened by a series of small, sparkling cascades.

Eventually, after another 40mins, you reach a scrubby riverside pasture known as **Komitski Chark** (Komitskoto), where, during the summer months, there is usually a herders' encampment and grazing cattle. Here, the E4 European long-distance hiking trail, which has been accompanying you from zaslon Tevno Ezero, breaks away east, bound for hizha Popovi Livadi and the Central and Southern Pirin. However, you keep straight on south, passing through a patch of ancient mixed forest. Finally, after about 15mins, you emerge from the trees to find yourself directly behind **hizha Pirin** (1640m).

Tucked in at the southeastern foot of Malka Kamenitsa, Mitrovo Ezero is considered by many to be one of the most beautiful lakes in the Pirin.

Hizha Pirin is an old but attractive hut, pleasantly located on a small meadow surrounded by ancient coniferous and beech forests. It is a three-storey building that can accommodate 78 people. During the main summer season it may be possible to obtain something to eat at the nearby café/bar.

DAY 3
Hizha Pirin to Melnik (via Rozhen Monastery)

Time	4hrs 30mins
Distance	18km
Ascent	255m
Descent	1535m
Highest point	1695m (Staro Lopovo)

This long yet fairly gentle stage leaves behind the high mountainous terrain of the Pirin National Park to enter a new landscape, dominated by low, scrub-covered sandstone hills and ridges. In summer the walk can be very hot, so ensure you have plenty of water. Much of the day is spent walking through the so-called Melnishki Piramidi (Melnik Pyramids), a labyrinth of strangely shaped sandstone ridges and gorges that are a paradise for naturalists. The region is not only an Important Bird Area, with 113 breeding species of bird, but also a Prime Butterfly Area, providing a refuge for species such as Lulworth skipper, sandy grizzled skipper, eastern baton blue, chequered blue, green-underside blue, zephyr blue, purple emperor, Freyer's purple emperor, scarce tortoiseshell and lesser spotted fritillary. It is also a paradise for reptiles, with both Hermann's tortoise and spur-thighed tortoise frequently sighted along the trail.

Set off west from **hizha Pirin** (1640m) on the green-blazed trail, crossing the bridge over the **Bashmandra** (Sredna Reka) directly below the hut, then looping down to reach a junction after about 5mins. Here fork left downhill, and after a couple of minutes cross a log bridge over the **Kelyova Reka** (Krayna Reka; Golitsa). Ignore the blue-blazed route that heads downstream bound for hizha Malina, and instead keep straight on along the green-blazed trail, following an old, somewhat grassy and sandy track.

A couple of minutes later, a faint path breaks off right into the forest, but you remain on the main track. Then 5mins after that another faint path, this time breaking off on the left, is likewise ignored. The main trail keeps straight on, crossing a brook, and then bending right, climbing steeply up an eroded path to meet a track after 5mins. Here, go straight on across and join a grassy path that bends right round the top edge of the forest, to arrive after another 5mins at **Staro Lopovo**, an expansive open saddleback some 25mins from hizha Pirin.

Ignoring the red-blazed trail that leads straight on northwest bound for hizha Kamenitsa, drop left towards the forest through mulleins and thistles, still following the green-blazed trail. The path then contours gently on and on via forest, mainly beech, crossing a succession of ferny brooks. After about 25mins, you emerge once again onto an open grassy ridgeback, and continue straight on down the right flank, getting your first views towards the maze of sandstone ridges and gullies in which Melnik lies hidden. ▸

Rising up on the far horizon beyond is the Belasitsa mountain range, with the town of Petrich nestled in at its foot.

The trail runs on and on along the ridge, which is sometimes referred to as **Vlashkiya Pat** ('the Vlachs' trail'), making its way on via a succession of minor tops. After about 40mins, some 1hr 30mins from hizha Pirin, you pass a feeble water source, Vlashkata Cheshma ('the Vlach's fountain'). The trail continues on along the right flank of ridge via forest before emerging again a little over 5mins later at Solunski Preslap, a saddle on which there is a shack and small cultivation.

Here, keep straight on along the track onto the left-hand flank of the ridge, running on beside a wooden fence. Some 5mins further on, ignore the forestry track that cuts back left, and keep straight on along the main ridge skirting **Petrova Tsarkva** (1443m). Within 10mins you then get your first distant view towards the Rozhen Monastery, and then 10mins after that, pass another feeble water source.

A few minutes later, a total of about 2hrs from hizha Pirin, you reach an important junction directly beneath a small domed peak known as **Kiselets** (1339m). Here, take the track that runs down the left flank of the peak beside a fenced cultivation and which leads through an area of sparse oaks. After 10mins, at the end of an open ridge spur, the

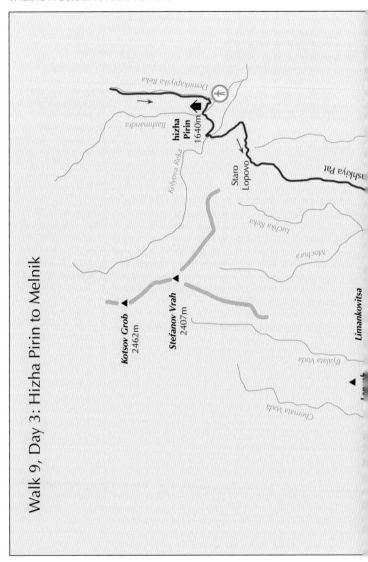

Walk 9, Day 3: Hizha Pirin to Melnik

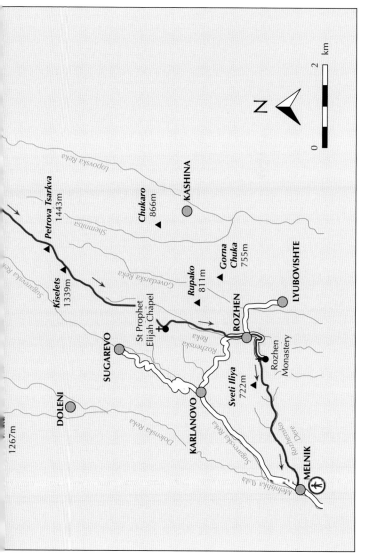

track makes a large bend, but you keep following the marked trail straight on along the spur, with the Rozhen Monastery clearly visible directly ahead.

Suddenly the trail splits. A green-blazed path, bound directly for the village of Rozhen, keeps straight on along the spur. It is possible to take that route, but I suggest following the blue-blazed trail that runs down slightly over to the right through more sparse oaks. Keep a careful eye on the blazes now, as there is a succession of junctions.

After about 5mins you meet a track and go straight on into a plantation of young pines, then 5mins later, at the foot of a small knoll, fork left, skirting round the left flank of the hill. A few minutes further on, you meet another track and start following it straight on. However, after a distance of only about 25m, take a marked path left, cutting off some of the bends.

Further on, the trail runs along a ridge spur, where most of the original oaks have been replaced with pines. Here, after about 15mins, you pass a small marble cross tucked away in the trees on the right, then just beyond, a total of 2hrs 40mins from hizha Pirin, reach the **St Prophet Elijah chapel**.

The St Prophet Elijah chapel was built in 1856 by villagers from nearby Sugarevo, and stands precariously right at the edge of a sandstone cliff, giving fabulous views. Directly ahead you can see the Rozhen Monastery, and to its right, just visible in a gorge, are the rooftops of Melnik. Close to the chapel, enclosed by metal railings, is the grave of **Todor Aleksandrov** (1881–1924). One of the leading figures in the Internal Macedonian Revolutionary Organisation (IMRO), he was murdered near here as part of the organisation's bloody internecine feuding.

The trail resumes by dropping down directly into the trees below the grave, quickly reaching a fine viewpoint at the start of a narrow knife-like crest. Don't be tempted by the goat path along the crest itself, but instead continue a steep zigzag descent left, following a sandy and often slippery path through the trees. Eventually, after about 15mins, you reach the bottom of the drop and find yourself in an open sandy channel.

Start following the channel down, but after a couple of minutes you should try to make your way out through the brambles and scrub on the left. Having done so, you then emerge into the broad dry valley of the **Rozhenska Reka,** through the middle of which runs an old track. Join this and follow it on right down the valley, once again resuming company with the green-blazed trail that you parted from some time ago.

The valley track is open and baked by the sun, but there are numerous beautiful butterflies to take your mind off the heat, as well as plenty of **interesting birds**, such as short-toed eagle, honey buzzard, European bee-eater, golden oriole and nightingale.

After about 5mins a signed path detours left to the grave of four German airmen who crashed here in April 1941. Then, 10mins further on, you reach an asphalt lane, and turning left along it, arrive in the centre of **Rozhen** village under 10mins later. ▶

En route, you will pass the Rozhen motel (0743-7282), whose shaded courtyard is a perfect place to pause for a drink and perhaps a bite to eat.

The House of the Gourds in Rozhen village

From the village square, fork right beside the so-called House of Gourds onto a small steep lane. After 5mins you can cut off one of the hairpins, before rejoining the road and following it straight on for another 5mins to the St Cyril and St Methodius church.

Beside the **St Cyril and St Methodius church**, shaded by an old fig tree, is the grave of Yane Sandanski (1872–1915), another leading figure in the Macedonian revolutionary movement who was assassinated in the Pirin as part of the spate of bitter internal feuds.

Following the road on for another 5mins, you finally reach the **Rozhen Monastery**, a total of about 3hrs 30mins walking from hizha Pirin.

Rozhen's monastic courtyard not only offers shade, but also a refreshing aura of tranquillity, and is, in my opinion, one of the most beautiful and atmospheric of all the Bulgarian monasteries. Although originally founded in the early 13th century, most of what you can see today

The Melnik Pyramids

dates from the 18th century. The southeastern wing of the monastery is obviously older, containing a refectory (*trapezariya*) whose internal walls preserve some fragments of 16th-century frescoes. Likewise, the fresco in the niche over the entrance on the western facade of the Nativity of the Holy Virgin church is inscribed with the date 1597. The interior of the church also harbours several other treasures, including an exquisitely carved 18th-century iconostasis, some unique stained-glass windows dating from 1715, and a miraculous Virgin and Child icon, which dates from 1670.

As you leave the monastery and come back out through the main gates, the trail to Melnik breaks off left on a faint path that runs west-northwest across the meadow. After a few minutes the path splits and you fork left, climbing up to a viewpoint from which there is a fine panorama over the monastery. Following a narrow path that skirts along the flank of a sandstone ridge, you then emerge on a wonderful crest about 15mins from the monastery.

> It is well worth making a detour to the **old oak tree** that stands at the very tip of the ridge, as the views over the surrounding sandstone formations are quite stunning, a rippling series of jagged knife edges, pinnacles and mushroom-like formations.

The onwards trail cuts straight over the ridge, and almost immediately starts to zigzag down a heavily eroded path which in places has been deeply cut by rain water. It seems hard to believe that this was once the main trackway between Melnik and the monastery at Rozhen. However, in a couple of places it is still possible to make out small surviving sections of the original cobbles.

Eventually, after a steep and slippery 10mins descent, you reach the bottom of a deep wooded gully, the **Rozhensko Dere**, which is then followed on downstream. Usually the gully bottom is dry and sandy, but occasional flash-floods turn it into a torrent of water. It takes about 30mins to make your way through the sandstone gorge and reach the outskirts of **Melnik**, and then about 5mins more before you find yourself in the centre of town.

The town of Melnik

MELNIK

In fact it is hard to think of Melnik as a town, for at first sight it seems little more than a cluster of picturesque houses squeezed soporifically into a sandstone defile. Indeed, today the permanent population of Melnik is less than 300 people. This does of course add to its appeal, and is partly what makes Melnik an ideal place to relax for a day or two at the end of the trek.

There is no shortage of places to stay, with half a dozen stylish hotels and countless guest-rooms in private houses to choose from. Then, when you have secured yourself a room and washed away the grime of the walk, what could be better than to sit back in the town's balmy warmth and enjoy a bottle of the local Melnik wine. Reputedly a favourite with Winston Churchill, it was this rich fruity treasure that once lured the packhorse men of old to embark on their treacherous journey across the mountains from Bansko.

Before leaving Melnik, it is well worth having a good look round, for the town has a long and illustrious history, and hides many interesting architectural and archaeological sites. During the medieval period, Melnik was one of the most important strategic centres in this part of the Balkan Peninsula, and at the beginning of the 13th century became the capital of a powerful independent feudal fiefdom ruled by Despot Alexei Slav. The ruins of his residence, known as the Bolyarska Kashta, rise up on the sandy spur in the centre of town.

Melnik's second golden age occurred during the 18th and 19th centuries, when it once again became a thriving economic centre, based around the flourishing trade in tobacco and wine. During this period the population boomed, reaching the almost unimaginable size of some 25,000 residents. Many of the richer merchants built themselves lavish mansions, a handful of which survive today, including the wonderful Kordopulova Kashta. Built in 1754 by Manolis Kordopolis, this towering four-storey house is one of the finest examples of National Revival Style architecture in Bulgaria. The building is open to the public, and after you finish looking round, you can then enjoy some wine tasting in its labyrinthine cellars.

Over the centuries, Melnik also developed into a leading spiritual centre, and according to some sources, as many as 78 churches and chapels sprung up in and around the town. Four have survived and are still in use today – the St Nicholas the Miracle-worker church, built 1756, the St Anthony church, the St Peter and St Paul church, and the St John the Precursor church. There are also several other ruined chapels dotted around the town, as well as the remnants of a couple of once-flourishing monasteries. The latter are located on the small sandstone plateau that rises up directly to the south.

GETTING BACK

When you need to move on, there is one direct bus a day from Melnik to Sofia, currently departing at 6.00am, and five others at 7.40am, 11.40am, 12.15pm, 3.30pm and 5.00pm to the avtogara in Sandanski (0746-22130), from where there are 15 buses each day to Sofia, the first departing at 5.00am and the last at 5.00pm.

WALK 10
The Yulen Reserve

18km/2 days

This beautiful two-day trek leads you over two high passes and through several large cirques that are studded with glacial lakes. The route snakes its way around the periphery of the Yulen Reserve, which was established to preserve a mix of forest, sub-alpine and alpine eco-systems, and the many rare and endemic plants and animals that are found within them. The reserve is split into two sectors by the Demyanitsa and Valyavitsa valleys. The western part is fairly small and lies on the northeastern flank of the Pirin's main ridge, while the larger eastern sector encompasses much of the mighty side ridge known as Polezhansko Bilo. In lower parts of the reserve there are ancient coniferous forests dominated by Macedonian pine, Scots pine and Norway spruce, while above the treeline are thickets of dwarf mountain pine as well as large areas of sub-alpine pasture. There are also numerous cliffs and rock outcrops, as well as extensive patches of moraines and scree. The flora of the reserve is very rich, with over 700 species of higher plants, while the fauna includes brown bear, wolf and Balkan chamois. The latter can often be seen as you cross over the high passes.

GETTING TO THE START

The starting point for this walk is hizha Bezbog, a large five-storey hut situated high in the mountains on the banks of Bezbozhko Ezero. The hut can accommodate 120 people, and meals are usually available from the kitchen. It is possible to reach hizha Bezbog on foot in about 5hrs following a green-blazed trail that climbs up from the village of Dobrinishte via hizha Gotse Delchev. However, this 1400m ascent has little to recommend it. Much of the first section between Dobrinishte and hizha Gotse Delchev follows an asphalt road, and it is far better to save your energy for the walk proper by getting a taxi from Bansko to drive you the 18km up to hizha Gotse Delchev (1450m). This hut and the surrounding wooden bungalows can accommodate about 100 people.

From hizha Gotse Delchev, the green trail continues climbing steeply up towards hizha Bezbog, still over 800m higher up the mountainside. However, again there is a good alternative to the long steep slog – a chair-lift whose lower station is located directly behind hizha Gotse Delchev and whose upper station lies just below hizha Bezbog. It is a pleasant 30mins ride, first gently up through the treetops, and then on across the open sub-alpine pastures.

DAY 1

Hizha Bezbog to Hizha Demyanitsa

Time	4hrs 30mins
Distance	10.5km
Ascent	400m
Descent	1250m
Highest point	2510m (Dzhengalska Porta)

This beautiful but fairly demanding walk includes some steep ascents and descents. The trail frequently alternates between springy pastures and rocky sections, and there are also some moraines and boulder fields to be crossed. During the first part of the day the trail passes a number of glacial lakes, where dragonflies such as moorland hawker, robust spreadwing, yellow-winged darter and small bluetail can be seen. There are also several interesting butterflies to look out for, including clouded yellow, common blue, Nicholl's ringlet, large ringlet, black ringlet and Cynthia's fritillary.

From **hizha Bezbog** (2237m) set off south along the western bank of **Bezbozhko Ezero** (2239m), passing beneath the steep northeastern flank of Bezbog (2645m), a dangerous avalanche zone in winter. On reaching the southern end of the lake, you start a short sharp climb, zigzagging your way out of the Bezbozhki cirque, and after 20mins arrive at an open saddle-like area known as **Bezbozhki Preval**. ▶

There is a fine view back over the lake and hut, with the Rila Mountains rising up imposingly on the far northern horizon.

From the saddle, follow the clear path straight on south into a thicket of dwarf pine.

Soon a wonderful view opens up into the **heart of the Pirin**, with the strikingly pointed peak Sivriya (2591m; Ostrets) standing out to the south-southeast. Tucked in directly below it to the east, you can just make out part of Dolno Kremensko Ezero, the second largest lake in the Pirin Mountains.

After 5mins, and having dropped down out of the dwarf pine onto a grassy area, ignore the faint cairned path

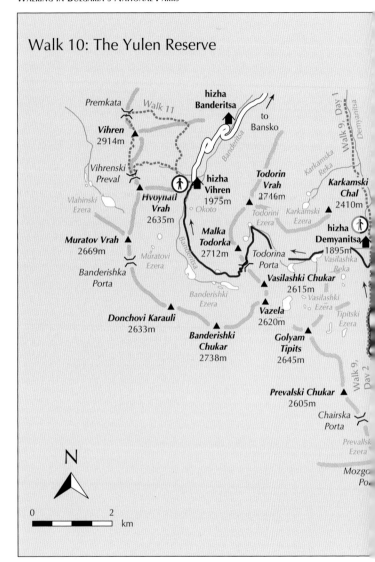

Walk 10: The Yulen Reserve

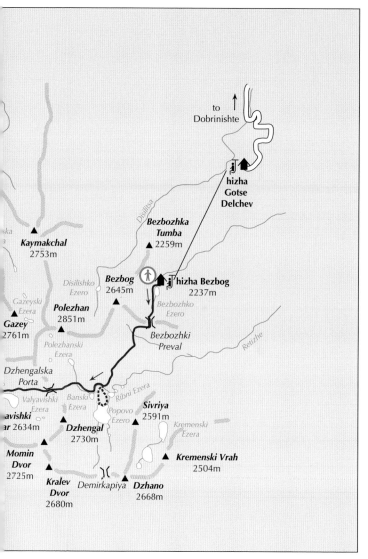

to
Dobrinishte

hizha
Gotse
Delchev

Dzhilitsa

Bezbozhka
Tumba
▲ 2259m

Kaymakchal
2753m

Disilishko
Ezero

Bezbog
2645m
▲

hizha Bezbog
2237m

Bezbozhko
Ezero

Gazeyski
Ezera

Polezhan
2851m
▲

Gazey
2761m
▲

Bezbozhki
Preval

Retizhe

Polezhanski
Ezera

Dzhengalska
Porta

Valyavishki
Ezera

Banski
Ezera

Ribni Ezera

avishki
ar 2634m

Popovo
Ezero

Sivriya
2591m

Kremenski
Ezera

Momin
Dvor
2725m
▲

Dzhengal
2730m
▲

Kremenski Vrah
2504m
▲

Kralev
Dvor
2680m

Demirkapiya

Dzhano
2668m
▲

breaking off on the right. This is bound for Polezhan (2851m; Mangartepe), the fifth highest peak in the Pirin. Instead, keep on the yellow-blazed trail, undulating on southwest to arrive after 20mins at a giant cairn.

> Directly below, in the valley of the Retizhe, lies the area known as **Govedarnika**, where cattle from the village of Obadim are traditionally pastured during the summer months. The view on down the valley is beautiful, with the Rodopi Mountains rolling away into the haze on the far horizon.

Another 20mins brings you to an important junction. The yellow-blazed trail that forks off right is the one you need, but it is worth making a 15mins detour along the green-blazed trail to visit **Popovo Ezero** (2234m; Papazgyol).

> Popovo Ezero is the **largest lake** in the Pirin, and also the deepest at 29.5m. In the northwestern part of the lake is a small island known as Kalimavkata. According to legend, a local priest drowned himself here after his beautiful daughter Kalina was kidnapped by a Turkish lord. As the priest's body disappeared beneath the water, his kamelaukion (*kalimavka*) rose up to the surface, forming the island. Since then, the lake has been known as 'the priest's lake'.

Returning to the junction, and resuming on the yellow-blazed trail for hizha Demyanitsa, you soon cross a lovely grassy terrace through which a stream gently meanders, and on which lie three small shallow pools known as the **Banski Ezera**. From here begins a long steep ascent, rocky in places, which finally, after 50mins, brings you up to **Dzhengalska Porta** (2510m; Samodivska Porta).

> This **rocky saddle** is situated between Dzhengal (2730m; Samodivski Vrah) to the south-southeast and Malak Polezhan (2822m) to the north-northwest. Gazing west from the col across the Valyavishki cirque you can see the main ridge of the Pirin, dominated by the imposing bulk of Golyamata Strana (2644m).

Crossing the saddle you now begin a long steep descent which, to start with at least, is very rocky. Steadily, as you drop further into the Valyavishki cirque, the terrain becomes more mellow and grassy, and finally after 25mins, you arrive at the eastern end of Golyamo Valyavishko Ezero (2280m), the third largest lake in the Pirin.

View back towards the crest Dzhengalski Greben from the Valyavishki cirque

> In Golyamo Valyavishko Ezero's northern part is an elongated **twin-topped island**. Sometimes, if the water level is especially high, the connection between the two becomes submerged, leaving them looking like two small independent islets.

The trail continues west along the northern bank of the lake, and in places you will need to scramble across large rocks and boulders directly at the water's edge. It takes about 10mins to reach the far western end, where the outflow from the lake forms the start of the river **Valyavitsa**.

Before continuing your descent, take a look back across the lake. Rising up on the skyline behind you is one of the most beautiful views in the Pirin – the jagged, alpine-style crest of **Dzhengalski Greben** (Samodivski Greben), which drops northwest from Dzhengal towards the Dzhengalska Porta.

From the outflow of the lake, continue your descent through the Valyavishki cirque, and having forded first a small stream known as the Prevalski Potok and then the Valyavitsa itself, you arrive after 20mins at an important junction at the northern end of Tiyatsite. Here, a blue-blazed trail bound for hizha Kamenitsa cuts back left, climbing via the Prevalski cirque towards the high col Mozgovishka Porta (Walk 9, Day 2). You, however, keep straight on north, following the yellow-blazed trail.

The path crosses the soft turf of Tiyatsite, then leads gently on down downstream through Dalgata Polyana, where you can see a few surviving poles of the former telephone-line which threaded right across the mountains between Bansko and Sandanski. Passing below Golyamata Strana (2644m), whose steep, avalanche-prone eastern flank rises up on the left, you will probably hear the sound of cowbells, for on the opposite side of the river is Govedarnika, where a herd of calves is usually grazed throughout the summer.

Eventually, after 45mins, you ford the Tipitska Voda and reach the start of the forest. Then, after another 20mins, you come to a junction where the green-blazed trail you will use tomorrow breaks off left for **hizha Vihren**. For now, keep straight on north, following the yellow-blazed trail through the forest on a broad and uncomfortably stony path that eventually, after 10mins, drops down to cross the Vasilashka Reka directly below **hizha Demyanitsa** (1895m).

The hut plus the adjoining 14 wooden bungalows can accommodate about 175 people. Hot meals can be ordered from the restaurant.

DAY 2
Hizha Demyanitsa to Hizha Vihren

Time	4hrs
Distance	7.5km
Ascent	680m
Descent	600m
Highest point	2575m (Todorina Porta)

This is a fairly tiring but enjoyable day that connects the Demyanitsa and Banderitsa valleys. The first half of the route involves a prolonged climb, but the going underfoot is mostly soft and pleasant. Having crossed the high pass Todorina Porta, there then follows a long steep descent, the first part of which can be quite jarring with a heavy pack.

Directly below **hizha Demyanitsa** (1895m), cross the **Vasilashka Reka**, then set off south on the green-blazed trail upstream along the river Valyavitsa, steadily climbing a stony track at the edge of the forest. After about 10mins you reach a junction where the blue-blazed trail by which you arrived at the hut yesterday keeps straight on south up the valley, bound for zaslon Tevno Ezero (Walk 9, Day 2). Here, fork off right on the green-blazed trail, zigzagging up into the coniferous forest.

The path is fairly steep, but there are some wonderful specimens of ancient Macedonian pine and abundant birdlife to take your mind off the ascent. After about 20mins the trail levels off at a point where a faint and almost indiscernible path splits off left, bound for the former Orlovo Gnezdo partisan camp. You, however, keep on along the main path, which just beyond, fords the stony bed of the Vasilashka Reka. Continue upstream, skirting some boggy glades at the edge of the forest.

This region is often referred to as **Zhabarnika**, on account of the numerous grass frogs that breed in the pools here. It is also a favoured breeding ground for mosquitoes, hence its other name, Komarnika. More pleasant are the beautiful dragonflies, which include blue hawker, moorland hawker, small bluetail and yellow-winged darter. It is also worth keeping an eye open for common bluet, which is also likely to be here.

The lake holds many fish, and has large patches of common water crowfoot forming beautiful white rafts on its surface.

Having climbed over a small rocky section, and on through a tunnel of dwarf mountain pine, you emerge after 15mins at the bottom end of Ribno (Dolno) Vasilashko Ezero (2126m), the lowest of the 10 lakes in the Vasilashki cirque. ◄ Keep on along the true left bank of the lake, and then at the far end begin a long steady climb through the Vasilashki cirque.

The trail runs on high above Gorno Vasilashko Ezero (2154m), which lies down to the left, and eventually, having surmounted a series of terraces and crossed over a stream, you find yourself ascending more gently up a broad high mountain pasture known as Vasilashki Chal. The trail follows the stream, crossing a boggy patch bejewelled by several species of beautiful damp-loving flowers.

Dolno Todorino Ezero is one of the Todorini Ezera, two small glacial lakes that are often referred to by walkers as Todorini Ochi or Ochite na Todorka ('the eyes of Todorka').

Just beyond, about 45mins from the lake, you reach a point where the green-blazed trail starts to bend steadily left towards the high saddle Todorina Porta. However, I recommend you make a slight detour here, and breaking off the marked trail, simply continue straight on up the valley for another 10mins to Dolno Todorino Ezero (2510m), a pretty little lake tucked right in at the southern foot of **Todorin Vrah** (2746m). ◄

Ribno Vasilashko Ezero

To resume from the lake, simply turn back towards the green trail, and by angling slightly up to the right, you can intersect it easily again after about 5mins. The trail then runs on over a section of fractured rocks and boulders, with Gorno Todorino Ezero (2536m), the upper and larger of the two Todorini Ezera, suddenly appearing directly below you to the right.

Having crossed the boulder field, you then cut across the steep eastern flank of **Malka Todorka** (2712m), and with a couple of final zigzags, emerge after 15mins at **Todorina Porta** (2575m), a total of about 2hrs 10mins walking from hizha Demyanitsa. ▸

From the saddle, the trail starts a steep zigzag drop towards the Banderishki cirque, the path deeply eroded into the side of the mountain. As you drop, the cirque opens out in front of you, revealing many of the sparkling Banderishki Ezera that lie scattered below amongst a chaos of granite boulders and large patches of dwarf pine. Eventually, after about 25mins, there is respite when you reach a small flat terrace containing Zhabeshko Ezero (2322m). The name means 'frog lake' and is a fitting title, since it is usually alive with grass frogs.

Beside the lake is an important junction, where a red-blazed trail breaks off left, bound for zaslon Tevno Ezero by

View over the Vasilashki Ezera from Todorina Porta

The saddle Todorina Porta lies on the ridge Todorino Bilo, between Malka Todorka to the northwest and Vasilashka Chukar (2615m) to the southeast.

225

way of Bashliyska (Glavnishka) Porta. However, you keep straight on the green-blazed trail along the left bank to the far end of the lake, before resuming your descent through the Banderishki cirque. The trail zigzags steeply down through thickets of dwarf pine and a succession of small grassy terraces, to arrive after 45mins at Ravnako, a large flat water meadow cut through by the **Banderitsa** river.

Here, on the right bank of the river, the path splits, and you are faced with a choice. Both branches are bound for hizha Vihren, but my recommendation is to take the left-hand path, which continues for 5mins along the right bank of the river to Ravnashki Brod, a point where you can ford across a couple of large boulders to the opposite bank. However, if water levels are high and the river running fast, it is safer not to try and leap across here, but instead you should go back to the junction and use the other path, which climbs its way up and over some rock outcrops and through thick dwarf pine to arrive directly at hizha Vihren in about 20mins.

However, assuming you can ford the river, make your way on down the left bank of the Banderitsa, and having dropped over a small rise, and skirted a large rock known as Puknatiya Kamak, you arrive within 15mins at the car park in front of **hizha Vihren** (1975m).

The hut stands on a rocky threshold on the left bank of the Banderitsa, with Vihren (2914m) rising up to the northwest and Todorin Vrah (2746m) directly to the southeast. Although the hut can accommodate about 190 people, be aware that in the height of summer it can sometimes be full. Hot meals are available from the kitchen.

GETTING BACK

During the summer there is a privately run mini-bus service (0749-88331) linking the hut to Bansko. This shuttles back and forth three times each day, currently departing hizha Vihren at 9.30am, 3.00pm and 6.00pm.

WALK 11
Mount Vihren

7km/1 Day

Vihren (2914m), the highest peak in the Pirin Mountains, may be slightly lower than Musala (2925m) in the neighbouring Rila range, but it is by far the more majestic and rewarding summit, offering walkers that perfect combination of beauty and challenge. The name Vihren derives from the older Turkish appellation 'Eltepe', implying 'windy peak', and is a fitting title for a mountain that was regarded in former times as the throne of the Slavic storm god Perun, after whom the Pirin Mountains get their name. The weather on Vihren can indeed be wild, especially in winter, when it is buffeted by gales and blizzards, and subject to frequent avalanches. The first successful winter ascent wasn't achieved until January 1925, and any winter mountaineering expedition on the peak remains a dangerous undertaking. However, in summer, given stable weather, ascending the peak is not difficult for walkers, although the route described below does require a head for heights and entails some simple scrambling. While most people opt to climb the peak as a more direct and monotonous out-and-back walk up its bleaker southern flank, this wonderful circular route offers a far more attractive and exciting alternative. By ascending the peak from the north, you have the chance to see Vihren in all its glory, skirting directly beneath its imposing northeastern face.

The opening part of this wonderful walk offers a succession of fantastic views, first down into the Banderitsa valley then up towards Vihren itself. The flora and fauna along the route are also exceptionally varied, and will delight both botanists and birdwatchers. Despite gaining considerable height, much of the trail is surprisingly undemanding, with the only real challenge being a short simple scramble to reach the Golyam Kazan cirque.

The remaining part of the ascent is steep and quite challenging, with the section above Premkata requiring the use of hands in places. However, the scrambling is very mild and there is little sense of exposure. The descent from the summit is very steep and jarring with a heavy pack, but is fairly straightforward.

GETTING TO THE START

The starting point for this walk is hizha Vihren, located on the left bank of the River Banderitsa, directly between Vihren and Todorin Vrah. The hut can be reached by a private mini-bus service (0749-88331), which currently departs from the avtogara in Bansko three times a day, at 8.30am, 2.15pm and 5.00pm. Alternatively you could make the 16km journey from the town by taxi. The hut can accommodate almost 200 people, but during the height of summer can sometimes be full.

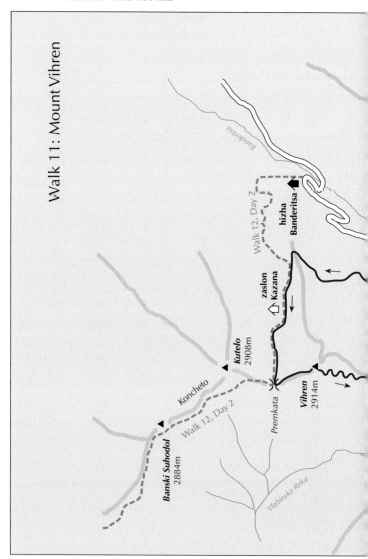

Walk 11: Mount Vihren

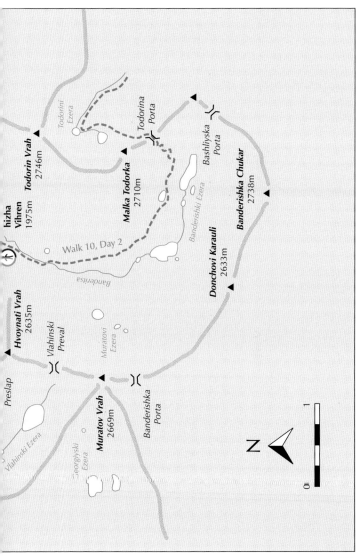

Todorini Ezera

Todorin Vrah 2746m

Todorina Porta

Bashliyska Porta

Banderishka Chukar 2738m

hizha Vihren 1975m

Malka Todorka 2710m

Banderishki Ezera

Walk 10, Day 2

Donchovi Karauli 2633m

Banderitsa

Hvoynati Vrah 2635m

Vlahinski Preval

Muratovi Ezera

Preslap

Muratov Vrah 2669m

Banderishka Porta

Vlahinski Ezera

Georgiyski Ezera

N

1

0

WALK 11
Mount Vihren

Time	4hrs 10mins
Distance	7km
Ascent	940m
Descent	940m
Highest point	2914m (Vihren)

Keep an eye open here for flowers such as yellow columbine (*Aquilegia aurea*), heart-shaped orchid (*Dactylorhiza cordigera*) and clustered bellflower (*Campanula glomerata*).

From **hizha Vihren** (1975m) set off northwest up the main red-blazed trail. This climbs steadily, crossing sections of boulders and pushing through some thickets of dwarf pine to arrive after 20mins at the small stream known as **Vihrenska Voda**. Having forded the stony streambed, the path splits. Both branches have red blazes, but ignore the left-hand trail, which continues steeply west towards the Kabata cirque, and instead take that which forks off right.

The trail climbs north through dwarf, ankle-scratching clumps of juniper, and then reaches a small flat grassy patch, beyond which, some 10mins from the Vihrenska Voda, you cross a second small stream, known as the Dalboko Dere. ◀

The trail climbs steadily on, with the valley of the Banderitsa dropping away ever deeper below you to the right. Eventually, after about 30mins, you come to a boulder patch and a small rock wall on the eastern flank of Vihren.

Geologically, this is an interesting spot, because it marks the **contact zone** between granite and limestone rocks, and if you search around you can see both types of boulders lying side by side. So not surprisingly, there is also a rich variety of beautiful alpine plants growing in this region, including several saxifrages, such as *Saxifraga ferdinandi-coburgi*, *Saxifraga luteo-viridis* and *Saxifraga exarata*, as well spring gentian (*Gentiana verna*), alpine aster (*Aster alpinus*), and two pretty flaxes, the bright-yellow-flowered *Linum capitatum* and the blue-flowered *Linum alpinum*. A number of interesting birds are also often spotted on the rocks above, including wallcreeper, alpine chough and alpine accentor, while parties of Balkan chamois also frequent these crags.

Climbing gently on for another 10mins, you then reach the back of a rocky side spur known as Dzhamdzhiev Rab. This is a beautiful viewpoint, but in bad weather can be quite bleak and windswept, a fact emphasized by the prostrate vegetation that is dominated by mountain avens (*Dryas octopetala*) and net-leaved willow (*Salix reticulata*), two species more characteristic of the arctic tundra.

The trail heads on up the back of the spur, but then almost immediately cuts across into the dwarf pine on the right flank. If visibility is poor, it is important you don't miss this. Over the years several people have gone wrong at this point, and simply kept on up the ridge, only to get themselves into trouble on the crags above, which are known as Dzhamdzhievi Skali ('Dzhamdzhiev's rocks'). The marked trail, along the flank of the ridge, needs some care itself, especially with a big pack, and in a couple of places you will be forced to use your hands to overcome short sections of rock, and haul yourself up between the clumps dwarf pine.

Eventually, after about 15mins, you reach a junction where a green-blazed trail breaks off right, descending via the Malak Kazan cirque towards hizha Banderitsa (Walk 12, Day 2). You keep left, following the main red-blazed trail for another 10mins into heart of the Golyam Kazan cirque.

Entering the Golyam Kazan cirque

231

Aptly named 'the large cauldron', the **Golyam Kazan cirque** is a dramatic spot – a wild hollow filled with a chaos of marbleised limestone blocks and a large permanent patch of *firn* snow, tucked in at the very foot of Vihren's towering 460m high northeastern wall. Perched up on a rocky elevation on the eastern side of the cirque is **zaslon Kazana** (2448m), a small metal refuge that can accommodate about half a dozen people. It was built in 1957 by researchers from the Bulgarian Academy of Sciences, who were carrying out studies in the region, but is now mainly used by alpinists and rock climbers.

Leaving Golyam Kazan, continue west, starting a steep zig-zag climb out of the cirque, first over large boulders, then smaller more fractured scree, where the path is somewhat slippery and eroded. Eventually the gradient eases slightly, and the footing improves as you follow on up a slight gully to arrive after 35mins at **Premkata** (2660m), a large saddle located on the main ridge of the Pirin between Vihren and **Kutelo** (2908m).

From Premkata (2660m) a trail breaks off north, climbing abruptly up the somewhat bleak flank of Kutelo (2908m) en route for the Koncheto ridge and hizha Yavorov (Walk 12, Day 2). However, you now turn south to begin the ascent of Vihren. Having reached the very foot of the peak, the gradient suddenly increases, and the path quickly changes from gravel to rock. As it does, the line of the route becomes a little less obvious, and in poor visibility it is very important to look for and carefully follow the red-blazes as you scramble up the rocks. Eventually, after about 30mins easy scrambling from the saddle, you will arrive on the summit of **Vihren** (2914m).

If you are lucky enough to be on the top of Vihren in fine weather, the **panorama** is stupendous – a labyrinth of peaks and ridges rippling away in all directions. Not only can you see almost the entire Pirin National Park stretched out below, you can also make out the silhouettes of several neighbouring mountain ranges. Far off to the north-northeast rise the Rila Mountains, while stretching away east towards the far horizon are the rolling folds of the Rodopi. To the south, marking the border with Greece, lie the Slavyanka and

Summit of Vihren (2914m)

Belasitsa ranges, while to the southwest and west are the Ograzhden, Maleshevska and Vlahina mountains, which stretch along the frontier with Macedonia.

From the summit, the trail drops steeply with many zigzags down Vihren's slippery and heavily eroded southern flank. It takes about 30mins to reach the saddle **Vihrenski Preslap** (2535m), which offers some brief relief to the knees.

Vihrenski Preslap separates Vihren from Hvoynati Vrah (2635m), and marks an **abrupt transition** from marble to granite rocks. Lying down in the cirque to the west you can see the Vlahinski Ezera, a tight cluster of four picturesque lakes.

After a few minutes gentle stroll south along the broad back of the saddle, the path suddenly bends east, resuming its descent as it drops down for 15mins into a small and surprisingly lush embryonic cirque known as Kabata. ▶

This is a pleasant place to rest and lie down on the soft grass, looking back up towards the imposing bulk of Vihren.

View over the Vlahinski Ezera from Vihren

Resuming, another jarring zigzag drop awaits, steadily taking its toll on the knees as it brings you back down after 30mins to the rocky streambed of the **Vihrenska Voda,** and the junction from which you broke off early on at the start of the day. From there, another 15mins descent through the dwarf pine and over the last of the boulders finally brings you down to the car park in front of **hizha Vihren** (1975m).

Hizha Vihren is a large hut situated on a rocky river threshold on the left bank of the Banderitsa. It can accommodate almost 200 people, but in summer is often full.

GETTING BACK

From the car park you can get the private mini-bus service (0749-88331) back down to Bansko. This currently departs at 9.30am, 3.00pm and 6.00pm.

WALK 12
The Bayvuvi Dupki–Dzhindzhiritsa Reserve and Koncheto

23.5km/2 days

Much of this beautiful but challenging walk is focused in and around the Bayuvi Dupki–Dzhindzhiritsa Reserve. On the first day of the walk, you will climb steadily up through ancient coniferous forests dominated by Macedonian pine. Many of the trees here are between 250 and 300 years old, with some individuals known to be over 550 years of age. The reserve also preserves some ancient Bosnian pines, including two specimens that are over 1000 years old. Higher up, the coniferous forests are replaced by thickets of dwarf pine, roamed by brown bear, wild boar and wolf. The second day of the walk then sees you climbing into the alpine zone, a region of rocky peaks and ridges that is amongst the most rugged and spectacular in Bulgaria. This is the realm of the Balkan chamois and golden eagle, and also the habitat for a whole array of wonderful alpine plants, which include many Bulgarian and Balkan endemic species. During this section of the walk you traverse the very crest of the Pirin, following a narrow marble ridge known as Koncheto, which requires both good weather and an excellent head for heights.

Trail through the Bayuvi Dupki–Dzhindzhiritsa Reserve (Day 1)

GETTING TO THE START

The starting point for this walk is Predela (1142m), the important mountain pass that separates the Pirin from the neighbouring Rila range. The highpoint of the pass, from which the trail begins, is located on the main road some 15km northwest of Bansko and 10km west of Razlog. There are seven buses each day from Sofia's tsentralna avtogara, which cross the pass en route to Bansko, currently departing at 7.30am, 8.30am, 9.45am, 11.25am, 1.15pm, 2.00pm and 4.45pm. These buses don't actually stop at the trailhead itself, but a little further down the road to the west, by a collection of cafés and snack bars. A further 1.5km down the main road is a junction where a lane leads left to hizha Predel (1050m), a small but pleasant mountain hut that can accommodate about 30 people.

235

Walk 12: The Bayuvi Dupki–Dzhindzhiritsa Reserve and Koncheto

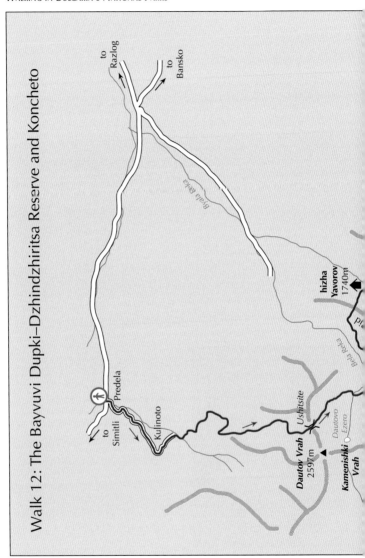

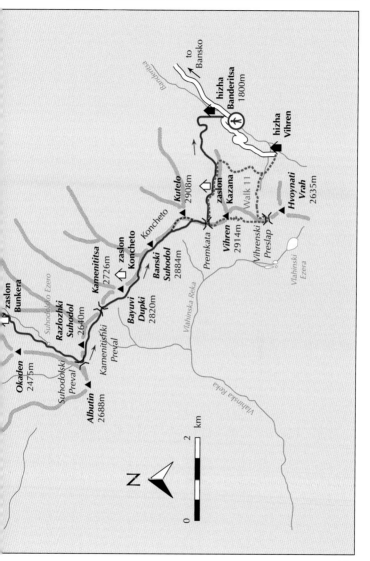

DAY 1
Predela to Hizha Yavorov

Time	4hrs 20mins
Distance	11.5km
Ascent	1220m
Descent	620m
Highest point	2250m (Ushitsite)

This opening stage is fairly tiring, as it involves significant ascent, and is quite steep in places. However, the walk is pleasant, taking you through the heart of the Bayuvi Dupki–Dzhindzhiritsa Reserve. There are opportunities to see many birds typical of the forest and sub-alpine zones. I have also, on occasion, encountered brown bear and wild boar along this trail.

From the highpoint of **Predela** (1142m), set off south towards the Pirin Mountains on the red-blazed trail, which for the time being is still a small crumbling asphalt lane.

A new garden centre has just sprung up at the trailhead, and you should also be aware that given the amount of **construction work** currently underway in this region, by the time this book is published, a whole conurbation of new hotels and apartments may well have appeared along this road, making any detailed description rather superfluous. However, you will soon reach Tisheto, where there is an old forestry base, and a memorial fountain built in 1981 to commemorate the 1300th anniversary of the Bulgarian state.

Keeping on along the main asphalt lane, shaded by beech, and ignoring a couple of forks off to the left, you then reach **Kulinoto**, some 30mins from the Predela pass. Here, having passed a dilapidated forestry rest-home that is almost certain to be redeveloped, the asphalt peters out, and within a couple of minutes you reach a junction where you follow the red-blazed trail east, running on along a track through the forest. The track soon crosses a ski-piste, and after 15mins reaches Ilyazov Dol, a small stream beside which is a humble partisan memorial.

Shortly beyond, when the track splits, keep straight on along the main lower branch, ignoring the fork up right. After 15mins you arrive at an important junction at a small glade and bend in the track. Here, fork off right onto a small path that immediately begins a very steep climb through the trees. After 10mins you pass a feeble water source and then, just beyond, the ruins of a wooden shack. Climbing on, you then emerge 5mins later at a grassy glade and track.

Cut straight across the glade and, having rejoined the track, follow it on left through the forest. Eventually, after 15mins, you reach another larger, somewhat scrubby clearing, where you fork off right on the clearly marked red-blazed trail that climbs into the forest, entering the boundaries of the Bayuvi Dupki–Dzhindzhiritsa Reserve. To start with the trail is somewhat narrow and overgrown, as it passes through a short section of scrubby beech wood, but as you gain height, you eventually climb into beautiful coniferous forest dominated by towering ancient trees.

Eventually, after about 35mins, you enter the dwarf pine zone, crossing a small flat lake-less cirque area, from which there is a wonderful view ahead towards the rocky northeastern flank of **Dautov Vrah** (2597m; Garbets). Keep zigzagging on up through the thick clumps of dwarf pine until, after about 25mins, you emerge at **Ushitsite** (2250m), a high windy col some 2hrs 30mins from the Pedela pass. ▸

From the col, start dropping steeply down via dwarf pine and lush glades. However, take care, for after about 20mins you reach a large open grassy area where you need to make a sudden sharp bend left. You then continue on down through more dwarf pine for another 5mins, before reaching the upper end of an extensive open scrubby area known as Konyarnika.

More care is needed here, as the path is faint and the red blazes hard to spot, as you push on through the ankle-scratching clumps of dwarf juniper. It takes about 15mins to reach the far end of the clearing, where the trail becomes more obvious again as it enters a stand of ancient storm-damaged pines. Emerging from these, you then head straight

In clear weather there is a fine, if somewhat daunting, panorama ahead towards the majestic ridge of the Northern Pirin, along whose jagged crest you will be walking the next day.

View south from the Ushitsite saddle

The name means 'white river' and refers to the fact that the riverbed here is formed of beautiful white marble rocks and stones.

on through the middle of a large patch of tall weeds, and having passed an old herders' hut (*koliba*), arrive at a small wooden footbridge over the river **Bela Reka**, a total of about 50mins from the Ushitsite col. ◄

Having crossed the river, keep on downstream along the red-blazed trail. In places this is steep and stony, but elsewhere more gentle as it passes through forests and grassy glades. After 15mins you cross through a broad open area, where the forest is steadily regenerating after having been destroyed by an avalanche, and then about 5mins later reach Badzhoro, where near a ruined brick building there is a junction of tracks.

Follow the main right-hand track straight on. After 10mins you come to a second junction, at a place known as Stalbata ('the ladder'), where you suddenly break off right from the track, following the red-blazed trail as it makes a steep zig-zag climb up through the forest. Eventually, after 15mins, you cross the back of **Okadenski Rid**, a side spur which breaks off north-northeast from the main backbone of the Pirin.

Dropping on down the other side, through beautiful ancient forest, it then takes only 15mins before you emerge from the trees directly behind **hizha Yavorov** (1740m).

The hut stands in the valley of the Razlozhki Suhodol, and is named after the famous poet and revolutionary, Peyo Yavorov. Hot meals can usually be obtained from the kitchen.

DAY 2
Hizha Yavorov to Hizha Banderitsa
(via Zaslon Koncheto and Premkata)

Time	5hrs 55mins
Distance	12km
Ascent	1100m
Descent	1040m
Highest point	2836m (Bezimenen Vrah III)

An exhilarating stage that leads along the narrow marble crest known as Koncheto, the most famous ridge-walk in Bulgaria. Although the most difficult sections have a metal cable for assistance, it is not a walk to be undertaken in bad weather, or by anyone with a fear of heights and exposure. Eventually, having reached the Premkata saddle, you have a choice of routes. You can either continue on along the ridge over the summit of the Pirin's highest peak, Vihren (Walk 11), or else descend steeply down to hizha Banderitsa, the trail described below.

From **hizha Yavorov** (1740m), set off southwest up the valley of the Razloshki Suhodol, following the red-blazed trail through ancient coniferous forest. After an easy start, the trail begins to climb quite steeply, until finally, after about 45mins, you arrive at **zaslon Bunkera** (2040m).

Zaslon Bunkera is a small stone refuge that can accommodate about 10 people. During the winter of 1943–44 it was used as a partisan hideout.

Pressing on from the refuge into the dwarf-pine zone, you pick up the first of the winter pole-markers, and having climbed across a section of boulders, zigzag your way up after about 45mins to the small lake **Suhodolsko Ezero** (2311m). From there, continue climbing steadily south-southwest through more dwarf pine, then rocks, to arrive after another 45mins on the main ridgeback at the saddle **Suhodolski Preval** (2540m).

A yellow-blazed path drops south over the saddle towards the valley of the Vlahinska Reka, from where it is possible to break off east-southeast to reach hizha Sinanitsa. However, you stick with the red-blazed trail, following it east-southeast along the ridge just below the crest. Having skirted south of **Razlozhki Suhodol** (2640m) and then across the southwestern flank of **Kamenititsa** (2726m), you arrive after about 30mins at another important saddle – **Kamenitishki Preval** (2675m).

An unmarked path drops north from the saddle, leading back down towards hizha Yavorov, but you continue southeast along the red-blazed trail, which follows a good path across the southwestern flank of **Bayuvi Dupki** (2820m), passing a memorial to a fallen climber. Finally, having skirted the peak, you arrive after 30mins at **zaslon Koncheto** (2760m).

This small white refuge can accommodate about 12 people and stands on the crest just above the trail.

Beyond the refuge, continue east-southeast along the red-blazed trail for 15mins to Bezimenen Vrah III (2836m), from which a wonderfully craggy side spur known as Koteshki Chal breaks off north-northeast. Then, bending gently southeast to skirt across the southwestern flank of **Banski Suhodol** (2884m), you climb up to arrive after 15mins at the start of the famous marble crest known as **Koncheto**, which links Banski Suhodol to the neighbouring peak Kutelo.

About 400m long and some 50 to 100cm wide, the **crest** is extremely exposed. Its northeastern flank forms an almost vertical 500m high wall above the Banski

Suhodol cirque, while the slightly less sheer southwestern flank plunges down some 600–700m towards the valley of the Vlahinska Reka.

The cable-assisted trail along the Koncheto ridge

The walk along the crest is breathtaking, leading over shiny smooth marble rocks that offer little in the way of grip for boots. However, thankfully there is a metal cable to cling on to, and this certainly provides some welcome reassurance, especially in wet or windy weather. After a while the cable route splits in two. The left-hand branch continues to climb along the crest. The other branch, the one recommended for anyone with a bulky pack, loops lower down across the southwestern flanks of **Kutelo** (2908m), before dropping steeply down to arrive after 30mins at the large well-formed saddle known as **Premkata** (2660m).

In good weather, those who feel like a final challenge, and who wish to prolong the ridge walk, can do so by continuing over the summit of Vihren (2914m) to **hizha Vihren** (Walk 11). However, the trail described here provides an alternative finish at hizha Banderitsa.

From the saddle, follow the red-blazed trail that drops directly east down a fairly gentle slope. After a while the

View back north-west towards the Pirins marble ridge from the Premkata saddle

path suddenly becomes steeper, zigzagging down over loose scree and rocks to arrive after about 30mins in the heart of the Golyam Kazan cirque, directly beneath Vihren's imposing northeastern wall. The trail continues straight on through the cirque, beneath **zaslon Kazana** (2448m), a small refuge that stands perched up high to the left, and after 10mins reaches a junction.

Here you have another choice. By continuing on the red-blazed trail that now slants off to the right, you could reach hizha Vihren in about 1hr 30mins (Walk 11). However, our route keeps straight on along the green-blazed trail, which almost immediately begins a steep zigzag drop into the Malak Kazan cirque. Unlike Golyam Kazan, which is wild and rocky, Malak Kazan resembles an elongated meadow.

Enjoying a short respite while you walk gently across the flat grassy bottom of the cirque, you then resume a steep descent, dropping down through thickets of dwarf pine and a couple of small lush glades, a region favoured by wild boar. There then follows a slippery zigzag drop down a short section of eroded scree into the Mecho Dere. ◄

The steep rocky mountainside hereabouts is studded with some wonderful, ancient, wind-warped specimens of Bosnian pine.

Continuing on down into denser forest of Macedonian pine, you finally emerge after about 1hr into the open beside **hizha Banderitsa** (1800m).

Situated on a terrace above the river Banderitsa, the hut comprises two buildings and a collection of bungalows, which together can accommodate a total of almost 200 people.

A few minutes walk away from the hut, either up the road or on an unmarked path through the forest, is **Baykusheva Mura**, an ancient Bosnian pine reputed to be over 1300 years old, and thus one of the oldest trees in the country. If you continue up the road for about 20mins you reach hizha Vihren, a walk that is highly recommended for butterfly enthusiasts. This part of the Banderitsa valley holds many interesting species, such as olive skipper, large grizzled skipper, clouded Apollo, Apollo, clouded yellow, scarce copper, Balkan copper, mountain argus, blue argus, Meleager's blue, Balkan fritillary, turquoise blue, false Eros blue, Arran brown, Ottoman brassy ringlet, large ringlet.

GETTING BACK

When you are ready to leave the mountains and descend back to Bansko, it should be possible to pick up a mini-bus (0749-88331) from the café/bar situated a few minutes walk down the road below hizha Banderitsa. The service to Bansko is currently scheduled to depart from hizha Vihren at 9.30am, 3.00pm and 6.00pm, and should pass by here a short time later.

APPENDIX 1
Route Summary Table

Walk	National Park	Start	Finish	Distance	Duration	Ascent	Descent	Page
1	Central Balkan	Divchovoto	Chiflik	42.5km	3 days	2110m	2050m	40
2	Central Balkan	Mazaneto	Cherni Osam	51km	4 days	1675m	2105m	58
3	Central Balkan	Kalofer	Karlovo	38km	3 days	1585m	1785m	76
4	Central Balkan	Lagat	Gabarevo	33km	3 days	3075m	2165m	9?
5	Rila	Rila Monastery	Rila Monastery	44.5km	4 days	2685m	2730m	118
6	Rila	Komplex Malyovitsa	Komplex Malyovitsa	22.5km	2 days	1380m	1380m	136
7	Rila	Borovets	Govedartsi	61km	4 days	3580m	3725m	149
8	Rila	Kostenets	Kostenets	26km	2 days	1785m	1785m	171
9	Pirin	Bansko	Melnik	45km	3 days	1960m	2500m	192
10	Pirin	Hizha Bezbog	Hizha Vihren	18km	2 days	1080m	1850m	216
11	Pirin	Hizha Vihren	Hizha Vihren	7km	1 day	940m	940m	227
12	Pirin	Predela	Hizha Banderitsa	23.5km	2 days	2320m	1660m	235

Approaching the saddle Vetroviti Preslap (1545m) and Boba Vrah (1707m) (Walk 1)

APPENDIX 2
English–Bulgarian Glossary and Pronunciation Guide

English	Bulgarian	Cyrillic
Conversation		
Good morning	*Dobro utro*	Добро утро
Good day	*Dobar den*	Добър ден
Good evening	*Dobar vecher*	Добър вечер
Good night	*Leka nosht*	Лека нощ
Hello	*Zdraveyte*	Здравейте
Yes (with shake of head)	*Da*	Да
No (with nod of head)	*Ne*	Не
Please	*Molya*	Моля
Thank you	*Blagodarya*	Благодаря
Excuse me!	*Izvinete!*	Извинете!
When?	*Koga?*	Кога?
Where?	*Kade?*	Къде?
Why?	*Zashto?*	Защо?
What?	*Kakvo?*	Какво?
Who?	*Koy?*	Кой?
How?	*Kak?*	Как?
How many/much?	*Kolko?*	Колко?
am	*sam*	Съм
is	*e*	е
are	*sa*	са
Numbers		
One	*Edno*	Едно
Two	*Dve*	Две
Three	*Tri*	Три
Four	*Chetiri*	Четири
Five	*Pet*	Пет
Six	*Shest*	Шест
Seven	*Sedem*	Седем
Eight	*Osem*	Осем
Nine	*Devet*	Девет
Ten	*Deset*	Десет
Eleven	*Edinadeset*	Единадесет
Twelve	*Dvanadeset*	Дванадесет

English	Bulgarian	Cyrillic
Twenty	*Dvadeset*	Двадесет
Hundred	*Sto*	Сто
Provisions		
What would you like?	*Kazhete!*	Кажете!
I am looking for	*Tarsya*	Търся
I want	*Iskam*	Искам
Have you got?	*Imate li?*	Имате ли?
We have/ There is	*Ima*	Има
We haven't/ There isn't any	*Nyama*	Няма
How much does it cost?	*Kolko struva?*	Колко струва?
Open	*Otvoren*	Отворен
Closed	*Zatvoren*	Затворен
Food supplies	*Hranitelni stoki*	Хранителни стоки
Market	*Pazar*	Пазар
Restaurant	*Restorant*	Ресторант
Inn	*Mehana*	Механа
Bill/receipt	*Smetka*	Сметка
Water	*Voda*	Вода
Wine	*Vino*	Вино
Beer	*Bira*	Бира
Herb tea	*Bilkov chay*	Билков чай
Coffee	*Kafe*	Кафе
Milk	*Pryasno mlyako*	Прясно мляко
Yoghurt	*Kiselo mlyako*	Кисело мляко
Vegetarian	*Vegetariansko*	Вегетарианско
Fruit	*Plodove*	Плодове
Bread	*Hlyab*	Хляб
Salad	*Salata*	Салата
Soup	*Supa*	Супа
Meat	*Meso*	Месо
Chicken	*Pile*	Пиле

English	Bulgarian	Cyrillic
Pork	*Svinsko*	Свинско
Veal	*Teleshko*	Телешко
Lamb	*Agneshko*	Агнешко
Fish	*Riba*	Риба
Accommodation		
Have you a room?	*Imate li staya?*	Имате ли стая?
Hotel	*Hotel*	Хотел
Guest-house	*Kashta za gosti*	Къща за гости
Private lodging	*Chastna kvartira*	Частна квартира
Mountain hut	*Hizha*	Хижа
Mountain refuge	*Zaslon*	Заслон
Room	*Staya*	Стая
Bed	*Leglo*	Легло
Sheets	*Charshafi*	Чаршафи
Blankets	*Odeala*	Одеала
Pillow	*Vazglavnitsa*	Възглавница
Toilet	*Toaletna*	Тоалетна
Bathroom	*Banya*	Баня
Shower	*Dush*	Душ
Dining room	*Stolova*	Столова
Kitchen	*Kuhnya*	Кухня
Transport		
Airport	*Letishte/ aerogara*	Летище/ Аерогара
Taxi	*Taksi*	Такси
Bus	*Avtobus*	Автобус
Bus stop	*Spirka*	Спирка
Bus station	*Avtogara*	Автогара
Train	*Vlak*	Влак
Railway station	*Gara*	Гара
Ticket	*Bilet*	Билет
Directions		
Where is?	*Kade e?*	Къде е?
How far?	*Kolko daleche?*	Колко далече?
Near	*Blizo*	Близо
Far	*Daleche*	Далече
Continue	*Prodalzhete*	Продължете
Cross	*Presechete*	Пресечете

English	Bulgarian	Cyrillic
Climb	*Izkachete*	Изкачете
Descend	*Slezte*	Слезте
Follow	*Sledvayte*	Следвайте
Turn	*Zaviyte*	Завийте
Left	*Nalyavo*	Наляво
Right	*Nadyasno*	Надясно
Straight on	*Napravo*	Направо
Back	*Nazad*	Назад
After	*Sled*	След
Before	*Predi*	Мреди
North	*Sever*	Север
South	*Yug*	Юг
East	*Iztok*	Изток
West	*Zapad*	Запад
Trail blazes/ markers	*Markirovki*	Маркировки
Junction	*Razklon*	Разклон
Path/trail	*Pateka*	Пътека
Track	*Pat*	Път
Bend	*Zavoy*	Завой
Bridge	*Most*	Мост
Lake	*Ezero*	Езеро
River	*Reka*	Река
Stream gully	*Dere*	Дере
Spring	*Izvor*	Извор
Drinking fountain	*Cheshma*	Чешма
Forest	*Gora*	Гора
Dwarf pine scrub	*Klek*	Клек
Rocks	*Skali*	Скалм
Scree	*Sipey*	Сипей
Mountain	*Planina*	Планина
Peak/Summit	*Vrah*	Връх
Ridge	*Bilo*	Било
Saddle/col	*Preslap/ preval*	Преслап/ Превал
Pass	*Prohod/porta*	Проход/ Порта
Meadow	*Polyana*	Поляна
Steep	*Stramno*	Стръмно
Easy	*Lesno*	Лесно
Difficult	*Trudno*	Трудно
Dangerous	*Opasno*	Опасно

English	Bulgarian	Cyrillic
Lost	*Zaguben*	Загубен
Map	*Karta*	Карта
Compass	*Kompas*	Компас
Weather		
Weather forecast	*Prognoza za vremeto*	Прогноза за времето
Sunny	*Slanchevo*	Слънчево
Rainy	*Dazhdovno*	Дъждовно
Cloudy	*Oblachno*	Облачно
Fog	*Magla*	Мъгла
Hail	*Gradushka*	Градушка
Snow	*Snyag*	Сняг
Avalanche	*Lavina*	Лавина
Thunder	*Gramotevitsa*	Гръмотевица
Lightning	*Svetkavitsa*	Светкавица
Storm	*Burya*	Буря
Wet	*Vlazhno*	Влажно
Cold	*Studeno*	Студено
Icy	*Ledeno*	Ледено
Warm	*Toplo*	Топло
Hot	*Goreshto*	Горещо
Health		
Help!	*Pomosht!*	Помощ!
I need	*Imam nuzhda ot*	Имам нужда от
Mountain rescue	*Planinska spasitelna sluzhba*	Планинска спасителна служба
Hospital	*Bolnitsa*	Болница
Doctor	*Lekar*	Лекар
Pain	*Bolka*	Болка
Injury	*Travma*	Травма
Wound/cut	*Rana*	Рана
Broken	*Schupen*	Счупен
Head	*Glava*	Глава
Leg	*Krak*	Крак
Arm	*Raka*	Ръка
Back	*Grab*	Гръб
Knee	*Kolyano*	Коляно
Ankle	*Glezen*	Глезен
Pharmacy	*Apteka*	Аптека
Medicine	*Lekarstvo*	Лекарство
Bandage	*Prevrazka*	Превръзка

Pronunciation Guide

Cyrillic		Latin	
Capital letter	Small letter	Transliteration	Pronunciation
А	а	A, a	m**a**n, b**a**r, b**u**t
Б	б	B, b	**b**it, **b**all
В	в	V, v	**v**ine, sto**v**e
Г	г	G, g	**g**ive, **g**o
Д	д	D, d	**d**im, **d**o
Е	е	E, e	**e**gg, g**e**t
Ж	ж	Zh, zh	mea**s**ure
З	з	Z, z	**z**eal, **z**oo
И	и	I, i	**i**ll, b**i**t
Й	й	Y, y	**y**es
К	к	K, k	**k**iss, **c**ool
Л	л	L, l	**l**ip, a**ll**
М	м	M, m	**m**iss, **m**an
Н	н	N, n	**n**o, **n**o**n**e
О	о	O, o	**o**dd, h**o**t
П	п	P, p	**sp**ill, **sp**oon
Р	р	R, r	**r**ear
С	с	S, s	**s**ince, **s**o
Т	т	T, t	**st**ill, **st**one
У	у	U, u	b**u**sh, p**u**ll, b**oo**k
Ф	ф	F, f	**f**ill, **f**ull
Х	х	H, h	lo**ch**
Ц	ц	Ts, ts	ha**ts**, bi**ts**
Ч	ч	Ch, ch	**ch**ur**ch**, tha**tch**
Ш	ш	Sh, sh	**sh**e, **sh**oe
Щ	щ	Sht, sht	pu**shed**, wa**shed**
Ъ	ъ	A, a	b**u**t, t**ou**ch, h**e**r
Ь	ь	Y, y	(softening sound)\
Ю	ю	Yu, yu	**you**
Я	я	Ya, ya	**ya**rd

APPENDIX 3
Further Reading

General Travel Guidebooks

Bulgaria: The Bradt Travel Guide by Annie Kay (Bradt, 2008)

The Rough Guide to Bulgaria by Jonathan Bousfield & Dan Richardson (Rough Guides, 2008)

Bulgaria Travel Guide by Richard Watkins & Chris Deliso (Lonely Planet, 2008)

Walking Guidebooks

The Mountains of Bulgaria: A Walker's Companion by Julian Perry (Cordee, 1995)

Historical Background

The Bulgarians: From Pagan Times to the Ottoman Conquest (Thames and Hudson, 1976)

A History of Bulgaria 1393–1945 by Mercia MacDermott (Allen & Unwin, 1962)

Natural History

The Birds of the Balkan Peninsula by Simeon Simeonov & Tanyu Michev (Petâr Beron 1991) (NB Written in Bulgarian)

Important Bird Areas in Bulgaria by Irina Kostadinova & Mladen Gramatikov (BDZP, 2007)

Pocket Field Guide to the Dragonflies of Bulgaria by Milen Marinov (Eshna, 2000) (NB Written in Bulgarian)

Prime Butterfly Areas in Bulgaria by Stanislav Abadjiev & Stiyan Beshkov (Pensoft, 2007)

Atlas of Bulgarian Endemic Plants by Ana Petrova et al. (Gea-Libris, 2006)

Flowers of Greece and the Balkans: A Field Guide by Oleg Polunin (Oxford, 1987)

View towards Smradliovo Ezero from Vodni Chal (Walk 7)

APPENDIX 4
Mountain Huts and Other Useful Contacts

Mountain Huts
Bulgarian Hiking Association
www.btsbg.org 02-9801285

The Bulgarian Hiking Association website is Cyrillic-only (including, naturally, the search facility) and so we include below the current full URLs for the mountain huts listed on it that do not have their own websites. If you use these in conjunction with a website translation tool, such as Google Translate, these pages will provide you with lots of useful information. If the structure of the website changes, the best way to get information will be by calling the (English-speaking) Bulgarian Hiking Association helpline on **02-9801285**. NB If contacting them to book a bed, it is a good idea to pre-order your evening meal and breakfast. If you plan to turn up at the huts without a reservation, then it is important to carry some of your own food supplies with you in case their canteens are not operating and meals unavailable.

Central Balkan National Park

Hut Name	Reservations	Website/web page
Hizha Benkovski	Bulgarian Hiking Association (02-9801285)	http://btsbg.org/modules/addresses/visit.php?cid=79&lid=252
Hizha Eho	Bulgarian Hiking Association (02-9801285)	http://btsbg.org/modules/addresses/visit.php?cid=121&lid=143
Hizha Kozya Stena	Bulgarian Hiking Association (02-9801285)	http://btsbg.org/modules/addresses/visit.php?cid=121&lid=144
Hizha Pleven	Bulgarian Hiking Association (02-9801285)	http://btsbg.org/modules/addresses/visit.php?cid=97&lid=206
Hizha Dobrila	0888-757578/032-511222	www.dobrila.eu
Hizha Dermenka	Bulgarian Hiking Association (02-9801285)	http://btsbg.org/modules/addresses/visit.php?cid=75&lid=247
Hizha Ray	Bulgarian Hiking Association (02-9801285)	http://btsbg.org/modules/addresses/visit.php?cid=104&lid=176
Hizha Vasil Levski	Bulgarian Hiking Association (02-9801285)	http://btsbg.org/modules/addresses/visit.php?cid=105&lid=185
Hizha Balkanski Rozi	0335-95373	http://btsbg.org/modules/addresses/visit.php?cid=105&lid=181
Hizha Hubavets	0335-95373	http://btsbg.org/modules/addresses/visit.php?cid=105&lid=182
Hizha Mazalat	Bulgarian Hiking Association (02-9801285)	http://btsbg.org/modules/addresses/visit.php?cid=64&lid=347
Hizha Sokolna	0887-435467/04363-442	http://btsbg.org/modules/addresses/visit.php?cid=160&lid=345

Rila National Park

Hut Name	Reservations	Website
Hizha Ivan Vazov	0887-727772	http://www.ivanvazovhut.info/
Hizha Malyovitsa	Bulgarian Hiking Association (02-9801285)	http://btsbg.org/modules/addresses/visit.php?cid=143&lid=343
Hizha Vada	0887-069466/048-815598	http://btsbg.org/modules/addresses/visit.php?cid=143&lid=83
Hizha Lovna	0707-2140/0707-2148	http://btsbg.org/modules/addresses/visit.php?cid=71&lid=268
Hizha Sedemte Ezera	Bulgarian Hiking Association (02-9801285)	http://btsbg.org/modules/addresses/visit.php?cid=143&lid=81
Hizha Musala	Bulgarian Hiking Association (02-9801285)	http://btsbg.org/modules/addresses/visit.php?cid=143&lid=80
Hizha Ledeno Ezero	Bulgarian Hiking Association (02-9801285)	http://btsbg.org/modules/addresses/visit.php?cid=143&lid=91
Hizha Granchar	Bulgarian Hiking Association (02-9801285)	http://btsbg.org/modules/addresses/visit.php?cid=33&lid=218
Hizha Ribni Ezera	048-836914/0887-939316	
Hizha Mechit	Bulgarian Hiking Association (02-9801285)	http://btsbg.org/modules/addresses/visit.php?cid=143&lid=79
Hizha Belmeken	0899-665685	http://btsbg.org/modules/addresses/visit.php?cid=140&lid=93

Pirin National Park

Hut Name	Reservations	Website
Hizha Demyanitsa	Bulgarian Hiking Association (02-9801285)	http://btsbg.org/modules/addresses/visit.php?cid=2&lid=19
Hizha Pirin	Bulgarian Hiking Association (02-9801285)	http://btsbg.org/modules/addresses/visit.php?cid=35&lid=319
Hizha Bezbog	Hotel 'Dobrinishte' (07447-2120)	http://hoteldobrinishte.com/
Hizha Vihren	Bulgarian Hiking Association (02-9801285)	http://btsbg.org/modules/addresses/visit.php?cid=2&lid=22
Hizha Yavorov	Bulgarian Hiking Association (02-9801285)	http://btsbg.org/modules/addresses/visit.php?cid=37&lid=324
Hizha Banderitsa	Bulgarian Hiking Association (02-9801285)	http://btsbg.org/modules/addresses/visit.php?cid=2&lid=17

Tourist Information	
Balkan Trek	www.balkantrek.com office@balkantrek.com
Foreign & Commonwealth Office Travel Advice	www.fco.gov.uk/en/travelling-and-living-overseas/travel-advice-by-country/europe/Bulgaria
The Embassy of the Republic of Bulgaria in London	www.bulgarianembassy-london.org
Central Balkan National Park	www.centralbalkannationalpark.org
Rila National Park	www.rilanationalpark.org
Pirin National Park	http://pirin.bg/
PAN Parks	www.panparks.org
Travelling to Bulgaria	
British Airways	www.britishairways.com
Bulgaria Air	www.air.bg/en
Easyjet	www.easyjet.com
Wizz Air	http://wizzair.com
Sofia Airport	www.sofia-airport.bg 02-9372211
Travelling within Bulgaria	
OK Supertrans Taxis	www.oktaxi.net 02-9732121
Sofia Central Bus Station	www.centralnaavtogara.bg
Bulgarian State Railways	http://razpisanie.bdz.bg/site/search.jsp
Mountain Maps	
Balkan Trek	www.balkantrek.com office@balkantrek.com
Mountain Rescue	
Mountain Rescue Services	www.pss.bg/base.html 02-9632000

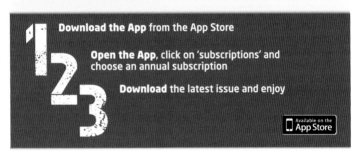

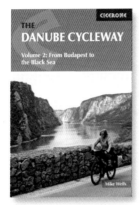
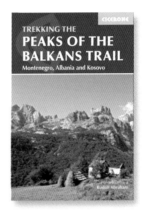

Walking – Trekking – Mountaineering – Climbing – Cycling

Over 40 years, Cicerone have built up an outstanding collection of over 300 guides, inspiring all sorts of amazing adventures.

Every guide comes from extensive exploration and research by our expert authors, all with a passion for their subjects. They are frequently praised, endorsed and used by clubs, instructors and outdoor organisations.

All our titles can now be bought as **e-books**, **ePubs** and **Kindle** files and we also have an online magazine – **Cicerone Extra** – with features to help cyclists, climbers, walkers and trekkers choose their next adventure, at home or abroad.

Our website shows any **new information** we've had in since a book was published. Please do let us know if you find anything has changed, so that we can publish the latest details. On our **website** you'll also find great ideas and lots of detailed information about what's inside every guide and you can buy **individual routes** from many of them online.

It's easy to keep in touch with what's going on at Cicerone by getting our monthly **free e-newsletter**, which is full of offers, competitions, up-to-date information and topical articles. You can subscribe on our home page and also follow us on **Facebook** and **Twitter** or dip into our **blog**.

Cicerone – the very best guides for exploring the world.

CICERONE

Juniper House, Murley Moss, Oxenholme Road, Kendal, Cumbria LA9 7RL
Tel: 015395 62069 info@cicerone.co.uk
www.cicerone.co.uk and www.cicerone-extra.com